New Century Local Government

Commonwealth Perspectives

Edited by Graham Sansom and Peter McKinlay

Commonwealth Secretariat

Commonwealth Secretariat
Marlborough House
Pall Mall
London SW1Y 5HX
United Kingdom

Published by the Commonwealth Secretariat
Edited by editors4change Limited
Typeset by Techset Composition
Cover design by Rory Seaford Designs
Printed by Hobbs the Printers, Totton, Hampshire

Views and opinions expressed in this publication are the responsibility of the authors and should in no way be attributed to the institutions to which they are affiliated or to the Commonwealth Secretariat.

Wherever possible, the Commonwealth Secretariat uses paper sourced from sustainable forests or from sources that minimise a destructive impact on the environment.

Copies of this publication may be obtained from

Publications Section
Commonwealth Secretariat
Marlborough House
Pall Mall
London SW1Y 5HX
United Kingdom
Tel: +44 (0)20 7747 6534
Fax: +44 (0)20 7839 9081
Email: publications@commonwealth.int
Web: www.thecommonwealth.org/publications

A catalogue record for this publication is available from the British Library.

ISBN (paperback): 978-1-84929-093-7
ISBN (e-book): 978-1-84859-149-3

Foreword

Research and policy investigations are important components of the Commonwealth Secretariat governance work that contribute to informed decisions taken by Commonwealth policy-makers. Our policy research on local governance not only outlines choices for member governments, but also endeavours to provide cutting-edge evidence for the design, implementation, and review of public policies, thereby contributing to broader development goals. The Secretariat portfolio of publications on local government includes four volumes under the *Local Government Reform Series*.

New Century Local Government: Commonwealth Perspectives seeks to cover current and future issues, including moves towards decentralisation in Commonwealth member states that have arisen since 2000, and which continue to present both challenges and opportunities for local government.

The world in which local governments operate is changing rapidly as a consequence of a confluence of forces, including demographic changes, the fall-out from the global financial crisis, shifts in the patterns and location of economic growth, and urbanisation in developed and developing countries alike. This offers scope for local government across the Commonwealth to respond in new and distinctive ways, especially in future within the architecture of the post-2015 global development framework.

'New Century' in the title of this publication refers to the evolving role of local government as the function of the State continues to change in the contemporary world. Distilled wisdom drawn from current thinking and international good practices is brought together in this book with contributions by fifteen distinguished authors from across the Commonwealth.

The future of local government depends in most cases upon the attitudes and decisions of national or provincial governments. The Commonwealth Secretariat seeks to play a constructive role in this context in supporting the goals of democratic decentralisation from both central and local perspectives; promoting fresh thinking about and among local governments; and ensuring that new ideas are explored, and that lessons from the varied experiences of member countries are widely disseminated and understood.

The Commonwealth collectively has also long subscribed that development and democracy are inter-related and mutually reinforcing. This is relevant at all levels of government and administration. This book aims to contribute to that endeavour.

We acknowledge all contributions in this publication for helping to carry forward the scholarly agenda on local government for the benefit of all Commonwealth governments and the citizens whom they represent and serve.

Kamalesh Sharma
Commonwealth Secretary-General

Contents

Abbreviations and acronyms

BC	British Columbia (Canada)
CapRD	Capital Regional District (Canada)
CCCLM	Council of Capital City Lord Mayors (Australia)
CCO	council-controlled organisation (New Zealand)
CSRD	Columbia Shuswap Regional District (Canada)
CLGF	Commonwealth Local Government Forum
DDAF	democratic decentralisation assessment framework
DOPP	Devolution of Power Plan (Pakistan)
GDP	gross domestic product
GLA	Great London Authority
IDP	integrated development planning (South Africa)
ILO	International Labour Organization
JNNURM	Jawaharlal Nehru National Urban Renewal Mission (India)
LGA02	Local Government Act 2002 (New Zealand)
LTCCP	Long-Term Council Community Plan (New Zealand)
LTFS	long-term financial strategy (New Zealand)
MP	Member of Parliament
MPRA	Municipal Property Rates Act 2004 (South Africa)
NAC	National Advisory Council (Jamaica)
OAG	Office of the Auditor General
OECD	Organisation for Economic Co-operation and Development
PDC	Parish Development Committee (Jamaica)
PRF	Parochial Revenue Fund (Jamaica)
RD	regional district (Canada)
SOE	state-owned enterprise (New Zealand)
TNRD	Thompson Nicola Regional District (Canada)
UNDP	UN Development Programme
USAID	United States Agency for International Development
WIEGO	Women in Informal Employment: Globalizing and Organizing

Chapter 1

Introduction and Overview

Peter McKinlay and Graham Sansom

In 2009 the Research Advisory Group of the Commonwealth Local Government Forum (CLGF) came together for its biennial research colloquium in the lead-up to the Commonwealth Local Government Conference. Discussion was shaped by an awareness not only of the many challenges facing local authorities across the Commonwealth, but also of underlying changes in the nature and perceptions of the fundamental role of local government. The latter reflected a number of drivers, including globalisation and economic imperatives; decentralisation policies and the evident failings of central governments to deliver desired outcomes at local and regional levels; the emergence of ever-larger metropolitan centres; fiscal constraints following the global financial crisis; and the need for local government to contribute more substantially to the delivery of the United Nations Millennium Development Goals.[1]

The colloquium also identified a number of key issues for local government across the Commonwealth, such as the need for transformational change, for a broad developmental model of local government and for structures which were 'fit for purpose' within their own local contexts. Participants acknowledged that 'Western' models of local governance would not always be appropriate; in some cases adapted systems of traditional governance may be the best way forward (as is substantially the case in parts of Africa and the Pacific).

Three basic propositions were developed which the colloquium considered were likely to shape the ongoing development of local government in Commonwealth countries. These reflected the combination of an increasing need for high-level expertise, on the one hand, and greater engagement with communities, on the other, the latter encompassing a shift from formal *local government* to the broader concept of *local governance*, facilitating community development and involving a wide range of citizens and stakeholders in decision-making.

Basic proposition 1

The shift from 'government' to 'governance' represents and requires an attitudinal change on the part of local government regarding its powers and responsibilities. These must be seen as more than delivering services and performing formal governmental functions. Rather, local governments should regard themselves as exercising their powers and holding their resources 'in trust' for local communities, to be used to support those communities in pursuing their preferred goals. The shift to governance should also be seen as transforming local government's underlying purpose from that of a subsidiary level within a hierarchy of governments to one of community leadership working with communities to enhance local well-being.

This proposition recognises that, regardless of whether the focus is on developed or on developing countries, the role of local government is now much more than that of an efficient deliverer of services. In developed countries, increasingly the issues confronted by local government demand a partnership approach working across institutions of government, the market and civil society (see Hambleton 2004 for an oft-quoted discussion of the shift from government to governance).

In developing countries, local government is often the only public institution of governance with an on-the-ground presence and at least some ability to support initiatives to develop social or economic capacity within communities. South Africa's constitution recognises the developmental role of local government. The 1998 White Paper on Local Government expressed this role as 'local government committed to working with citizens and groups within the community to find sustainable ways to meet their social, economic and material needs and improve the quality of their lives' (Department of Constitutional Development 1998: 17).

Basic proposition 2

Local government is potentially the single most critical catalytic resource for change at the community level, but unleashing its potential requires a rethinking of its role and this may be best realised through practical demonstration of what can be achieved.

This proposition specifically recognises both the magnitude of the necessary changes in local government's role and the way it operates, plus the importance of demonstrating what can and should be done through practical experience. This involves 'learning by doing', and in particular creating the means for individual local authorities to learn from their fellows both within their own jurisdictions and across the Commonwealth. Complex questions need to be addressed, such as how local governments can more effectively represent and reflect a wide range of community interests; how they are resourced and can be given (or can develop) the capacity to take on additional functions; and whether a shift in their role will be supported and respected by central governments.

Again, these are questions that face local government in both developed and developing countries, and they are explored in different ways in several of the chapters that follow. There is extensive scope for an ongoing exchange of practical experience and lessons learned among Commonwealth countries.

Basic proposition 3

An essential precondition is the shift from formal consultation to effective engagement with communities.

This proposition recognises the changing nature of the way in which many local governments work with their communities. It points to the need for a shift from the formal consultation processes often required by the statutory frameworks under which local governments operate, to a much more collaborative approach to working with local communities. In developed countries in particular, research has highlighted the changing ways in which people wish to engage with their local council: many no longer wish to rely on electing council members as their principal means of engagement, instead seeking a variety of forms of consumer, network and participatory governance (Haus and Sweeting 2006; Schaap et al. 2009).

Adoption by the colloquium of these three propositions led to the decision to put together a collection of papers that would illustrate some of the challenges being faced in different parts of the Commonwealth, ways in which the role of local government is evolving, and practical examples of 'new' local government at work. In due course, 15 authors (in three cases two or more working in collaboration) accepted the invitation to contribute. CLGF offered encouragement, and the Commonwealth Secretariat agreed to publish the book and contribute to the costs of bringing it together, including a workshop for the authors held in early 2011.

The result is a series of chapters which contribute to understanding the changing role of local government and its relationships with central governments, and also discuss a number of initiatives aimed at improving local government's capacity and performance, as well as strengthening the bond between local government and its communities. Insights are provided into both the differing and similar challenges confronting local governments in developed and developing countries across the Commonwealth, establishing a basis for greater collaboration, especially in helping build capability in emerging systems of governance.

1.1 The emerging context

New Century Local Government may seem an ambitious title, with its implication of major change from what has gone before. The title was chosen deliberately, partly in recognition that there is indeed very significant change taking place across much of the Commonwealth, and partly with an aspirational focus. The world in which local government operates is changing dramatically as a consequence of a confluence of forces, including demographic change, the fallout from the global financial crisis, significant shifts in the patterns and location of economic growth, and the fiscal stress facing governments in most developed and many developing countries. There is both need and opportunity for local government across the Commonwealth to take stock and to play its part in leading the response.

As one example of the changing environment, it is now virtually a cliché to argue that the twenty-first century is the century of the city. In 2007 the percentage of the world's population living in urban centres passed 50 per cent. By 2050 it is expected to grow to approximately 70 per cent (United Nations Department of Economic and Social Affairs 2012). By itself, this growth in urban populations presents major challenges for local government across most of the Commonwealth. In some jurisdictions, principally in developing countries, it will be the challenge of coping with rapid urbanisation and providing the basic services needed to maintain an acceptable quality of life. In others, especially in more developed countries, it will be coping with the realisation that cross-border relations are now increasingly between major metropolitan centres rather than country to country. This has significant implications for relationships between central, subnational and local governments.

The challenges of urbanisation will be compounded by widely varying growth rates of population and economic development within individual countries, as major urban centres continue to draw in population at the expense of regional and rural areas. There is a need for effective place-based strategies in order to address the very different needs of individual communities.

This is just one change among many, but a change that underlies an important shift in perceptions of the role of local government. The growth of urban and especially metropolitan centres, and what that means in terms of the distribution of population and economic activity, has highlighted the new reality that local government cannot be treated as a broadly homogeneous set of subnational government arrangements delivering services designed to achieve broadly similar outcomes within predetermined national standards. Instead, we now increasingly realise that local government has responsibility for a wide range of highly diverse communities, facing different needs and opportunities, and requiring different locally developed strategies to address those needs.

In turn, this suggests that something more is required in terms of policies, legislation and programmes of reform than just the ongoing tinkering with local government structures that has characterised the approach of central governments (including state or provincial levels) across much the Commonwealth. Although there are still jurisdictions that evince a somewhat narrow view of the role of local government as primarily about local public services, infrastructure and regulation (evidenced, for example, by recent amendments to the *Local Government Act* in New Zealand), it is now becoming more common to see local government policy focused on the delivery of the broader outcomes which its communities seek.

Thus, in several Commonwealth countries we are seeing a growing recognition of 'local' as the pivotal node for co-ordinating delivery of a wide range of services. This is occurring for a number of reasons, including the need for cost savings, the often ponderous nature and silo mentality of centralised bureaucracies, and the scope to draw on local knowledge and networks, to encourage co-design and co-production, and to strengthen the community's own institutions. The concept is very much one of a partnership between the state, the private sector and civil society.

England has been one of the archetypes for this approach, and reveals the inherent tensions between central and local associated with it. Change began with the successive initiatives of the Blair/Brown Labour government, which came to office in 1997. These included the creation of the Greater London Authority with an elected executive mayor for London; the introduction in 2000 of a broad power for local authorities to promote community well-being, plus the establishment of Local Strategic Partnerships; and later a series of pilots of 'Total Place', the idea that public sector agencies within both central and local government should be jointly planning and resourcing local service delivery.

The coming to office of the Conservative/Liberal Democrat coalition government saw an even stronger emphasis – at least in rhetoric – on 'localism', including continued support for devolved and locally co-ordinated service delivery, but also a new emphasis on the 'Big Society', at the heart of which was a view that government had intruded too far into the lives of citizens and it was time to hand responsibility back. This was followed by 'Open Public Services', with its argument that responsibility for service delivery should be devolved, not just from the centre to the local level, but further to individuals and community groups. Thus, while the 'local' is normally conceived as local government plus a range of other formal and informal institutions, sometimes it may not involve local government at all. Under the coalition government's policies, local government could be bypassed, and some of its services could also be taken over by community organisations.

This exemplifies the tensions that arise between levels of government competing for scarce resources, and for the electoral approval of the same local and regional communities. In this book evidence of such tensions is presented in several chapters, including those on England, India, Pakistan and the Caribbean. They seem to afflict any form of decentralisation that involves a meaningful transfer of resources and decision-making authority from central to local governments, and constitute a major barrier to strengthening local governance.

A related source of tension in pursuing new directions for local government is that between continuing pursuit of the concepts and prescriptions of the New Public Management, with its focus on efficiency and the role of managers, and emerging awareness of the need to foster community governance. Efforts to ensure increasingly efficient delivery of services have seen the use of practices drawn from the corporate sector, including casting elected councillors in the role of a 'board of directors' responsible for policy and strategy, with management delegated full responsibility and a high degree of autonomy to go about implementation.

However, local government's role as an institution of local democracy, and an enabler of community governance, points to a different approach from the corporate model. In this context, elected members are expected to have an intimate knowledge of the communities they serve and the way services are being delivered. Communities, in turn, look to have a say on decisions that affect them directly – something which cannot be achieved through the normal electoral process alone. This has been emerging as an important shift for local government in a number of Australian states (McKinlay et al. 2012).

A further manifestation of changing perceptions of its role has been a heightened interest in restructuring local government, partly in response to the rise of metropolitan centres and other shifts in the distribution of population, but increasingly as a means of enhancing the strategic capability of local governments – their ability to cope in an increasingly complex and challenging environment. The latter is seen to require more robust organisations that command a broader array of resources, and that can assemble the knowledge and high-level skills needed to understand and address 'wicked' issues and problems (Aulich et al. 2011).

Compulsory restructuring of local government has been widespread across the Commonwealth, either focused on a small number of authorities or across an entire sector. A few examples follow:

- In Canada, the provinces of Ottawa and Québec have both undertaken comprehensive restructurings, best known for their impact on the major metropolitan centres of Toronto, Ottawa and Montréal, and raising important questions about the nature and functioning of metropolitan governance.

- In England, the most significant initiative has been the creation of the Greater London Authority with a powerful, popularly elected executive mayor. Successive British governments have maintained a commitment to elected mayors with greatly enhanced authority as a means of strengthening political leadership, streamlining decision-making and imparting a stronger focus on strategy. However, the shift to elected mayors has been made voluntary, requiring a local referendum, and few have succeeded.

- In Australia, most states have undertaken extensive restructuring of their local government sectors. Queensland's was the most recent, completed in 2008. Like England, Queensland has also sought to extend the powers and responsibilities of mayors, and the Local Government Act was again amended accordingly in 2009. Mayors now lead policy development, play a significant role in formulating budgets and may direct both the chief executive and the next level of senior managers. For many years all mayors in Queensland have been popularly elected, while the Lord Mayor of Brisbane has long wielded executive powers.

- In New Zealand, following a major royal commission, the government implemented a radical restructuring of local government in the Auckland region in 2010, replacing a number of authorities with a single unitary council now responsible for all local government functions for one-third of New Zealand's population. The new mayor has what might be described as 'semi-executive' powers (see Chapter 12). More recently the Local Government Act has been amended to streamline the process of local government amalgamations, with the obvious intention of reducing the number of councils, and to give all mayors power similar to those of the Auckland mayor. As in Queensland, all New Zealand mayors have been popularly elected for several decades.

- In the Caribbean, local government reform has seen both consolidation and fragmentation of local government areas (see Chapter 2). The establishment of the Portmore Municipality in Jamaica is a particularly interesting case, involving partial excision of an area and transfer of some local government functions from an existing, much larger parish, as well as creating the position of a new, popularly elected mayor. This reflects a desire both to strengthen local leadership and to improve engagement with the local community and other key stakeholders.

- South Africa, rebuilding its institutions with the ending of apartheid, consciously adopted a new developmental model of local government, as described earlier. This move also involved a complete restructuring of local government areas, and a major reduction in their number. A key objective was to enhance the capacity of local government to support disadvantaged communities by combining previously under-serviced townships and rural areas with affluent 'white' towns and suburbs.

1.2 Issues, experience and findings

The following chapters are arranged in three sections. The aim is to link chapters that explore similar or related themes and to build up a picture of the different ways in which local government across the Commonwealth is responding to the basic propositions set out earlier. Inevitably several chapters deal with more than one of those propositions. The three sections cover:

- decentralisation, localism and intergovernment relations;

- local government finance and economic development; and

- new approaches to governance.

1.2.1 Decentralisation, localism and intergovernment relations

This first section looks at recent moves to implement policies of decentralisation and localism, including empowering both local governments and their communities as agents of local governance and development, in the very different contexts of the Caribbean, Pakistan and England.

Eris Schoburgh and Bishnu Ragoonath analyse recent moves towards democratic decentralisation and local government reform in a number of smaller Caribbean states (Jamaica, Trinidad and Tobago, St Lucia, and Antigua and Barbuda) over the past two decades. They highlight the tensions in central–local relations mentioned earlier: how decentralisation is promoted by international agencies as a way forward for developing countries, but is often seen internally as a zero-sum game in which devolution means a loss of power and resources at the centre and is therefore resisted. Central government dominance thus remains intact with only marginal reform, and continued paternalism and lack of respect towards local government and its role.

However, Schoburgh and Ragoonath also assert that an effective reform process requires more than just the development of policy by central governments. It needs engagement by local government itself, by the private sector and by civil society. In their view local governments can be criticised for failing to articulate an authoritative position on their future, and failing to seek and incorporate the views of their citizens. They argue that local governments in the region must assume a greater share of the responsibility for reform outcomes – or the lack of progress. In particular, they make the case that local government must look beyond simply calling for additional funding and persuade the private and not-for-profit sectors in the region to become more involved in local affairs.

These are important lessons for local government in other jurisdictions, emphasising the need for local government itself and other local stakeholders to lead the debate about the future of local governance, rather than simply waiting for the centre to develop its proposals. They also reflect one of this book's central themes: that local government must develop new ways of working to respond to the challenges it now faces.

In the second chapter of this section, Munawwar Alam provides an overview of the history of local government in Pakistan post-independence, drawing lessons from the alternation between civilian and military governments. He finds that military governments have been far more willing to embrace decentralisation and strengthening of local government, perhaps because they are less fearful of the loss of their own power than are elected civilian governments, and also welcome the legitimacy to be gained by nurturing democracy and citizen participation at the local level. Alam notes that this phenomenon is not unique to Pakistan, quoting comparable experience in Ghana and The Gambia.

Alam focuses in particular on the Devolution of Power Plan (DOPP) introduced by the Musharraf military government, which he sees as the first major and thoroughgoing attempt at decentralisation in Pakistan's history. The DOPP embraced the concept of subsidiarity, with a significant transfer of power from the provinces (Pakistan being a federation) to the districts and lower levels. This was matched by electoral reform (notably encouragement of women's participation), and reforms to the civil service and police. A further important element was the establishment of Citizen Community Boards (CCBs) as a form of community governance, promoting local input to development planning and self-help initiatives. The DOPP also saw the emergence of local government associations as a vehicle for advancing the sector.

Alam concludes that decentralisation is inherently neither good nor bad. It can improve the efficiency and responsiveness of the public sector, and also contribute to significant social change, but strong political will and leadership are needed to create and maintain conducive conditions for institutional change. Thus the success or failure of decentralisation programmes depends on a country's broader democratic and political culture. Parallel institutional development needs to be ongoing, and in Pakistan military governments have been more willing to accept this challenge. Since the return to civilian government in 2009, the provinces have reasserted their power over local government, and local elections have been repeatedly deferred. Albeit in a very different context, there are some obvious echoes of the Caribbean experience.

The next two chapters consider the recent history of local government reform in England and, as foreshadowed earlier, here too can evidence be found of the inter-government tensions inherent in the pursuit of decentralisation, devolution and localism. Nigel Keohane considers the lessons that can be learned from the latest development in more than a decade of endeavours to achieve a measure of devolution from central government to local government within England, namely community-based budgeting. He sets this in the context described earlier: the 1997–2010 Labour government's various initiatives aimed at a degree of devolution to local government and 'joined-up' delivery of services; followed by the Conservative/Liberal Democrat coalition's pursuit of localism and the Big Society, with its focus on far-reaching devolution that goes beyond local government to community organisations and potentially even individuals. In part, this more radical approach reflected the failure of Labour's reforms to make any significant impact on England's highly centralised system of government, especially when compared with the progress made through devolution of real power to the new Scottish parliament and Welsh assembly. The pursuit of 'joined-up' government had been frustrated by the imposition of uniform national targets, despite increasing differentiation of local needs, and by departmental and professional silos.

Keohane reviews what is very much work in progress, but which reveals the practical and cultural difficulties of managing complex change involving a number of different elements of the public sector bureaucracy. He also highlights the research evidence suggesting that greater devolution and interagency collaboration in service delivery can both achieve significant savings and produce better outcomes. The former is a key motivating factor in the coalition government's approach: grants to local government have been cut by 28 per cent over four years. The English experience may thus be seen on the one hand as a cautionary tale highlighting the difficulty of achieving 'real' devolution; but on the other as an insight into the scale of the potential benefits – if new ways of delivering services can avoid the downside risks of such severe funding cuts. Keohane concludes that, in times of economic hardship and fiscal constraint, UK governments appear to think that the potential benefits justify any risk involved.

Mike Bennett and Kevin Orr then seek to place the challenges of localism in a long-term historical context. They view the tension between central and local as a permanent state of affairs, taking on different colourations depending on the ideology of the age, but persistent nonetheless. Looking back several centuries, this is illustrated by Henry VII's endeavours to bring local governance more under the control of the central state, rather than individual feudal lords. It is an experience that highlights a common theme: the interplay between the centre's need to control and its dependence on local compliance – with an element of discretion always present because of the inherent limitations associated with managing from the centre.

Bennett and Orr carry their discourse forward to what they see as the present ambivalence around localism. This is explored by contrasting the persistent promotion of 'localism', as a mantra for decentralisation, with a programme of implementation that is seen by some as reinforcing central control. The associated legislation gave local government a general power of competence, but also incorporated some 136 new opportunities for the Secretary of State to intervene in local affairs, prompting the president of the Local Government Association to observe that the bill actually centralised more powers than it localised. Bennett and Orr conclude that in all likelihood 'politics as usual' will continue between central and local actors and institutions in the ongoing struggle to promote their own ideas and interests. That effectively sums up the key messages of all four chapters in this first section.

1.2.2 Local government finance and economic development

The second section comprises three chapters. They focus first on how local government is funded. This remains one of the most fundamental issues for the sector's future, whether in terms of supporting the infrastructure needed to underpin the growth of modern cities and regions, or finding new ways to use property taxes to promote developmental objectives. This developmental theme also encompasses the further issue of how local government relates to the informal economy.

Om Prakash Mathur considers the prospects for adequate funding of Indian municipalities in a context of rapid urban growth and a significant infrastructure deficit. As is typically the case with federal polities, in India local government is primarily the responsibility of the states, but it is the federal government that commands the resources necessary to support development and in particular to provide essential urban infrastructure and services. Increasingly, this is leading to tensions between all three spheres, as the states have been slow to implement national policies (sanctioned by a constitutional amendment and supported with considerable funding) that tend to shift the balance of power towards local governments.

Meanwhile, municipalities simply cannot cope with the pressures they face. Their taxation base is inadequate and they have failed to realise the revenue potential created by rapid economic growth. As a result, their own-source revenues are minimal relative to their expenditure needs. This deficiency is exacerbated by poor financial management and limited accountability for their actions.

Mathur thus points to one of India's major dilemmas as it seeks to maintain economic growth and improve living standards. In highly urbanised societies, economic growth is crucially dependent on the quality and functioning of the urban environment, which in turn depends on municipal governments both having and utilising own-source revenues – in addition to grants – that match their responsibilities to provide infrastructure and services. This requires a concerted multi-tier effort to bring about speedy implementation of India's established financial reform agenda, and to ensure that local government can play its proper role in the management of the country's burgeoning metropolises.

Jaap de Visser considers a different but related aspect of local government financing, namely the potential to use local rates (property tax) as a tool for achieving socio-economic goals within the South African framework of 'developmental local government'. This is articulated in South Africa's constitution and by the 1998 White Paper on Local Government. The objective is a system of local government committed to working with citizens and communities to find sustainable ways to meet their social, economic and material needs and improve the quality of their lives. There is a clear expectation that municipalities will apply property taxes in such a way as to achieve developmental goals such as reducing poverty, facilitating access to economic opportunities and encouraging sustainable use of resources – as well as to generate essential revenue.

De Visser reviews the rating policies of South Africa's 20 largest municipalities in order to assess the effectiveness of their use of property taxation as a developmental instrument. His overall finding is that, although the concept has merit, implementation can be extremely challenging. Among the many problems he identifies are the absence of a consistent approach to property valuation (with some municipalities effectively having no data) and the lack of sufficient technical expertise both to develop and to implement sophisticated rating policies and systems (are they well targeted and likely to achieve the intended results?). Skills shortages also lie at the heart of broader deficiencies in financial management across local government.

Simpler initiatives appear to work well, such as the exclusion from rating of low-value residential property, and there is evident potential to explore a number of other options, such as use of differential rating to redistribute wealth and to help achieve land-use planning objectives. Nonetheless, there is also a risk that overcomplicated rating systems will result in loss of transparency and accountability, and that offering too many concessions will significantly reduce revenues.

On the whole, however, de Visser concludes that technical and policy-making capability is a dominant issue, and one that should not be underestimated:

> *A key lesson for other jurisdictions would be that the successful deployment of property rating as a developmental instrument is contingent on the provision of strong support to municipalities. This should include a robust legal framework that provides the necessary tools to creatively use property rating, insists on transparent policy-making and demands good administration. However, because expertise in rating administration is hard to come by, particularly in a developmental context, support needs to go further.*

Alison Brown explores a different aspect of the developmental role of local government, but one that also raises the issue of capability as a central concern: local government's role in respect of the informal economy. She presents three case studies of experience in Durban, Dar es Salaam and India. Clement Stone's urban regime theory is used as a lens through which to examine experience, drawing particularly on his insight that lower-status groups are weakly positioned to contribute to governance. This leads to two questions: first, how can lower-status populations mobilise as active partners for change; and, second, under what conditions can local government and non-government actors partner to expand opportunities?

All three case studies highlight the problem of the natural alliance between local politicians and local elites whose interests often run counter to, for example, supporting and enabling the informal economy, especially in highly visible activities such as street vending. Brown points to the often-held view among civic leaders that the international status and image of their cities demands that they be 'cleaned up', notably when they are about to host major events. This subverts the vital contribution of the informal economy to city life and community welfare.

Her work identifies a number of practical issues whose resolution should contribute a great deal to the willingness and capability of local councils to facilitate informal economy activity. First is addressing the absence of data: without an awareness of the significant contribution the informal economy can make, the incentive to support it may be lacking. Next is the question of council revenue: local street traders may be able to pay a relatively high proportion of their income in fees, but the absolute amounts may be small, requiring cost-effective collection systems which may be beyond the capability of individual local authorities. A third issue concerns the placement of responsibility for regulating the informal economy within the local authority's organisation: place it with the division responsible for traffic management, and street trading becomes a problem to be solved rather than an economic opportunity to be grasped.

Brown concludes by proposing that local government requires an attitudinal shift in the exercise of its powers and responsibilities, so that it grasps the potential value of the informal economy and how it can facilitate its development as part of global value chains. This links back to the idea that local government's role goes beyond service delivery, to holding powers in trust for communities and supporting them in pursuing their goals. It also means a shift from positioning local government as an outpost of central administration to one of community leadership in enhancing local well-being.

1.2.3 New approaches to governance

The book's final section includes four chapters that examine experience from more developed Commonwealth countries in what may broadly be termed 'new approaches to governance'. These cover the need for effective regional co-operation, the increasing focus on strategic planning, new frameworks for service delivery and the evolving role of mayors.

Brian Walisser, Gary Paget and Michelle Dann and reflect on the experience of four decades of the development of British Columbia's regional districts – flexible groupings of municipalities that have come together to undertake shared services and other forms of mutual co-operation. They also consider the complexities and challenges that arise when matters which need to be addressed regionally entail a clash of local interests, and thus cannot be addressed purely on the basis of co-operative action to achieve mutual benefit.

British Columbia's regional districts are one of the lesser-known success stories of intra-local authority collaboration in the development of shared services. Walisser and colleagues explain how and why regional districts have evolved into quasi-governmental providers of a wide range of services to their local authority members (and occasionally beyond).

However, not all region-wide decisions necessarily result in mutual benefit for the parties involved. Walisser and colleagues offer valuable reflections on what should happen when the incentive of mutual benefit is insufficient to overcome legitimate differences, observing that, if forms of governance are designed solely to optimise outcomes for individual localities, horizontal and vertical bonds between the relevant institutions at a regional scale usually remain weak and fragile. They conclude by proposing that future pathways to effective regional governance must focus on enhancing regional leadership and co-ordination, expanding the regional decision-making 'toolkit' and developing new techniques of 'meta-governance' – the orchestration of complexity and plurality.

Michael Reid considers local government's use of strategic planning, concentrating on New Zealand experience since the restructuring of local government in 1989, but making extensive comparisons with practice in Australia, especially New South Wales, England and South Africa. He observes that New Zealand's 1989 reforms created larger, more capable local governments, which were willing and able to adopt new approaches to governance. By the mid-1990s most had voluntarily developed strategic plans.

Since then, successive New Zealand governments have legislated to require councils to prepare a range of long-term strategies. Legislation in 1996 introduced long-term financial strategies (LTFS); these had a minimum ten-year timeframe, but were largely unconnected with other forms of strategic planning. A new government came in to office in 1999. One of its objectives was a thorough overhaul of local government legislation, and its concerns included this lack of connection between the LTFS and broader social, cultural and environmental agendas for local government.

This led to a new Local Government Act, which came into force in 2002. The Act replaced the LTFS with the Long-Term Council Community Plan (LTCCP), still including financial forecasts but now to integrate the broad spectrum of a local government's activities based on 'community outcomes'. These were long-term goals for each locality identified through extensive community and stakeholder consultations led by the council, but not confined to local government's responsibilities. The idea was to promote a 'whole-of-government' and 'whole-of-community' approach to achieving desired outcomes. This echoes similar initiatives in the UK and South Africa.

Practice in identifying community outcomes varied widely. Some councils adopted comprehensive processes, sometimes run independently, which were effective in engaging a wide cross-section of their communities. Others went through a much more formalistic process with little real practical engagement. Experience with implementation of LTCCPs has been similarly diverse, but marked by a widespread failure to secure sufficient commitment from other parties, especially central government agencies.

However, Reid's primary concern is increasing emphasis of both legislation and practice on accountability and compliance in the processes of strategic planning. He highlights the risks involved in seeking to use strategic plans, both to articulate community aspirations and visions, and as a means of ensuring sound management. He notes, for example, that the statutory requirement for draft LTCCPs to be signed off by the council's auditor resulted in highly complex documents dominated by the demands of transparency and accountability and a focus on prudent stewardship of assets. Thus, when long-term strategic plans are seen as mechanisms for accountability and financial management, their core purpose – that of innovative engagement with citizens about possible futures – may be squeezed into the background.

Peter McKinlay also draws on recent New Zealand experience, in this case relating to the use of local government-owned companies, and other arms-length entities, to manage local government assets and services in Westminster-tradition countries. He identifies the opportunities these instruments provide, not only for service delivery but also to enhance local democracy.

The chapter begins with a review of experience in a number of other jurisdictions, notably European countries where the use of local government-owned companies is by and large routine, and with little focus on them as a special case requiring enhanced monitoring or compliance arrangements. McKinlay then explores experience in selected Westminster jurisdictions, including England, British Columbia and Australian states. Typically, their focus has been on the conditions precedent to establishing an arms-length entity, rather than on post-establishment governance and accountability.

The remainder of the chapter examines the unique New Zealand model for managing relationships between local councils and arms-length entities. McKinlay argues that the strength of the model lies in its focus on the importance of post-establishment governance, including clear specification of the respective roles of elected members representing the council as owner, and members of the governing body of the arms-length entity. This includes the evolution of good practice, which emphasises relationship management rather than compliance. He concludes that the New Zealand model arguably represents the most successful regime among Westminster jurisdictions for post-establishment governance of local authority-owned or controlled arms-length entities, not just in the commercial sphere but as a means for improving community engagement and facilitating co-production. It is certainly an approach that could be applied in many Commonwealth countries.

In the book's final chapter, Graham Sansom considers the evolving role of mayors, with a particular emphasis on recent developments in Australia. He notes the extent to which executive or 'semi-executive' mayors are now common in local government, both in developed jurisdictions within Europe and North America (principally the United States), and in a number of developing-country jurisdictions such as South Africa, and goes on to examine emerging practice in England, New Zealand and Australia itself.

Sansom seeks to place recent developments in the role of mayors within a conceptual framework of governance, strategic planning and leadership. His overarching theme is that there is a need for new approaches to political governance, recognising among other things the need for effective community leadership to safeguard and advance local interests, and the benefits which a mayoral mandate can bring to the formulation and consistent implementation of strategic plans and budgets. Mayors can also lead community engagement, facilitate new approaches to community governance and speak with authority in intergovernmental relations.

Directly or indirectly, the chapter discusses the impact of New Public Management on the governance of local authorities, with its emphasis on the separation of the policy role of the governing body from the implementation role of management. Sansom questions whether this reflects reality, and joins others in suggesting that in practice the shift in the 'balance of power' towards management may have detracted from good governance. In particular, Australian experience highlights the importance of the mayor–chief executive relationship, and the need to review and restate their respective roles so that their efforts are more effectively combined. Sansom's chapter rounds off the book's exploration of its three central propositions. It reflects a view that the core role of local government lies in facilitating the good governance of its communities, including providing sound leadership in articulating and promoting the achievement of important community goals. In doing so, it concludes that those objectives cannot be achieved unless the political arm of local government has the capacity to discharge its responsibilities effectively alongside those of management. To build that capacity, the role of the mayor seems a good place to start.

1.3 Fresh ideas for a new century?

This book by no means pretends to offer a comprehensive and coherent picture of all the issues facing local government across the Commonwealth: it can fairly be described as a 'patchwork quilt' of information and ideas. However, collectively the chapters present most of the key challenges and suggest many ways forward.

An overriding message is the need to contemplate quite radical changes – in some instances revolutionary rather than evolutionary – to ensure that local government becomes or remains 'fit for purpose'. Whether democratic decentralisation, localism, responsive local and regional governance, and efficient and effective service delivery can be pursued successfully through what might be described as 'conventional' institutions of local government is open to question. This applies equally to well-established and seemingly robust systems of local government in some Commonwealth countries, and emerging systems in others.

Challenges to current orthodoxies may arise from financial pressures and lack of resources, from questioning of local government's democratic legitimacy and representativeness, from failings in leadership and local policy development, from a clash of local interests within regions, and from difficult central–local relations. There are also signs of a growing belief in some quarters that, all too often, local government has failed to realise its potential, and that there may be better ways of achieving societal goals.

Across much of the Commonwealth, the later years of the twentieth century saw the enthusiastic embrace by both central and local governments of the precepts of economic rationalism and New Public Management. In many cases, the result has been significant improvements in the way local governments are managed, although perhaps at some cost to the values of local democracy. However, it appears the time has now come for a more far-reaching stocktake and reappraisal of the purpose, role and prospects of local government as it faces the changing dynamic of a new century. Its 'toolkit' needs to be expanded to give greater weight to emerging ideas about community governance; to address complex, 'wicked' problems; to cope with scarce and often declining resources in the public sector; and to achieve better outcomes for local communities through more productive intergovernment relations, as well as partnerships with the private sector and civil society.

Several recent reports on local government reform in Australia have focused on the concept of building 'strategic capacity'. In 2007, the Queensland Local Government Reform Commission argued that the challenges facing that state '… require governments of all levels to be high capacity organisations with the requisite knowledge, creativity and innovation to enable them to manage complex change…' (Local Government Reform Commission 2007: 5). This theme was picked up in a subsequent overview of 'consolidation' in local government by the Australian Centre of Excellence for Local Government (Aulich et al. 2011; Aulich et al. 2013). The centre's work pointed to other key dimensions of strategic capacity explored in this book, notably an adequate financial base; sound governance practices; and the ability to undertake effective strategic planning, regional collaboration and intergovernment relations.

A further – and critical – dimension suggested in this book is that local governments require the skills and capacity to facilitate community governance and self-help, based on an understanding of their role as stewards of community values, authority and resources. In the final analysis, local government needs engaged stakeholders and constituents to underpin its very existence. If councils cannot build successful local coalitions, they are vulnerable to being bypassed by central governments seeking solutions to their own problems. And if local government is bypassed, who can speak with any authority for local communities?

This is an issue not just for local governments and their constituents, but also for state, provincial and national governments. The chapters that follow include evidence of the unique role which local government could play in facilitating the better design, targeting and delivery at a community level of services provided by those 'higher' levels. This applies especially to the 'wicked problems', which have resisted most attempts at top-down solutions. In addition, the fiscal challenges faced by central governments throughout the Commonwealth should give them a vested interest in strengthening local government to help find and deliver better ways of meeting community needs.

However, while there is a growing realisation that the structures and modus operandi of central governments have severe limitations when it comes to dealing with many of society's problems, the opportunity this may provide for local government must be tempered by the recognition that it too has work to do before it can credibly present itself as integral to new solutions.

This chapter began with three propositions. To conclude, we pose three questions about the future of local government as we head through seemingly troubled times towards the middle of the century:

- Will local government more or less as we know it prosper by adapting to a changing environment and by making itself indispensable to its citizens, to central governments and to other key partners; or by failing to adapt will it instead decline in significance where it is already well established, and fail to flourish where it is still in its infancy?

- Can local governments think creatively and find their own solutions to the challenges they face, or will they continue to have solutions imposed on them? Will they make the necessary effort to enhance their leadership and managerial skills, strengthen their knowledge base and become high-capacity learning organisations?

- Will there be a 'New Century Local Government' that is recognised as being far more than the provider of basic services; that becomes the primary agent and true leader and representative of its communities, responding creatively to local and regional needs? Or will local governments be just one of many local and regional organisations competing for legitimacy, for scarce resources and for central government support?

Of course, local government's future is not entirely – or in some cases even largely – in its own hands. Everywhere it is subject to the attitudes and decisions of central governments (national or provincial), and in developing countries much depends on how local government ranks in the eyes of international agencies and donors. In this context, the Commonwealth can play a critical role in supporting the goals of democratic decentralisation and localism from both central and local perspectives; promoting fresh thinking about and among local governments; and ensuring that new ideas are explored and that lessons from the varied experiences of member countries are widely disseminated and understood. Hopefully this book will make a worthwhile contribution to that endeavour.

Note

1   Viewed at: www.un.org/millenniumgoals (accessed 25 May 2013).

References

Aulich, C, M Gibbs, G Gooding, P McKinlay, S Pillora and G Sansom (2011), *Consolidation in Local Government: A Fresh Look, Volume 1 – Report*, Australian Centre of Excellence for Local Government, University of Technology, Sydney, available at: www.acelg.org.au/upload/program1/1320885841_Consolidation_Final_Report_Vol_1_web.pdf (accessed 25 May 2013).

Aulich, C, G Sansom and P McKinlay (2013), 'A Fresh Look at Municipal Consolidation in Australia', *Local Government Studies*, May, available at: www.tandfonline.com/doi/abs/10.1080/03003930.2013.775124 (accessed 25 May 2013).

Department of Constitutional Development (1998), *White Paper on Local Government*, Government Printers, Pretoria, South Africa.

Hambleton, R (2004), *Beyond New Public Management – City Leadership, Democratic Renewal and the Politics of Place*, paper to the City Futures International Conference, Chicago, Illinois, USA, 8–10 July 2004.

Haus, M and D Sweeting (2006), 'Local Democracy and Political Leadership: Drawing a Map', *Political Studies*, Vol. 54 No. 2, June, 267–288.

Local Government Reform Commission (2007), *Report of the Local Government Reform Commission – Volume 1*, LGRC, State of Queensland, Australia.

McKinlay, P, S Pillora, SF Tan and A Von Tunzelmann (2012), *Evolution in Community Governance: Building on What Works*, Australian Centre of Excellence for Local Government, University of Technology, Sydney.

Schaap, L, C Geurtz, L de Graaf and N Kirsten (2009), *Innovations in Sub-National Government in Europe: A quick scan*, Netherlands' Council for Public Administration, available at: www.rob-rfv.nl/documenten/migratie/innovations_in_subnational_government_in_europe.pdf (accessed 25 May 2013).

United Nations Department of Economic and Social Affairs (2012), *World Urbanisation Prospects: The 2011 Revision – Highlights*, United Nations, New York, available at: http://esa.un.org/unup/pdf/WUP2011_Highlights.pdf (accessed 25 May 2013).

PART I. DECENTRALISATION, LOCALISM AND INTERGOVERNMENT RELATIONS

Chapter 2

Democratic Decentralisation in the Commonwealth Caribbean: Is There a Case for New Roles and Relationships?

Eris D Schoburgh and Bishnu Ragoonath

Local government reform in the Commonwealth Caribbean[1] is a manifestation of experimentation with democratic decentralisation or 'democratic local governance' (Blair 2000), which is sweeping political and administrative systems worldwide. Central to the debate is the identification of a 'democratic deficit' and a general consensus that greater citizen activism and more responsive state institutions are positively correlated (Gaventa 2004; Narayan et al. 2000; Commonwealth Foundation 1999; Ward et al. 2010).

Democratic decentralisation may fairly be described as a 'social movement' in that fundamental transformations are being wrought in institutions, organisations, policy outlook and strategies (Conyers 1986). However, specific goals and objectives differ from one country context to the next, and these diverse expressions reflect the differing ideational stances of its adherents. For instance, proponents of neoliberal ideas see democratic decentralisation as a means of reducing the erstwhile command and control orientation of the state, frequently cited as the primary source of self-serving behaviour that contributes to maladministration (Grindle 2007; Manor 1999).

The development community attaches the goal of poverty reduction to democratic decentralisation, complementing communitarian approaches and empowerment models of development. According to Blair, 'much of [democratic local governance's] attraction as a development strategy lies in its promise to include people from all walks of life in community decision making' (2000: 23). Marginalised groups such as women, cultural minorities, small business owners and small farmers are promoted as important beneficiaries of decentralisation policies. In addition to making local political office more accessible to these constituencies, democratic decentralisation widens the scope for participation. This leads to positive socio-economic outcomes such as provision of infrastructure that meets local needs, improved living conditions and enhanced economic growth (Blair 2000). Hickey and Mohan point out that this participatory approach to development 'asserts the importance of placing local realities at the heart of development interventions' with a transformative effect in that agents of development shift roles from acting as 'directive experts' to 'facilitators of local knowledge and capabilities' (2005: 8; see also Chambers 1983).

For pluralists, democratic renewal remains the essential function of decentralisation, permitting citizens to 'become more effective at rewarding and punishing the behaviour of local officials' (Grindle 2007: 7). Fung and Wright conceptualised these types of decentralisation reforms as 'empowered deliberative democracy' based on 'their potential to be radically democratic in their reliance on the participation and capacities of ordinary people, deliberative because they institute reason-based decision making and empowered since they attempt to tie action to discussion' (2001: 7). Thus democratic decentralisation is associated with skills of deliberation, consensus building and conflict resolution (Grindle 2007).

In terms of public management practice, devolving tasks performed by central government to a lower level is expected to result in higher levels of responsiveness to citizens' needs, as well as improved efficiency and effectiveness in service delivery. Grindle summarised these sentiments:

> When government administration is brought closer to those who receive services … beneficiaries of these services would become active in demanding good quality. Because those responsible for the quality of services are local, citizens will be more motivated to complain and demand improvements if services fail or decline in quality. Moreover, civil servants will have incentives to orient their behaviour toward good service provision because of the potential for public disruption and complaints from dissatisfied 'customers' (2007: 9–10).

Clearly decentralisation is at the core of contemporary state reforms and, where its democratic component is emphasised, local government reform follows closely as it offers an enabling institutional framework for deeper citizen participation and improved social outcomes.

In the Commonwealth Caribbean, local government reform takes place against a background of a growing disconnect between citizens and government, evidenced in mistrust of elected representatives and a citizenry indifferent to its rights and duties (Schoburgh 2010a). Policy overtures in the region confirm generally that one of the most enduring orthodoxies concerning local government is its perceived value as an 'enhancer' of local democracy. Although the objective realities of democratic practices cast considerable doubt on this orthodoxy, pressures for reform emanating from international agencies are based on the premise that local government is not merely necessary, but is also the most convenient realm for the practice of democratic governance (Schoburgh 2010a). Caribbean policy-makers have thus evinced a strong commitment to 'shoring up the fortunes' of local government. This translates into addressing the outstanding matter of local government's rickety status in intergovernmental relations in the region. The democratic value of local government has found expression in official policies signalling both the philosophical basis of reform and strategic directions for implementation.

The intended directions of democratic decentralisation are clear:

- a shift from unicentrism in which central government dominates all political and policy interactions, to polycentrism in which there is a multiplicity of actors, each assuming a leadership role at different points in the process;

- clarification of the status and role of local government;

- a new role for the centre (central government); and

- a shift from central–local relations to intergovernmental relations in which local government is treated as an equal partner in a web of institutional interactions.

The crucial questions are:

- To what extent have reform policies and strategies demonstrated these values?

- Have local governments used the 'window of opportunity' created by reform proposals to press their claim for a change in roles and relationships?

- Is civil society, the new entrant and the actor on which democratic governance rests, seduced by the new policy direction?

- How does central government envision its place in the new context of democratic decentralisation?

These questions will form the basis of a comparative analysis of the attempts by Caribbean governments to institute democratic decentralisation. Using local government reform proposals and policies as our frame of analysis, we examine policy formulation and implementation in Jamaica, Trinidad and Tobago,[2] St Lucia, and Antigua and Barbuda. The chapter seeks to provide useful insights into the political economy of reform in the region, and to generate further debate about alternative strategies to achieve sustainable reform outcomes.

2.1 Analytic method

Table 2.1 sets out a 'democratic decentralisation assessment framework' (DDAF) to guide our analysis of local government reform proposals, policies and programmes in the country cases. This draws on Brinkerhoff and Crosby's (2002) implementation task framework; the assessment by Blair and the United States Agency for International Development (USAID) (1997) of democratic local governance; and Rondinelli, McCullough and Johnson's (1989) political economy framework.

The DDAF uses a set of indicators that are grouped under four headings:

- *Policy design and interpretation* concerns the technical scope of the policy.

- *Policy orientation* gauges the degree of congruence between action (implementation) and intention (pronouncement).

- *Political motivation* concerns the rationale for the policy.

- *Institutional setting* examines the task environment.

Assessment was carried out by applying a nominal rating scale with values from –5 to +5 depending on the extent to which an indicator is reflected in actual policies and programmes. The framework thus permits us to compare and contrast the disparate reform experiences under common themes. Results are presented in Table 2.2, later in this chapter.

Table 2.1 Democratic decentralisation assessment framework

Indicators	Measures
Policy design and interpretation	
Policy meets causal and contextual best-fit criteria	• Appropriate definition of problem • Principal causal linkages to problem are understood • Realistic performance indicators and timelines established • Policy marketed for support by key principals (funders; implementers; beneficiaries)
Policy includes fundamental elements for goal attainment	• Political, administrative and fiscal decentralisation articulated
Policy orientation	
Support and commitment to reform by line ministries	• Implementation plan developed and activated • Technical expertise provided and continuous assessment conducted • Programme reformulated
Willingness to transfer functions to local level	• Identification and commencement of divestiture of functions • Local problem-solving enabled
Willingness to assist in capacity building efforts at local level	• Identification and commencement of divestiture of functions • Local problem solving enabled
Political motivation	
Strong and committed political leadership (bi-level)	• Steady course of implementation of activities • Ventilation of local perspective
Willingness to share power, authority and financial resources	• Principles of co-governance (competence, subsidiarity) explored • Supportive institutional mechanisms established
Facilitation of civil society groups' participation in local planning and management	• Participatory mechanisms established and operational • Participatory mechanisms integrated into local policy process
Institutional setting	
Mechanisms that foster accountable local leadership	• Quality of local electoral process • Complementary measures established, e.g. participatory budgeting, citizens' juries, mandatory consultative processes
Community empowerment	• Perceptions of empowered citizenry as zero-sum or positive sum game[3]
Nature of political competition	• Degree of influence of party politics on local government
Constitutional amendments	• Amendments in support of reform goal
Orientation of private and civil sectors	• Strong and independent civil society organisations • Level of private sector interest in local government

2.2 The varied dimensions of democratic decentralisation

Democratic decentralisation is a multidimensional process that is geared towards specific outcomes or *ends*, but it is also a *means* to these ends. In the first instance it is the most widely perceived end-state of a broad range of actions taken in the name of 'decentralisation', which seek to redistribute power, authority and responsibility between levels of government and administration (Schoburgh 2006; Alfonso 1997; Handler 1996; Rondinelli et al. 1989). Within the broad ambit of decentralisation, such actions have typically embraced:

- *de-concentration*, which involves a redistribution of administrative responsibilities and some authority to regional offices of central government;

- *delegation*, which entails the transfer of management authority for specific functions to semi-autonomous agencies; and

- *devolution*, which implies the creation of autonomous governmental bodies at a lower level.

As a means to an end, democratic decentralisation may be interpreted as either 'part of an administrative mentality or as part of a democratic way of thinking' (Blair 1995, cited in Manor 1999: 53–54). Here the logic of democratic decentralisation is its contribution to long-term goals such as improved welfare, and its potential to enhance capacity in local government. Both the *ends* and *means* interpretations are evident in Blair's discussion:

> Through participation [democratic local governance] promises to increase popular input into what local government does, and through accountability it bids to increase popular control over what local government has done or left undone ... it can improve local service delivery ... it can contribute significantly to poverty reduction (2000: 22).

Following Jun and Wright (1996), Schoburgh categorised decentralisation into (a) *administrative decentralisation* – flexibility in administrative organisation to facilitate delegation of authority and responsibility – and (b) *political decentralisation* – power sharing between levels of government. She then argued that, although administrative decentralisation compared with political decentralisation may appear to be 'soft' in terms of the degree of power and authority that is transferred to a lower level, it may nonetheless 'be linked with complex aims such as democracy-building and social control' (2006: 9–10). The prevailing paradigm of governance on which current reforms are based necessarily entails the simultaneous pursuit of political and administrative changes, propelled by globalising economic, social and political forces that challenge conventional approaches to state and governmental organisation. Thus decentralisation processes can be seen to have evolved from an emphasis on de-concentrating hierarchical structures of government and bureaucracies, through power-sharing models that promote democratisation and market liberalisation as an intermediate stage, to the current position of facilitating wider participation of the private sector and civil society organisations. Hence Blair (2000) argues that participation and accountability are the concepts that make democratic decentralisation distinguishable from earlier forms.

This evolution represents a response to the concepts and ideas advocated by the public choice school, and the doctrines of 'new public management' that have vigorously promoted citizen participation as a common thread. Political decentralisation is underpinned by a view of governance reform in which governments will aim to create channels and mechanism for public participation in decision-making, abide by the rule of law, increase transparency in public procedures and hold officials accountable (Cheema and Rondinelli 2007: 6). The new administrative mandate rides on the belief that governments should create the context for local citizens to solve their own problems, through deregulating and privatising those activities that could be carried out more efficiently and effectively by the private and civil sectors (Cheema and Rondinelli 2007: 4; Osborne and Gaebler 1992).

However, although the concept of democratic decentralisation embraces both political and administrative processes, it does not erase the likelihood of conflict emerging between the two. Different actors may pursue different courses depending on the assumptions on which their actions are based. For example, central government officials often prefer administrative decentralisation, while local policy and administrative leaders support political decentralisation. While both subscribe to the critical purpose of democratic decentralisation as a means to promote development and nurture participation and accountable governance, this does not diminish the likelihood of stalemate when they pursue their goals independently (see, for example, Shah and Thompson 2004).

Furthermore, although there is much enthusiasm about democratic decentralisation, the unsatisfactory rate of success with these reforms, especially in developing countries, suggests an important reality – as observed astutely by Manor:

> Devolution or democratic decentralisation on its own is likely to fail. Democratic authorities at lower levels in political systems will founder if they lack power and resources – meaning both financial resources and the administrative resources to implement development projects (1999: 7).

Hence democratic decentralisation must be both a process of *transferring* power, authority and responsibility from a higher to a lower level of government and administration, and one of *sharing* of authority and resources for collective goals. Administrative and political changes need to be supplemented by fiscal decentralisation,[4] which encompasses revenue sharing between central and local governments and increased fiscal autonomy at subnational levels, as well as economic decentralisation that promotes market liberalisation, deregulation, privatisation and public–private partnership arrangements (Cheema and Rondinelli 2007; Manor 1999). Taken together, these varying types of decentralisation hold out the promise of sustainable outcomes.

Figure 2.1 seeks to capture the many dimensions of democratic decentralisation, confirming that it is indeed a complex process. Irrespective of the overarching scheme a government adopts – whether political or administrative decentralisation – a combination of many factors will influence the ultimate nature and extent of discretionary decision-making at the local level. Figure 2.1 also highlights the reality

Figure 2.1 The process of democratic decentralisation

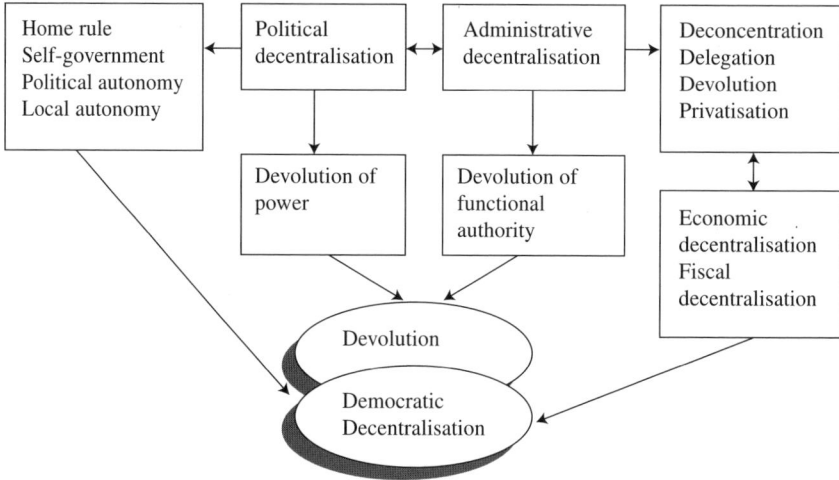

that political power-sharing is at the core of any scheme of decentralisation, and that reluctance to share power in any meaningful sense will in many instances lead to failed reforms.

2.3 Goals and strategies in the Caribbean

If reforms were to be assessed in terms of whether visions and goals for democratic decentralisation are in synchrony with global trends and respond to domestic priorities, then Caribbean governments would score highly. Consider the following extracts from policies and programmes. We start with Jamaica, which in 1993 commenced a comprehensive programme of local government reform as part of a broader and deeper process of state and governmental modernisation (Ministry of Local Government [Jamaica] 2002). The contemporary period of local government reform is outlined in Ministry Paper 8 of 1993 and Ministry Paper 7 of 2003.

The policy envisions:

> … strong and vibrant local government as essential to the attainment of a society in which all citizens enjoy real opportunities to fully and directly participate in and contribute to the management and development of local communities (Ministry of Local Government [Jamaica] 2003: 1).

However, this declaration must be placed against the backdrop of a history of institutional neglect of, and negative policy encroachments on, local government. This prompted the Jamaican government to state an unequivocal position on the value of local government, and to acknowledge that dismantling or downgrading local government is not the best approach to dealing with its past poor performance. The preferred strategy is to identify the issues that contribute to local government's problems and to devise appropriate solutions (Ministry of Local Government [Jamaica] 1993: 3). Nevertheless, as discussed later, the political environment in Jamaica is not always characterised by consensus among major political parties on the value and role of local government.

Trinidad and Tobago's local government reform policy dates from a 1990 proposal – *The Decentralisation Process: Regional Administration and Regional Development*. It aims to:

> … free the people at the community level to serve and assist each other and to better organise themselves to serve their communities and make their country a better place to live (Ministry of Works, Infrastructure and Decentralisation [Trinidad and Tobago] 1990: 2).

Local government is valued as a medium through which to channel co-operative community and economic development using a regional strategy. Initially the emphasis was on administrative decentralisation, but the draft 2009 *White Paper on Local Government Reform* left little doubt about the long-term intent of the policy, namely to 'facilitate the transformation and modernisation of local communities by empowering citizens to participate in the decision-making process' (Ministry of Local Government [Trinidad and Tobago] 2006: iii). And, like Jamaica, Trinidad and Tobago locates local government reform in a national programme of socio-economic transformation geared towards achieving developed-country status by 2020.

In St Lucia the uneasy accommodation of local government along with failed attempts at 'decentralisation' led in 1997 to the development of a *Green Paper on Local Government Reform*, which announced a new vision for that level (Ministry of Community Development, Culture, Local Government and Cooperatives [St Lucia] 2000). The goal of 'a highly autonomous, democratic community institution' sits on five pillars:

* accountability to the community;

* responsiveness to local needs and demands;

* provision of a wide range of services to local citizenry;

* partnership with central government in the processes of socio-economic development and poverty eradication;

* contribution to overall socio-economic welfare.

Among the values that inform the government's philosophy of local government is its role in facilitating citizens' understanding of, and appreciation for, the purposes of government generally, and in enabling democratic choices at the local level.

Similarly, the benefits of a decentralised system of government that is 'democratically controlled by local communities' have been seized upon in Antigua and Barbuda, where the government has outlined plans to restructure the local government department and district councils and to enact legislation to effect what is described as 'decentralised administration' (Ministry of Labour, Public Administration and Empowerment [Antigua and Barbuda] undated). This is to take place in a context where there is no formal local government system and the Barbuda Council is the only recognisable local government body on the island.

The preceding text has provided just a few instances of policy shifts being made in respect of the subnational level across the region. Activation of these reform policies demonstrates a dramatic about-face on the part of Caribbean governments, which now designate local government as the most appropriate medium through which communities can exercise both *voice* and *choice* in how they wish to deal with local problems and issues. In addition, irrespective of precisely how democratic decentralisation or a revitalised system of local government is interpreted, four values are observed to be common across the region. These accord a new status to local government as:

- a stratagem for democratic renewal;

- a means through which to maximise social and economic welfare;

- a component of public sector modernisation; and

- a legitimate partner and viable actor in intergovernmental processes.

However, vision and goals are just the start of a potentially conflictual policy process that entails both redistribution of functions and perceived threats to the organisational, policy and political status quo. This reality becomes evident in the strategies that are employed to effect reform programmes and the outcomes that are achieved.

2.4 A focus on structures

As noted above, for Caribbean governments the ultimate measure of democratic decentralisation is empowered communities that nurture the development and institutionalisation of norms of citizen participation in local decision-making and local self-management. The approach to achieving this ideal 'local state' varies between countries and vacillates between two poles: *fragmentation* and *consolidation* of local government structures. The foremost examples of these alternative strategies are, respectively, the municipal experiment in Jamaica (Schoburgh 2010b) and regional councils in Trinidad and Tobago. To varying degrees each country's programme bears on aspects of financial and legislative reforms, institutional and organisational strengthening, and demarcation of administrative boundaries and jurisdictional authority. However, the strategic choice guiding which series of activities are implemented first depends on what is deemed most urgent.

In Jamaica, Ministry Paper 8 of 1993 accorded priority to the restoration of functions and responsibilities to local authorities, which were removed during the 1980s. This included rebuilding the representational and service delivery capacity of parishes (the principal local authorities) through a US$50 million Parish Infrastructure Development Programme, funded by the Jamaican government and the Inter-American Development Bank (Ministry of Local Government [Jamaica] 1993). Rehabilitation of parish infrastructure was not merely a necessary step in reversing institutional decline and poor performance, but also a precursor to local authorities' assumption of the leadership of the local planning and development process and thus a transformation of their role (Ministry of Local Government [Jamaica] 1993: 6). As a result, local authorities have since resumed oversight of most local services, and laws and regulations have been amended, updated and consolidated where appropriate.

Legislative action has included drafting a Local Governance Act, which along with two other pieces of legislation, the Unified Services Act and Local Government Financing and Financial Management Act (frequently referred to as the three *strategic laws*), is expected to advance the reform process.

Ministry Paper 7 of 2003 appears more discerning of the complexities involved in assigning local government a developmental role:

> The process of reform since then has led to detailed analyses of the development environment in the country and resulted in a better understanding of the complexity of the issues to be resolved in this fundamental process of governance reform (Ministry of Local Government [Jamaica] 2003: 1).

The new priority of Ministry Paper 7 of 2003 is the creation of municipal management mechanisms for discrete urban and rural 'Development Areas'. Schoburgh defines these as 'localities that exhibit great potential for economic take-off, and where social and economic activities cause spillover across functional areas of local administrative units' (2007: 169). She argues that introducing the concept of Development Areas highlights questions about the utility of the parish as a viable unit of local government in the face of changing social and economic circumstances, and may be seen as an attempt to resolve the representational problems that have arisen (ibid).

The *Jamaican Municipalities Act of 2003* was promulgated in response to these concerns. It established the Portmore Municipality as an experiment in 'community self-management, construction of norms of co-governance, and ultimately democratic local governance' (Schoburgh 2009: 110). Municipalities are a new form of more participatory local government, established within parishes and assuming some of their functions. Thus municipalisation tends towards fragmentation of current local government units in order to respond more effectively to differing local needs and aspirations. It is also a process through which to facilitate direct local democracy and responsive local political leadership, as evidenced by the adoption in Portmore of a directly elected mayor.

Parish Development Committees (PDCs) parallel the municipal experiment. In addition to their democratic mandate, they are seen as instruments for promoting local development in partnership with other state agencies as well as the private and civil sectors. Ministry Paper 7 of 2003 describes PDCs as 'mechanisms of participatory local governance' created to promote strategic planning, enhance business competitiveness and promote economic development for job creation (Ministry of Local Government [Jamaica] 2003: 7). The problem is that PDCs have not functioned in the manner anticipated. Nor have other structures such as city and town councils or area committees, which were established as standing committees of parishes to broaden participation, brought any observable change to the local policy process. Meanwhile, Business Improvement Districts, tagged as the device for business development and retention, are still at the conceptual stage. Thus, while these various mechanisms might signal important structural shifts, to date they have failed to make either the democratic or the developmental impact envisioned. Moreover, local officials appear unwilling for the most part to accommodate interventions of any form from these new entities, despite the obvious negative impact on achievement of reform goals.

Trinidad and Tobago's 1990 proposal for reform described the local government system in that country as obsolete (Ministry of Works [Trinidad and Tobago] 1990: 4). Establishment of effective local government structures emerged as an urgent activity because it could offer a means to pursue regional development. According to the proposal for reform:

> It is not enough to increase the overall level of economic activity or social facilities available in the country; it is also necessary for each area of the country to play its part in national social and economic life (ibid: 3).

Thus at the outset reform was concerned principally with defining local government boundaries. The *Municipal Corporations Act 1990* consolidated all the existing laws governing local government in Trinidad and Tobago, and was seen as 'a catalyst for transforming the local government system into relatively autonomous, financially self-sufficient, efficient and effective corporate entities, providing quality services to burgesses within a participatory framework' (ibid: 5).

In 2006 a *Draft White Paper on Local Government Reform* again placed local government structure at the top of a list of priority issues within the development agenda (Ministry of Local Government [Trinidad and Tobago] 2006). But this time 'structure' had a broader connotation than defining geographic boundaries: it was interpreted as new management systems to be developed in tandem with the new role envisaged for local government. The White Paper espoused a transformational development paradigm in which local government becomes 'a harmonising agency for local development' (ibid: 12). However, apart from the Municipal Corporations Act 1990 and Amendment Act 8 of 1992, which organised local government into nine regions, two cities and three boroughs, there has been hardly any tangible outcome. The 2006 Draft White Paper notes that local government has operated under new legislation for more than 14 years, but reform goals have not materialised (ibid: 5); hence the decision of central government to review the process within new perspectives on local government reform.

In St Lucia there is evidence of a broader agenda. The 2000 Green Paper conceptualises basic principles on which effective local government is predicated, allied to a belief that 'mere reorganisation of structures, functions and boundaries' is an insufficient base on which to give substance to these principles and thus 'radical constitutional change' is considered necessary (Ministry of Community Development [St Lucia] 2000: 9). While constitutional reform is a consideration in other local government reform programmes in the region, it is not treated with the urgency implied in St Lucia's Green Paper, which perhaps reflects the non-existence of a democratic system of local government in that country for most of the 1990s.

St Lucia's reform programme also gives primacy of place to definition of the roles and functions of local authorities, central government and civil society organisations. For reformers in St Lucia, realisation of the vision of local government as the centre of communities means clarifying both the scope and nature of intergovernmental relationships, as well as bridging the gap between government and the third sector. At the same time the manifesto that 'no control or decision should be exercised or taken by central government if such controls or decisions can be exercised/taken at the local level, with equal or greater effectiveness' (ibid: 12) offers a perspective on the principle of subsidiarity that is slowly gaining momentum across the region.

Given the absence of a formal system of local government in Antigua and Barbuda (apart from the Barbuda Council), it is difficult to locate current thinking about reform, except to suggest that concerns about over-centralisation of the policy process and the need for democratic control by local communities are gaining momentum. There have been 'talks' about establishing district councils throughout Antigua to facilitate the democratic process, better understanding of the workings of government and co-operation for social transformation at the local level. Structural reform appears to be at the top of the agenda, with early attention being paid to the Department of Local Government within the Ministry of Social Transformation. Ensuring alignment of district councils with constituency boundaries appears to be a significant objective in order to maintain the powers of Members of Parliament (MPs).

Why is reorganisation of local government structures so often the foremost concern in reform, even though it arguably has the least impact on local autonomy? Perhaps the answer lies in three factors:

- it is the easiest activity to undertake, as it poses less potent threats to established power relations;

- being the most visible, it is the shortest route to legitimising the reform process; and

- the existing institutional framework may be more accommodating, although structural change is usually accompanied by new legislation.

Regardless of the reason, structural reforms – whether to organisations or to boundaries – are certainly the most prolific output to date of attempts at democratic decentralisation in the Caribbean.

2.5 Financial reforms

The next priority in local government policy papers are financial reforms, especially for countries that have well-developed systems of local government. However, financial reform has emerged as the most contentious aspect of policy in light of its transformative potential, and because the perspectives of central government and local government officials differ as to how it should be undertaken. Generally, implementation of financial reforms is defined by incrementalism, to the chagrin of local government officials who advocate a more decisive approach to resolving the funding problems that have plagued this level of government for so long. Instead the approach has been to focus on 'maximisation of own-source revenue, enhancement of loan-raising capability and adjustments in the level of central government subvention' (Schoburgh 2007: 167). Improved asset management, loan raising and municipal bonds, as well as an appropriate formula for local government financing, are among the steps under consideration in Caribbean countries to help meet local service needs, but to date the outcomes of reform have been modest.

In Jamaica, for instance, Ministry Paper 7 of 2003 gives prominence to steps taken towards achievement of 'financial autonomy' (Ministry of Local Government [Jamaica] 2003). The establishment of the Parochial Revenue Fund (PRF), through which revenues from property taxes and motor vehicle licences are distributed so as to ensure equitable access to funding at the local level, is presented as a beacon of success. So too are the measures taken to improve revenue flows to the PRF, and to maximise local government's own-source revenues. The paper notes that inflows to the PRF from property taxes increased from 475.9 million Jamaican dollars (J$) in 1998/99 to J$645.0 million in 2001/02, while adjustments to user fees and charges saw revenues to local authorities grow from J$80.0 million in 1997/98 to J$131.7 million in 2002/02. Additionally, administrative changes to the management of local authorities' commercial portfolios produced further revenue increases, from J$10.5 million in 1998/99 to more than J$124.0 million in 2001/02. However, despite these positive results, revenues remain insufficient to meet current service needs, prompting reformers to contemplate conducting a 'revenue survey' to determine the existing revenue base for each local authority, as well as to assess the potential for increased municipal taxation (ibid: 4).

In Trinidad and Tobago, the 1990 reform proposals involved central government retaining responsibility for financing the routine operations of local authorities, providing an annual subvention to each corporation based on an approved revenue and expenditure budget (Ministry of Works [Trinidad and Tobago] 1990: 12). The concern was to formulate revenue-sharing arrangements and to identify the most equitable cost-recovery schemes for certain services such as markets, abattoirs and rental of assets. Subsequently, the 2006 Draft White Paper acknowledged that this method of financing was inadequate to support the proposed new role of local government (Ministry of Local Government [Trinidad and Tobago] 2006)). Yet the strategies outlined for redressing the funding gap appear incongruent with the vision. The plan is to develop a funding formula using demographic and infrastructural criteria; to make block funding available; and to introduce accrual accounting and more effective auditing systems to reduce waste. Also among the proposed measures are institutional arrangements to strengthen property tax collection systems, but not devolution of tax powers. Little has been achieved thus far.

Jamaica may have made greater strides in financial reform, but shares Trinidad and Tobago's muted policy stance on tax-raising powers for local government. The combined experience of the two countries suggests that financial reforms in the Caribbean at this juncture are not to be seen as a precursor to fiscal decentralisation. Reforms are meant to make local authorities more economically viable entities, thus reducing the fiscal burden on central government to fund local services, but not to lead to full local autonomy. Policy settings do not involve cessation of central government influence over budget and financial decision-making in local government, even in the face of consensus that democratic decentralisation or greater local autonomy is unattainable without fiscal reforms. Rather, the code phrase in the policies is that local authorities will be given 'greater control' over funds or sources of revenue allocated to them. Sustainable financing of local government remains an elusive objective.

Nonetheless the incremental approach to financial reforms is understandable. For not only are these reforms mightily transformative if undertaken in their entirety, but they are also complex and could lead to outcomes that derail distributional and macro-economic objectives in small vulnerable states. These considerations inform, for example, Schoburgh's examination of the application of the principle of subsidiarity to local government reform processes in the region (2010c), as well as the broader debate surrounding fiscal relations and decentralisation in developing countries (Prud'homme 1995; Ter-Minassian 1997; Tanzi 1996).

2.6 Institutional strengthening

Another key element of local government reform in the Caribbean is the state of the institutional framework. Institutional strengthening appears lower in the hierarchy of local government problems, but is still a significant dimension owing to its catalytic function in the overarching process of transformation. For example, legislative changes are critical to enable realignment of physical boundaries, as well as improvements in revenue generation. Capacity enhancement strategies, such as human resource development and increased uptake of information and communications technology, relate both to the short-term objective of improved service standards and quality, as well as to the long-term goal of the strategic repositioning of local government as an agent of development.

Unfortunately reformers still grapple with how best to resolve the seemingly perpetual dissatisfaction of communities with the performance of local authorities. Some argue that the solution resides in constitutional status for local government to protect it from the whim and fancy of central governments. Public pressure for constitutional reform has increased, but it is difficult to decipher central governments' stance on the matter, and responses vary. Of the countries under study, Jamaica appears to accept the entrenchment of local government 'in principle' as an important element of reform, but the process continues to languish. Guyana has been the sole archetype of constitutional status for local government since the 1970s, and its experience has not been a particularly good one. Local government is as marginalised in that country as it is in others where constitutional reform is now being contemplated. One may conclude that there exist more powerful forces in the operational environment that stymie the impact of constitutional status.

2.7 Does size matter?

Clearly, local government reform policies in the Caribbean are at different stages of implementation. Our assessment of outcomes thus far suggests a simple division between *starters* and *non-starters*. The former comprise those countries that have effected adjustments, however minimal, in accordance with policy pronouncements. Jamaica and Trinidad and Tobago are the most advanced of this group, but as noted earlier their programmes have been afflicted by 'stops and starts', raising doubts about the stated goal of democratic decentralisation. The *non-starters* are those countries that since assessing the problems and proffering 'best' solutions have not progressed beyond concept papers or proposals. They are exemplified by St Lucia and Antigua and Barbuda, where reforms have been aborted.

It is difficult not to see *size* as one of the limiting factors for democratic decentralisation in the Caribbean context: the description of its countries as 'small island states' suggests a myriad of difficulties in policy development and implementation (Tendler and Freedheim 1994; Fox and Aranda 1996). Smallness of area and population was the justification for dissolving local government in Barbados in 1967. On the other hand the Commonwealth of Dominica, which has an area of just 751 square kilometres and a population of around 70,000,[5] is perhaps the most successful example of democratic decentralisation. Duncan (2004: 54) describes Dominica as having 'credible structures upon which to build a truly participatory democratic system with a renewed and reconceptualised local government system as a decisive partner with central government and other non-state actors'.

Perhaps it is more the size and structure of economies that pose the greatest threat to democratic decentralisation. Caribbean countries have recorded low growth rates (real GDP growth of less than 2 per cent per annum), and since the financial crises of 2008–09 growth targets have been missed, leading to tighter fiscal controls and little scope to action reform plans. The contradiction here is that Trinidad and Tobago has a large and well-performing economy, but the evidence suggests that its relative economic strength has not supported any significant push towards substantive decentralisation.

Thus key questions about the success and failure of reform processes for democratic decentralisation remain unanswered. Nonetheless reform outcomes thus far provide important clues about the nature of the process and whether programmes are composed of the 'right' ingredients for goal achievement. This is the subject of the next section.

2.8 Assessing reform outcomes

The normative values of democratic decentralisation have been promoted as a formulaic 'cure-all' for governmental problems, but there are a number of studies that have shown that implementation of these policies has not been easy or entirely successful (Nickson 1998; Manor 1999; Blair 2000; Bardhan 2002; Hickey and Mohan 2005; Grindle 2007; Cheema and Rondinelli 2007). Where positive outcomes have been realised, proponents are quick to claim success, but the failures and partial successes have been grist for the mill for sceptics, who quickly point out the limitations of decentralisation policies. Moreover, the fact that results may vary so much between countries points not only to the disparities that exist between ideas and action, but also to the complex framework of political, socio-technical, historical and cultural factors that have to be taken into account and which determine the 'rhythm, modalities and potential viability' of decentralising reforms (Alfonso 1997: 171). Decentralisation outcomes are unpredictable, because at the core of the process is redistribution of power, which involves substantial trial and error to achieve the correct balance. This is especially a problem for developing countries.

Notwithstanding this complexity and the nuanced lenses through which democratic decentralisation programmes must be assessed, international experience teaches us that there are key factors that can facilitate the process (Cheema and Rondinelli 2007; Brinkerhoff and Crosby 2002; Blair 1997). These factors establish the content of our analytic framework as described earlier, and form the criteria against which the outcomes of local government reform policies in the Caribbean can be evaluated. The results are set out in Table 2.2.

Our analysis highlights the many similarities among local government reform policies in the Caribbean – notably in the way they seek to address obvious deficiencies in structures, finance and capacity as constraints to local autonomy – as well as their basis in the amorphous realm of politics, where power and political partisanship have an awkward nexus. Politics have been the bane of local government reform programmes in the region, exemplified in the cases of Jamaica and Trinidad and

Table 2.2 Assessment of democratic decentralisation in the Caribbean – select country cases

Criteria	Country and nominal rating scale −5 to +5			
	Jamaica	Trinidad and Tobago	St Lucia	Antigua and Barbuda
Policy design and interpretation				
Policy meets causal and contextual best-fit criteria	+4	+4	+4	−5
Policy includes fundamental elements for goal attainment	−5	−5	−5	−5
Policy orientation				
Support and commitment to reform by line ministries	+5	+3	−5	−5
Willingness to transfer responsibilities to local level	+3	+3	−5	−1
Willingness to assist in capacity-building efforts at local level	+4	+2	+1	−5
Political motivation				
Strong and committed political leadership (bi-level)	+3	+1	−5	−5
Willingness to share power, authority and financial resources	−3	−5	+1	−5
Facilitation of civil society groups' participation in local planning and management	+4	−1	−1	−5
Institutional setting				
Mechanisms that foster accountable local leadership	−1	−1	−1	−1
Perception of community empowerment	+4	+4	+4	+4
The nature of political competition	+5	+5	+5	+5
Constitutional amendments in support of reform vision	−3	−5	−3	−5
Orientation of private and civil sectors	+1	+1	+1	−5

Tobago, where problem definition has focused on administrative issues, when in truth the real source of local government problems is its low status in central–local relations. Rather than being seen as a separate and distinct sphere of political influence, there is a tendency for the operations of local government to be fused with the centre. Thus local government is valued for the political leverage it offers the ruling central administration, more than for its representation of community interests.

Perhaps reformers recognise the political complexities involved in full democratic decentralisation, as evidenced by their use of the term 'greater autonomy', a compromise between the current state of local government and the ideal of local autonomy. This tension may explain why, even with established timelines and identifiable outputs, implementation of reform programmes appears to be in constant drift, making the process unusually open-ended and subject to political and administrative manipulation (Schoburgh 2007; Ragoonath 2009). Rondinelli et al. warn that 'if decentralisation policies are to be implemented successfully they must be designed carefully' (1989: 59). One criterion of 'good' design is to recognise the salience of political factors to successful reform outcomes. In our assessment, all countries score poorly against the criterion '*policy includes fundamental elements for goal attainment*'.

Table 2.2 reveals considerable variations in the degree to which central governments' policy orientation supports reform. For instance, Jamaica scores higher than Trinidad and Tobago in '*support and commitment to reform by line ministries*' and '*willingness to assist in capacity-building efforts at local level*', but the two countries attain the same score when it comes to '*willingness to transfer responsibilities to the local level*'. Two actions taken by reformers in Jamaica give them the edge over their Caribbean counterparts. The first was the establishment of the National Advisory Council (NAC) in 1993 (subsequently dormant for lengthy periods but revived in 2004 and again in 2007, both times under new leadership). The NAC serves as a 'thought leader' on local government reform and seeks to build critical mass interest in reform activities, as well as to evaluate the progress of implementation. Importantly, it has promoted bipartisan and multisectoral consensus on the new paradigm of local governance. In its 2009 report, the NAC acknowledged the level of institutional support for local government reform, and recommended that the 2007 Report of the Joint Select Committee on Local Government Reform be formally adopted as a gesture of consensus, as well as a record of the bipartisan agreement to the entrenchment of local government in the Jamaican Constitution (Department of Local Government [Jamaica] 2009).

Jamaica's second important step was the downgrade in 2007 of the Ministry of Local Government to that of a department within the Office of the Prime Minister (OPM), with a mandate to see to the complete devolution of functions to local government by June 2009.[6] However, this target was not reached and under the new government elected in 2011 priorities have changed; the department has now reverted to its original status as a ministry. Nonetheless measures were implemented to build capacity in local authorities in preparation for the proposed devolution.

Other countries receive mostly negative scores for policy orientation due to their status as 'non-starters' in reform. It should also be noted once again that, while moves towards reform in Jamaica are positive when assessed in terms of policy design or in relation to the rest of the Caribbean, there remains a disjuncture between reform rhetoric on the one hand and effective implementation on the other. This point has general applicability across the region.

Given this disjuncture, political motivation becomes a critical factor in understanding both the content and pace of reforms. In Table 2.2 the political motivation indicator is assessed using three measures: (a) *'strong and committed political leadership (bi-level)'*; (b) *'willingness to share power, authority and financial resources'*; and (c) *'facilitation of civil society groups' participation in local planning and management'*.

Jamaica has taken some steps towards (a), notably in terms of the directive issued to local authorities in 2007 to offer their perspective on the reform direction. Ministry Paper 7 of 2003 was quite blunt:

> Within twelve months all local authorities will be required to develop a reform plan in accordance with the new policy guidelines. If this plan is not forthcoming … at the expiration of the agreed time period, the Ministry of Local Government, Community Development and Sport reserves the right to intervene to establish such a plan (Ministry of Local Government [Jamaica] 2003: 16).

All countries scored negatively on (b) with the exception of St Lucia, which outlined a programme of co-governance based on the principle of subsidiarity in its 2000 *Green Paper on Local Government Reform* (Ministry of Community Development [St Lucia] 2000), but with little subsequent evidence of the policy being activated.

In relation to (c), implementation of parish and community development committees gives Jamaica a strong positive score. Once again, however, this action has had little demonstrable impact in achieving reform objectives: it is unclear whether the perspectives of local leaders and the deliberations of development committees are being integrated into either the reform programme or decision-making in local authorities.

A key factor in weakening political motivation for reform is that the institutional setting is devoid of both functioning systems that hold local leaders accountable, as well as institutional arrangements to protect local government from the self-interested behaviour of policy officials (see indicators in Table 2.2). Deficiencies in the local electoral process are a case in point. In Jamaica, for example, local elections are rarely held when they fall due, illustrating the low regard in which community preferences are held. Party politics are the most influential factor in the management of local electoral processes, and by extension the degree to which reform goals are achieved. While successful in other ways, the NAC seems powerless to arrest the practice of local elections being used for political expediency.

The impact of party politics is also evident in Trinidad and Tobago's experience with local government reform. The National Alliance for Reconstruction (NAR) came to power in 1986, subsequently winning the 1987 local government elections and later framing the revolutionary *Municipal Corporations Act of 1990*. However, in 1991 the People's National Movement (PNM), which dominated Trinidad and Tobago's politics from 1956 to 1986, was returned to government. It then won the 1992 local government elections on a manifesto of greater local autonomy for municipal corporations. The PNM subsequently kept its election promise to reduce the number of regions from 13 to 9 by means of *Amendment Act 8 of 1992*, but, while it emphasised accountability and value for money, it made no substantive changes to local government reform policy, nor did it advance the implementation process. This remains the situation after further changes of government in 1995 and 2010.

The conclusion may be drawn that, where local government serves the purpose of the ruling party, there is little compulsion to change the system. The obverse is also true: whenever local government is perceived as a political liability, then reforms take on a degree of urgency. Essentially, however, the political climate in the Caribbean appears antithetical to democratic decentralisation. This is compounded by weak systems of accountability, lack of strong civil society organisations and networks that might advocate for change, and the limited resources available for reform efforts in economically vulnerable small island states. The result has been an incremental 'stop-start' approach to reform, which is centrally managed and consolidates the power of national government. As argued elsewhere, 'because local government is valued as an instrument of political ascendancy rather than a tool of democracy, local government reform is a tool of central control' (Schoburgh 2007: 162).

All this means that 'success' in local government reform has to be seen not so much in terms of 100 per cent achievement of the indicators, but rather in whether such reforms remain part of the overarching agenda of government and continue to make progress. The importance of monitoring progress has been highlighted by Jamaica's NAC, which has recommended the formulation of a new ministry paper to indicate 'the course of action being pursued and outcomes that are to be achieved' (Department of Local Government [Jamaica] 2009: 79), noting the time that has elapsed since Ministry Papers 8 of 1993 and 7 of 2003. It has further proposed that the new paper integrate local government reform with other programmes aimed at social transformation (2009: 72).

2.9 New roles, new relationships

The country cases reveal that most central governments in the Commonwealth Caribbean have taken some worthwhile steps towards the goal of democratic decentralisation. This is so especially for those countries designated as *starters*. However, the rate of progress has been uneven with little real advancement of local government systems. Part of what is now required to deepen the process is a new outlook for the triad of actors – central government, local government and the non-governmental sector (profit and not-for-profit) – based on a common understanding of their role in goal attainment. There is no denying that reform policies in the Caribbean have already to some extent narrated new roles and relationships to support modern local government systems, encapsulated in concepts such as *local governance, public–private partnerships* and *networks*. But confusion persists in the role of the centre and the relationship between the national and subnational levels.

Democratic decentralisation via the route of local government reform has been a central government project. It is conceptualised and executed as such with little contribution from the beneficiaries of the reforms or other actors internal to the state. Unarguably the international development community has a stronger presence in these negotiations than local government or other sectors, and as a result the ministries under whose portfolio local government falls have been at the forefront of implementation. This is understandable, especially at the initial stages, but their continued predominance might explain the reason for the difficulty in crossing each reform threshold. Since there is no evidence to suggest that local government itself objects to the content or the direction of proposed reforms, then it makes sense that central ministries of local government should shift their role from *steering* to *enabling* the process of transformation. This would reduce the level of paternalism that presently characterises central–local relations, creating instead a context for local government to leverage support from independent actors such as the private sector. It could also build local problem-solving capacity by virtue of increased potential for self-correction and learning.

A criticism that could be levelled at local authorities is their seeming distance from the reform debate, evidenced by their failure to articulate an authoritative position on the future of local government and to seek and incorporate the views of their citizens. Put simply, local governments in the region must assume a greater share of the responsibility for reform outcomes. Their tendency to focus primarily on limited funding and resources regurgitates policy thinking from a previous era, and fails to present any creative ideas about local government's role as a harbinger of local democracy and agent of development.

Nor does the solution to local government's problems rest purely in constitutional status, though admittedly this would be an important 'value add'. Policy is about argumentation and what gets implemented depends on skills of persuasion and the mobilisation of influence. In order for local government to command central government's respect in the region, the lack of which is at the heart of the issues, local policy officials must play a role in shaping the reform discourse. They can do this by providing an independent interpretation of the problems; by conducting their own *prospective* analysis; and by providing considered feedback on policy strategies and outcomes. Local authorities are the sites of change and are thus endowed with first-hand knowledge of impacts. It is imperative that they become learning organisations, both to bring about better reform outcomes and to ensure their own viability in the long run.

Clearly, new legislation has not fundamentally altered central–local relations characterised by a dominant central government. In fact, both Jamaica's Municipalities Act of 2003 and Trinidad and Tobago's Municipal Corporations Act 1990 and its subsequent amendment have given the respective ministers for local government final veto power in local decisions. A similar arrangement applies in the case of services that local government provides and which fall under the purview of a central government ministry or department. Antigua and Barbuda, even at the stage of contemplating the best institutional fit between the Department of Local Government and decentralised governance and administration, thought it necessary to maintain the status quo by proposing that district councils be in the 'line of sight' of MPs. It could be construed that central governments are cautious in reform because of the implications that a transformed local government may have for their own operations (Ragoonath 2009).

Possibly the most pressing role change to be wrought is in the dimension of human resources, often blamed for the incapacities that attend local government. While current attempts to build human capacity are commendable, something more fundamental is required. The cue lies in the developmental role of local government, which suggests a shift in orientation of the local policy and administrative executive. Reforms have to be seen as a process of institution building that demands committed and competent leadership. Commitment comes from being vested in the process, and competence not only from education and training but also an appropriate match between skill sets and scope of work.

This highlights the importance of developing a modern human resource strategy in local government in the Caribbean, one which improves on the current practice of recruiting staff via municipal services commissions that are under-resourced and ill-equipped to match local authority needs with managerial skills and competencies. In addition, the benchmarks of professionalism in local government have to keep pace with emerging ideas, such as those of the 'new public management', and with organisational and institutional adjustments presently taking place at the national level. This point is of particular relevance to the position of chief administrative executive, whose professional legitimacy in the past has derived mainly from the ability to deliver local services efficiently and effectively, including advising councils, ensuring continuity in business processes and organisational stability, as well as balancing 'political' and 'public' interests (Nalbandian 1999). While these attributes remain important, the paradigm of *community* to which all local government reform policies in the region subscribe, together with the developmental role of local government, suggest that professional legitimacy must now also be grounded in new tasks, relationships and attitudes at the core of which are individual rights and equity as the basis of empowerment.

Another key challenge for democratic decentralisation resides in the extent to which the profit and not-for-profit sectors in the region are convinced that their involvement would make a significant difference to the state of local affairs. The signs are that neither sector is sufficiently enthralled by the reform programmes; this may be because of what are perceived as negligible results. Civil society groups have advocated for constitutional status for local government, as well as gender equity in local electoral processes, but both issues remain unresolved. Private sector involvement in reform debates has been non-existent, despite some attempts to create a conduit for business input (such as the parish development committees in Jamaica). While civil society organisations may be spurred at intervals to act based on their social conscience and their ability to gain the attention of the international development community, business is less likely to do so without incentives. Just as individuals prefer to associate with successful persons, the same applies to organisations: local authorities have to demonstrate that they can manage their portfolios effectively and efficiently in order to engage the private sector.

Democratic decentralisation relies on critical resources such as high-quality and committed leadership, information, knowledge and skills to improve policy and implementation. Among other things, this suggests that efforts to draw on the resources of civil society and the private sector need to transition from discretionary to mandatory, accompanied by measures to remove the threat of political manipulation (Department of Local Government [Jamaica] 2009). However, even if institutional frameworks are established to involve these sectors in local decision-making, much depends on whether this is seen by the political leadership as a zero-sum game in which their own influence and room to act is reduced. Regrettably, there is a preponderance of evidence to suggest that this is the case.

Finally, a lesson to be taken from the Latin American experience with democratic decentralisation is that perhaps the time has come for the Caribbean to initiate its own 'quiet revolution' by acting independently of the 'advice' of aid agencies and moving ahead energetically with reform plans. Campbell (2003: 8–9) ascribes the success of Latin America to political decisions that ran counter to conventional wisdom:

> governments moved quickly, not with slow deliberations as they were advised. They enshrined decentralisation in national constitutions, not in easily modifiable national laws. They transferred revenues to local authorities long before the true costs of delivering services were known and they were soft on spending rules throughout political liberalisation … Local governments in the region … invented through trial and error new ways of doing political business.

The Caribbean reality is that much of what is interpreted as 'lack of political will' is actually lack of finances to support reforms, and thus independent thinking comes with its own costs. However, to ensure necessary reforms, Caribbean policy-makers must be prepared to accept responsibility and find the resources required. Given a willingness to experiment and learn from the results, the obstacles to democratic decentralisation might not be so daunting.

2.10 Conclusion

For all intents and purposes the process of democratic decentralisation in the Commonwealth Caribbean has become synonymous with changes to subnational governance, and especially the orientation and activities of local government. Current tendencies towards local government reform originate in the conviction that this level of government is a viable medium through which to craft solutions to societal problems. As a consequence, the democratic and functional values of local government have found expression in policy documents that variously signal both the philosophical bases of reform and strategic directions for implementation.

However, democratic decentralisation involves much more than effective local service delivery or improved citizen participation in decision-making. It is fundamentally about curtailing the power of the centre (government, ministries and departments) to permit the evolution of community empowerment and local self-management. This is the crux of the matter and what is apparently missing from otherwise well-intentioned policies. The tentative way in which implementation activities have been handled suggests that reformers are hesitant to confront the issue of just how much power to devolve.

When local government reform is attached to the goal of democratic decentralisation, it becomes clear that local power is both conditioned and limited by its institutional setting and that decentralisation is a political process rather than an administrative one. Gaventa's précis is instructive:

> new forms of participatory governance create uncertainty about roles and new ways of doing things. For participatory governance to work, old rules of engagement need to be replaced by new ones that outline clearly the processes for inclusion and decision making, and the new roles, rights, and responsibilities of the various parties. Otherwise, old procedures are likely to kick in, even if the process looks more inclusive and participatory (2004: 23).

Democratic decentralisation is a process of negotiation and is thus inextricably linked to the broader political economy: social inequities and power asymmetries are fundamental considerations. The quest for a new order of local governance in the Caribbean requires consistent commitment on all sides, a willingness to experiment with new ways of addressing the challenges and obstacles involved, a stronger effort on the part of local government itself and, ultimately, agreement on significant changes to current roles and relationships.

Notes

1 Accounts of the region's local government systems may be found in Commonwealth Local Government Forum (2004, 2009, 2011), Ragoonath (2004), Duncan (2004), Singh (1972) and King (1990).
2 Local government reform policies and programmes pertain directly to Trinidad, as Tobago already enjoys a level of devolution facilitated by the *Tobago House of Assembly Act 37 of 1980*.
3 A zero-sum game is where citizens gain power while political representatives lose power. In a positive sum game both citizens and political representatives benefit.
4 Much of the analysis of fiscal decentralisation is done under the rubric of fiscal federalism. This is covered by a large body of literature, the starting point of which is Tiebout's (1956) model but which has been expanded into a robust debate by, for example, Oates (1972) and Bird and Vaillancourt (1998).
5 Dominica Population Census 2001.
6 This action was taken by the Jamaica Labour Party (JLP), which came to office in 2007 but lost to the People's National Party (PNP) in the 2010 national elections.

References

Alfonso, HD (1997), 'Political decentralization and popular alternatives: a view from the south', in Michael, K and HD Alfonso (Eds.), *Community Power and Grassroots Democracy: The Transformation of Social Life*, Zed Books, London, 170–188.

Bardhan, P (2002), 'Decentralization of governance and development', *Journal of Economic Perspectives*, Vol. 16 No. 4, 185–205.

Bird, RM and Francois Vaillancourt (Ed.) (1998), *Fiscal Decentralization in Developing Countries*, Cambridge University Press, Cambridge.

Blair, H (1995), *Assessing Democratic Decentralisation: A Center for Development Information and Evaluation (CDIE) Concept Paper*, United States Agency for International Development, Washington, DC.

Blair, H (1997), 'Spreading Power to the Periphery: A USAID Assessment of Democratic Local Governance', available at: http://pdf.usaid.gov/pdf_docs/PNACA904.pdf (accessed 15 January 2011).

Blair, H (2000), 'Participation and accountability at the periphery: democratic local governance in six countries', *World Development*, Vol. 28 No. 1, 21–39.

Brinkerhoff, DW and BL Crosby (2002), *Managing Policy Reform: Concepts and Tools for Decision-makers in Developing and Transitioning Countries*, Kumarian Press, Inc, Bloomfield, CT.

Campbell, T (2003), *The Quiet Revolution: Decentralization and the Rise of Political Participation in Latin American Cities*, University of Pittsburgh Press, Pittsburgh.

Chambers, R (1983), *Rural Development: Putting the Last First*, Intermediate Technology Publications, London.

Cheema, GS and DA Rondinelli (2007), *Decentralizing Governance: Emerging Concepts and Practices*, Ash Institute for Democratic Governance and Innovation, John F. Kennedy School of Government: Harvard University, Cambridge, MA.

Commonwealth Foundation (1999), *Citizens and Governance: Civil Society in the New Millennium*, Commonwealth Foundation, London.

Commonwealth Local Government Forum (2004), *Commonwealth Local Government Handbook*, The Forum, London.

Commonwealth Local Government Forum (2009), *Commonwealth Local Government Handbook*, The Forum, London.

Commonwealth Local Government Forum (2011), *Commonwealth Local Government Handbook*, The Forum, London.

Conyers, D (1986), 'Decentralization and development; a framework for analysis', *Community Development Journal*, Vol. 21 No. 2, 88–100.

Department of Local Government (Jamaica) (2009), *Final Report of the National Advisory Council on Local Government Reform*, Department of Local Government, Kingston, Jamaica.

Dominica Population Census May 2001.

Duncan, N (2004), 'Local government and governance for the twenty-first century', in Local Democracy and Good Governance in the Caribbean, Report of the Regional Symposium held in Montego Bay, Jamaica, April 2004, Commonwealth Secretariat, London, 43–66.

Fox, J and J Aranda (1996), *Decentralisation and Rural Development in Mexico*, Center for U.S.–Mexican Studies, University of California, San Diego, La Jolla.

Fung, A and EO Wright (2001), 'Deepening democracy: innovations in empowered participatory governance', *Politics & Society*, Vol. 29 No. 1, March, 5–41.

Gaventa, J (2004), 'Strengthening participatory approaches to local governance: learning the lessons from abroad', *National Civic Review: Making Citizen Democracy Work*, Vol. 93 No. 4, Winter, 16–27, available at: www.ncl.org/publications/ncr (accessed 29 August 2012).

Grindle, MS (2007), *Going Local: Decentralization, Democratization, and the Promise of Good Governance*, Princeton University Press, Princeton, NJ.

Handler, JF (1996), *Down from Bureaucracy: The Ambiguity of Privatization and Empowerment*, Princeton University Press, Princeton, NJ.

Hickey, S and G Mohan (2005), 'Relocating participation within a radical politics of development', *Development and Change*, Vol. 36 No. 2, 237–262.

Jun, JS and DS Wright (Eds.) (1996), *Globalization and Decentralization: Institutional Contexts, Policy Issues and Intergovernmental Relations in Japan and the United States*, Georgetown University Press, Washington, DC.

King, V (Ed.) (1990), *Perspectives on Local Government Reform in Trinidad and Tobago*, Department of Government: University of the West Indies, St Augustine.

Manor, J (1999), *The Political Economy of Democratic Decentralization*, The World Bank, Washington, DC.

Ministry of Community Development, Culture, Local Government and Cooperatives (St Lucia) (2000), *Green Paper on Local Government Reform*.

Ministry of Labour, Public Administration and Empowerment (Antigua and Barbuda) (undated) Local Government Department Documentation on the Restructuring of Local Government Department and District Councils.

Ministry of Local Government (Jamaica) (1993) Ministry Paper 8 of 1993.

Ministry of Local Government (Jamaica) (2002) Ministry Paper 56 of 2002. *Government at Your Service: Public Sector Modernisation Vision and Strategy 2002–2012*.

Ministry of Local Government (Jamaica) (2003) Community Development and Sport Ministry Paper 7 of 2003.

Ministry of Local Government (Trinidad and Tobago) (2009) Draft White Paper on Local Government Reform.

Ministry of Works, Infrastructure and Decentralisation (Trinidad and Tobago) (1990) The Decentralisation Process: Regional Administration and Regional Development in Trinidad and Tobago, Proposal for Reform, October 1990.

Nalbandian, J (1999), 'Facilitating community, enabling democracy: new roles for local government managers', *Public Administration Review*, Vol. 59 No. 3, 187–197.

Narayan, D, R Chambers, MK Shah and P Petesch (2000), *Voices of the Poor: Crying Out for Change*, World Bank, Washington, DC.

Nickson, RA (1998), 'Where is local government going in Latin America? A comparative perspective', International Centre for Local Democracy. Working Paper No. 6 (2011): 1–36, available at: http://works.bepress.com/andrew_nickson/18 (accessed 14 March 2011).

Oates, W (1972), *Fiscal Federalism*, Harcourt Brace Jovanovich, New York.

Osborne, D and T Gaebler (1992), *Reinventing Government: How the Entrepreneurial Spirit Is Transforming the Public Sector*, Plume, New York.

Prud'homme, R (Ed.) (1995), 'The dangers of decentralization', *World Bank Research Observer*, Vol. 10 No. 2, 210–220.

Ragoonath, B (2004), 'Local democracy and good governance in the Caribbean: an agenda for regional cooperation', Report of the Regional Symposium held in Montego Bay, Jamaica, April 2004, Commonwealth Secretariat, London, 67–85.

Ragoonath, B (2009), 'Yes to local government, no to participatory democracy: the local governance reform dilemma in Trinidad, St Lucia and St Vincent', *Commonwealth Journal of Local Governance*, No. 3, May, available at: http://epress.lib.uts.edu.au/ojs/index.php/cjlg pp. 32–50 (accessed 14 March 2011).

Rondinelli, DA, JS McCullough and RW Johnson (1989), 'Analysing decentralization policies in developing countries: a political-economy framework', *Development and Change*, Vol. 20, 57–87.

Schoburgh, ED (2006), *Local Government Reform: The Prospects for Community Empowerment in Jamaica*, University of the West Indies, SALISES, Mona.

Schoburgh, E (2007), 'Local government reform in Jamaica and Trinidad: a policy dilemma', *Public Administration and Development*, Vol. 27, 159–174.

Schoburgh, E (2009), 'Paradigm shift or rhetorical flourish? The "New Orthodoxy" of local governance in the Caribbean', *Social and Economic Studies*, Vol. 58 No. 1, 95–124.

Schoburgh, E (2010a), 'Balancing democratic governance, populism and patronage via popularly elected mayor: the case of Jamaica', paper presented at the 14th International Research Symposium on Public Management, University of Bern, Switzerland, 7–9 April 2010. Unpublished.

Schoburgh, E (2010b), 'Modernising local government structure by fragmentation: lessons from the Portmore Municipal Council – Jamaica', *Commonwealth Journal of Local Governance*, March, 102–125, available at: http://epress.lib.uts.edu.au/ojs/index.php/cjlg (accessed 14 March 2011).

Schoburgh, E. (2010c), 'Is subsidiarity the Panacea for local government problems in the Caribbean?', *Social and Economic Studies*, Vol. 59 No. 4, 27–66.

Shah, A and T Thompson (2004), 'Implementing decentralized local governance: a treacherous road with potholes, detours and rapid closures', World Bank Policy Research Paper 3353.

Singh, P (1972), *Local Democracy in the Commonwealth Caribbean*, Longman, Caribbean, Port of Spain.

Tanzi, V (1996), 'Fiscal federalism and decentralization: a review of some efficiency and macroeconomic aspects', World Bank Conference on Development Economics, 1995, World Bank, Washington, DC.

Tendler, J and S Freedheim, (1994), 'Trust in a rent-seeking world: health and government transformed in northeast Brazil', *World Development*, Vol. 22 No. 12, 1771–1791.

Ter-Minassian, T (1997), 'Intergovernmental fiscal relations in a macro-economic perspective: an overview', in TerMinassian, T (Ed.), *Fiscal Federalism in Theory and Practice*, International Monetary Fund, Washington, DC, 3–24.

Tiebout, CM (1956), 'A pure theory of local government expenditures', *Journal of Political Economy*, Vol. 64 No. 5, 416–424.

Ward, P, RH Wilson and PK Spink (2010), 'Decentralization, democracy and subnational governance: comparative reflections for policymaking in Brazil, Mexico and the US', *Regional Science Policy and Practice*, Vol. 2 No. 1, 51–62.

Chapter 3

Pakistan's Devolution of Power Plan 2001: A Brief Dawn for Local Democracy?

Munawwar Alam

Local government is not a new concept in Pakistan. Since the founding of the country in 1947, Pakistan has always had local governments as the lowest-tier political structure. However, grassroots democracy has been eclipsed at different times in the country's history. As we write this chapter, there is no elected local government in Pakistan. The chapter documents the recent history of decentralisation and local government in Pakistan, with special reference to the 'Devolution of Power Plan' (DOPP) introduced by the military government of General Pervez Musharraf in 2001. The author was closely involved with the DOPP at both the policy and implementation levels.

Public administration literature provides an enormous number of studies on decentralisation, but research focused on decentralisation in Pakistan within the context of military rule is limited. Some researchers, mostly belonging to international development agencies, have studied different aspects of the DOPP – sectoral, political etc. – but these do not comprehensively cover the breadth of the local government reforms of 2001. The main thrust of this chapter is that the DOPP was not simply another local government system per se, but rather a major attempt at decentralisation accompanied by a comprehensive package of reforms that had several strands – electoral reform, local government structures and processes, and changes to the police and bureaucracy – all aimed at modernisation and social change.

Pakistan's political history has been characterised by intermittent military rule. Since independence in 1947, there have been four periods of martial law under different dispensations, and three constitutions have been enacted (1956, 1962 and 1973). Cumulatively, military governments have ruled for almost half of Pakistan's existence since 1947. The alternating pattern of political and military governments[1] has not only affected the structure and design of local government systems, but more importantly had significant implications for the development of grassroots democracy. It has at times strengthened and at other times jeopardised the sustainability of local government in the country. In broad terms, local democracy has been nurtured by military governments, whereas during civilian governments it has been replaced by non-participatory, unelected local structures that are run by government-appointed civil servants. Thus, as far as local government is concerned, it may be said that the country has experienced both 'dictatorial democracy' and 'democratic dictatorship'.

According to Briscoe (2008), the formal state structure in any society may have a parallel or 'shadow' set of institutions that hold real power. This is especially true in the case of Pakistan. Every military government in Pakistan has introduced its own brand of local government. Cheema et al. (2005) have used the term 'non-representative governments' for these military regimes. They have attempted to analyse the Pakistani experience to find answers to the question of why non-representative regimes have been willing proponents of decentralisation to the local level.

In developing countries decentralisation may be either externally driven (e.g. through Structural Adjustment Programmes, donor pressure etc.) or internally motivated (e.g. by governments seeking to strengthen their legitimacy and gain popularity), though the country context is different in each case. In Pakistan's case decentralisation has always been internally driven, and Cheema et al. (2005) conclude that the military's need to legitimise its control appears to be a prime reason behind the recurring attempts at local government reform.

Bhave and Kingston (2010) view the military in Pakistan as a separate actor with its own interests. It can, however, be argued that institutional 'interest' and institutional 'role' are two different things, and that the course taken will vary according to the institution's interpretation of the context in which it has to operate. According to Sivaramakishnan (2000) local government in South Asia often tends to be stronger during eras of authoritarian rule than in times of democratic rule. He suggests that during democratic regimes elected local government is less attractive because it provides an additional platform for citizen participation, and hence may to some degree rival the centre.

The patronage of local governments under military regimes is not unique to Pakistan. In many countries military governments have attempted to create grassroots popularity and support, and to secure their legitimacy and a better external (and internal) image by nurturing local governments. In the Commonwealth, there are at least two more instances, Ghana and The Gambia, where army rulers introduced local government reforms. In Ghana, a major change in the governance system was introduced in 1988 by Flight Lieutenant Jerry John Rawlings, the organiser of the fourth coup in the country, in 1981. Writing about Ghana, Ahwoi (2010) argues that decentralisation of national administration, particularly in unitary states, works best in the presence of a strong central government. Although Pakistan is a federation, Ahwoi's thesis seems to apply.

The remainder of this chapter is divided into four sections. The first looks briefly at local government models in Pakistan before 2001 – all creations of military regimes. This is necessary if one is to distinguish the DOPP from previous waves of local government reform. The following sections then explore the DOPP of 2001–09 to examine what was new compared with previous attempts at decentralisation, and analyses some of the social factors evident in the two local government elections (2001 and 2005) which were a hallmark of the DOPP. The final section reviews the experience of the DOPP, looks at the current situation and future prospects, and draws some general conclusions.

3.1 Local government in Pakistan until 2001

In 1947, on the eve of independence, Pakistan inherited the local government system of colonial India. The British Administration had introduced the concept of 'local self-government' by creating a separate tier to administer civic functions, initially through appointed local administrators and then through elected municipal and district boards for urban and rural areas respectively. This system was first introduced in Bengal and Madras, followed by Bombay, Punjab and other colonial states. Separate laws were enacted in each state for large cities, municipal cities and towns, and rural areas (Alam 1999). During the independence movement in India, national political parties stood for greater representation at central and provincial levels rather than local government. This prompted the British government to grant autonomy at the provincial level (Cheema et al. 2005), and was a major factor in the weak development of local governments in the areas that later became Pakistan (Ali 1980).

The history of local government in Pakistan from 1947 to 2001 can be broadly divided into four periods:

- 1947–1958;

- 1958–1969, the 'Basic Democracy' system of General Ayub Khan;

- 1969–1979;

- 1979–1988, the local government system introduced by General Zia-ul-Haq.

3.1.1 1947–1958

As explained above, at the time of independence the areas that constituted Pakistan had few developed systems of local government, and the local bodies were mostly run by government-appointed administrators. The early years of independence were marked by limited constitutional development and the extreme pressures on limited resources brought about by partition. The partition of India in itself was phenomenal, and perhaps unique in the British Empire, as no other colony was partitioned at the time of granting independence. In Pakistan, migration of millions of Muslims from the Indian states and their settlement was in itself enough for the newly created country to handle with minimal infrastructure and resources, without trying to focus on other developmental issues such as establishing democratic local government.

Around 1956 some progress began to be made towards creating an adult franchise and electing local office bearers, but this was confined mainly to the Bengal (now Bangladesh) and Punjab provinces. In 1957–58 half the municipal councils in West Pakistan (the present Pakistan) were still managed by government-appointed administrators, as in most cases elections had not been held after the expiry of their terms of office. Waseem (1994) points out that, even where elections were held, there was only a limited franchise and massive malpractice.

3.1.2 1958–1969: The 'Basic Democracy' system of General Ayub Khan

This was the first period of martial law in Pakistan, which brought with it a 'first wave' of local government reform. The 'Basic Democracy' (BD) system was the first experimentation with local government in Pakistan under the auspices of a military regime. Field Marshal Ayub Khan introduced a system of 'controlled democracy' at all levels of government. Under this system, local government institutions were created in rural and urban areas through separate legislation. All urban and rural councils, as well as provincial and national assemblies, were elected indirectly through an electoral college consisting of 40,000 'Basic Democrats' popularly elected in each of East and West Pakistan.

3.1.3 1969–1979

After the imposition of the 'civilian² martial law' under Zulfiqar Ali Bhutto in 1971, all local bodies were dissolved and the functions and powers of local governments were vested in official administrators. This state of affairs continued throughout the reign of Mr Bhutto and the early years of the following period of the martial law regime of General Zia-ul-Haq, which began in 1977. By this time East Pakistan had seceded from Pakistan, and West Pakistan had been divided into four separate provinces: Punjab, Sindh, Balochistan and the North-West Frontier. According to the 1973 constitution (still in place), local government is a provincial subject. Thus all four provincial governments enacted their respective local government legislation in 1979.

3.1.4 1979–1988: The local government system of General Zia-ul-Haq

This period marked the 'second wave' of local government reform under a military regime. The system of local government introduced in 1979 by General Zia-ul-Haq was the most representative in nature since independence. For the first time in the history of Pakistan, elections to all local councils in both rural and urban areas were held simultaneously on the basis of adult franchise and under the aegis of independent provincial election authorities.

The special features of the 1979 local government system can be described as follows:

- local government laws relating to rural and urban areas were unified and harmonised;

- representation was given to peasants, workers, women and minorities in pursuance of principles laid down under the 1973 constitution;

- elections to local councils were held on a non-party basis;

- local governments had elected officer bearers (chairmen, mayors, etc.) and there were no appointed members; and

- local councils had significant autonomy, for example, they could approve their own budgets and taxation proposals.

Tables 3.1 and 3.2 summarise some of the key features of the three systems of local government introduced under military rule, and the intervening 'political' (civilian) governments.

3.2 The Devolution of Power Plan: What was new?

Although the coup of 1999 was the precipitating cause of devolution, movement towards local government reforms had begun earlier at the behest of international

Table 3.1 Local government systems under military rule

Period	No. of years	Military leader	Name of system	Distinguishing feature(s)
1958– 1969	11	General Ayub Khan	Basic Democracy	National law; local governments comprised both elected and appointed members, and served as an electoral college for the election of the national president
1979– 1988	9	General Zia-ul-Haq	No specific name	Elected local governments under provincial laws; no appointed members; 3–4 successful terms completed under this system
1999– 2008	9	General Pervez Musharraf	Devolution of Power Plan	Based on the principle of subsidiarity; radical departure from all previous systems; devolution accompanied by taxation, civil service, electoral and police reforms

Table 3.2 Local government under 'political' governments

Period	Political situation	Remarks
1947– 1958	No constitution, no elected government in the country	Urban councils and district boards in urban and rural areas respectively, continued according to laws left by the British government
1971–76	First elected national/ provincial governments	Despite promulgation of a local government law, no elections held throughout this period and local councils were managed through official administrators
1988– 1999	Several elected national governments held power	All elected local governments dismissed. Local government elections never held though announced and scheduled several times; elections held in certain provinces in 1998, but elected representatives never assumed office

donors and lenders, particularly the World Bank. On the global scene, pressure for decentralisation, especially market-based decentralisation, had already been brought to bear in developing countries as a result of the Structural Adjustment Programme of the International Monetary Fund in the 1980s and 1990s. Based on World Bank reports (1996, 1998), Cheema et al. (2003) argued that, although multilateral pressure for decentralisation in Pakistan had developed since the mid-1990s, no major attempts at decentralisation were initiated in Pakistan before General Musharraf took power in 1999. Therefore it can be said that the coup of 1999 was a turning point for local government reform, and that without the coup the course of decentralisation in Pakistan would have been further delayed.

In Pakistan, like any other developing country, public service delivery was characterised by a concentration of powers in the federal and provincial governments. Most service delivery was therefore under bureaucratic control, without any contribution from elected politicians at the local level. This meant that provincial and central governments carried out the policy-making and district authorities[3] acted as the implementation agency with little say in decision-making – a system of deconcentrated administration rather than decentralised authority.

To address this situation, General Musharraf established a National Reconstruction Bureau (NRB) as a 'think tank' to help transform an over-centralised and ineffective service delivery system into a decentralised and responsive one. After an extensive process of consultation, his government introduced its programme of devolution of power and authority under the aegis of the NRB in 2001. This began the 'third wave' of decentralisation in the country. The Devolution of Power Plan (DOPP) of 2001 was a radical departure as it was based on the concept of subsidiarity, involving transfer of power from provinces to districts and other lower levels. Before the DOPP, subsidiarity was not a commonly used term in developmental discussions and in the corridors of power in Pakistan.

The DOPP had two main elements: decentralisation and electoral reforms. Devolution was also accompanied by reforms to the civil service and police. Features introduced for the first time in the history of Pakistan are summarised in Table 3.3.

The following sections provide further detail on some of the key features of the DOPP reforms.

3.2.1 Application of subsidiarity

As noted previously, the 2001 system sought to apply the principle of subsidiarity.[4] Even though this was not fully implemented and many details were not resolved, especially in relation to financial decentralisation and relationships between provincial and local governments, the DOPP can be said to have brought about some of the most fundamental changes in governance and local governance in Pakistan since independence in 1947.

Under the 2001 system, district governments (the upper tier) were given responsibilities in agriculture, health, education, community development, information technology, finance and planning, together with revenue previously held by the provinces, and became financially competent through transferred funds and local taxes. Town/*taluka* governments (the middle tier) were assigned most of the functions of the former municipal authorities as the main providers of essential services (e.g. water, sanitation, roads and waste disposal). The union councils (the lowest/third tier) were envisaged as providing monitoring and oversight of service delivery, as well as undertaking small developmental projects. Union councils received funds directly from the district and collected some local taxes.

3.2.2 Abolition of the rural–urban divide

One of the important distinguishing features of the DOPP was that it abolished the previous rural–urban divide in local government. Under the British system of administration, urban local councils were established to provide essential municipal

Table 3.3 Innovative features of the DOPP

Electoral	• Voting age reduced from 21 to 18 years to bring youth into mainstream politics • Minimum educational qualification prescribed for candidates for *nazims* (mayors) • Manifesto mandatory for candidates for district and town/*taluka nazims* (mayors) • Elections conducted by (central) Election Commission of Pakistan instead of provincial election authorities • Local government elections held in phases for better management and co-ordination
Gender	• Reserved seats for women increased to 33% in all tiers of local government
General	• Divisional tier (between districts and provincial government) abolished • Office of the Deputy Commissioner (a colonial legacy of deconcentrated administration) abolished and replaced by senior district co-ordination officer (DCO) reporting to *nazim* (mayor); interaction of DCO with provincial government through mayor • Magistracy abolished; in Pakistan's context this was important, as provincial governments extended their reach through district officers who also had judicial powers that could be exploited through the district bureaucracy • Mayor made chief executive of the respective local government, with wide-ranging administrative and financial powers • Elaborate mechanism for internal and external recall of elected representatives prescribed under law; similarly, officials enabled to seek recourse against motivated or illegal orders of *nazims* (mayors)
Finance	• Provincial Finance Commission constituted for allocation of resources from provinces to districts, based on population, fiscal capacity, fiscal effort and specific needs etc. of districts
Police	• *Police Act 1861* replaced after nearly 150 years; law and order became the responsibility of *zila nazim* (district mayor), but the district police chief was responsible to their own professional hierarchy in matters of crime prevention, investigation and personnel management of force. This was intended to check patronage by political leadership and high-handedness on the part of police, while facilitating dispensation of justice • District Public Safety Commissions constituted, comprising elected and appointed members, to act as a safety valve providing recourse for both police chief and district mayor in cases of conflict • Police Complaint Authority introduced to deal with serious complaints against police
Community development	• A new grassroots institution developed – Citizen Community Boards – to engage local people in service delivery

services. By contrast, the capacity of rural councils in service delivery was far less (Siddiqui 1992), and they provided only limited representation, often strengthening the local elite.

3.2.3 Reform of bureaucracy

The DOPP was a bold attempt to transform an over-centralised bureaucracy, especially in terms of the established elite. The district co-ordination officer (DCO) of the district government, equivalent to a chief executive officer, was placed under the authority of the elected mayor. Likewise, the superintendent of police of the district reported to the mayor on the overall maintenance of law and order.

3.2.4 Developmental planning

Before the DOPP, the planning system was centralised and development funds were distributed to provincial departments through a top-down mechanism. The identification, appraisal and approval of development projects had no relationship to local priorities. The element of community participation was missing from the process, which was non-transparent and inequitable. Politicians, mainly parliamentarians of national and provincial assemblies, were provided with development funds to be spent according to their wishes.

The DOPP provided for Citizen Community Boards (CCBs) to mobilise the community in the development and improvement of service delivery through voluntary and self-help initiatives. CCBs played a major role in the transformation of development planning by creating a sense of ownership. They were given the legal right to enable citizens to actively participate in development activities, plus an earmarked budget that could be carried over from year to year. This also introduced transparency and accountability to the development process, as communities became active participants in projects instead of being passive beneficiaries.

3.3 Organised local government – a new phenomenon in Pakistan

Before and during the greater part of the DOPP period, local government associations (in the commonly understood sense) did not exist in Pakistan. However, under the DOPP there was a growing awareness and empowerment of local government that promoted a greater sense of unity and common purpose among its elected representatives. The first initiative came from Punjab province with the creation of the Local Councils Association of the Punjab (LCAP) in 2007. Since its inception, LCAP has become a leading national organisation, not only in its lobbying of provincial and national governments, but also in paving the way for a louder voice for local democracy across the whole country. Following LCAP, new local government associations were created in the other three provinces in Pakistan: Sindh, Balochistan and the North-West Frontier (Khyber-Pakhtunkhawa). Later, in November 2009, a national local government association was launched.

In the immediate post-Musharraf period, the local government associations established under the DOPP sought to mobilise public support from across civil society, business and the political spectrum to call for the protection of local democracy in Pakistan and for further local government elections. The international community expressed concern about the future of local democracy in Pakistan, while the associations' efforts were supported by local government leaders, including the Commonwealth Local Government Forum (Local Government Alliance 2009) – but at this point to no avail.

3.3.1 Social dimensions

One of the significant features of the DOPP was the attempt to make social change part of the reforms. According to Randall and Hermann (1981) 'social changes' are those that mark the transition from one stage or phase of a construed cycle of development to another. They designate as 'significant' those changes that evolutionary theorists associate with the movement of social forms or a whole society from a 'less advanced' state towards a durable 'advanced' state, or from one level or epoch to another. The definition of 'significant' will depend on the aspect of society or the segment of social reality that is seen to be of strategic importance. For example, reforms in local government institutions may be significant both as a process of strengthening local democracy and as a way of providing better and more efficient services for economic, social and cultural development. Montiel (1988) argued that the institutional development of local government is politically and culturally bounded, therefore its context and process need to be considered accordingly.

Against that background, this section examines some of the social factors and trends exhibited in the two local government elections – 2001 and 2005 – held under the DOPP. For this purpose reliance has been placed on secondary data and published sources. Pattan Development Organisation (Pattan) carried out substantial work in collecting data from the two elections, and here we rely on their data (Pattan 2006) plus other sources where available (see also Bari 2001).

As shown in Table 3.3, the DOPP incorporated significant electoral reforms. First and foremost, the voting age was reduced from 21 to 18 years in order to increase the involvement of young people.

Second, minimum educational qualifications were established, including having reached matriculation in order to take the position of district mayor (*nazim*). Pattan's analysis shows that, in the 2005 elections, most of the candidates indicated they had first or higher degrees. Approximately 46 per cent claimed to be graduates, while 30 per cent said that they had higher or professional degrees. About 15 per cent had completed their FA/FSc – equivalent to 12 years of schooling – while only 10 per cent were educated below that level (see Table 3.4).

Alam (unpublished) provides supplementary data from a study of 16 district and 102 town/*taluka* mayors elected in Sindh province in 2001. District mayors were more likely to be highly educated than their town/*taluka* counterparts (see Table 3.5).

Alam's study (unpublished) also indicated that a younger leadership came through in the 2001 elections. In 2001, among town/*taluka nazims* the largest number were 46–50 years of age (about 25 per cent), followed by those aged 41–45 years (19 per cent).

Table 3.4 Education of district and *tehsil nazims*

Education	Number	Percentage
Less than FA	48	9.7
FA/FSc	72	14.6
BA/BSc	225	45.5
Higher than BA/BSc	150	30.5
Total	495	100.0

Table 3.5 Qualifications of mayors elected in Sindh province in 2001

Qualification	District mayors (N = 16)		Town/*taluka* mayors (N = 102)	
	No.	%	No.	%
Matriculation	3	18.8	24	23.5
Intermediate	2	12.5	10	9.8
Graduate	5	31.3	33	32.4
Masters	3	18.8	10	9.8
MBBS (medical)	1	6.35	5	4.9
LLB (law)	1	6.3	7	6.9
BBA	1	6.3	2	–
Diploma	–	–	3	2.9
B.Engineering	–	–	3	2.9
MSc	–	–	3	2.9
MBA	–	–	2	2.0

Source: Alam (2001)

The numbers aged 56–60, 66–70 and 71–75 years were low – less than 5 per cent combined. Pattan data shows a similar picture for 2005. Nationwide approximately 15 per cent of the successful district and town/*taluka* candidates were in the age group 25–30 years, while 35 per cent were 31–40 years. Some 30 per cent of candidates were aged 41–50 years and approximately 20 per cent were older than 50 years.

Pattan data also suggests that the DOPP reforms encouraged new entrants to local government. In 2001, 57 per cent of candidates for *nazims* and 75 per cent for *naib nazims* (deputy mayor) contested elections for the first time. In 2005 similar trends continued: approximately 70 per cent of those elected as union councillors were new faces, and few of these had previously been members of town/*taluka* or district councils.

Alam's study (2004) of the 2001 elections in Sindh province again provides supporting evidence. Out of 16 district mayors elected in Sindh province, none had any past experience in local government, but 12 out of 16 had been a member of a provincial or the national parliament. This in itself may be seen as a reflection of empowerment at the local government level, attracting national/provincial or mainstream politicians to contest local government elections. In the category of town/*taluka* mayors, only 3 per cent had previous experience in local government, while one mayor had been a senator. Overall only 14 out of 102 town/*taluka* mayors (13.7 per cent) had previous political experience. This suggests the emergence of a new leadership, as envisioned in the devolution plan.

In Pakistan, women have been contesting elections for national and provincial assemblies, as well as local governments, since independence. However, their representation remained low because of socio-religious factors. In order to bring women into politics, the DOPP increased the number of reserved seats to 33 per cent at all levels. Previously only 5 per cent of seats were reserved for women in local councils. Thus the DOPP created about 24,000 seats for women in local governments across the country. In some parts of the North-West Frontier Province (NWFP) and Balochistan, women were not allowed to take part in the elections as a result of social conservatism. However, such cases were few. Election figures showed that on the whole the provision of reserved seats had encouraged women to participate in the political affairs of the country, with nearly 22,000 women elected (including those returned unopposed) (Pattan 2006).

Between 2001 and 2005 there was a 100 per cent increase in women candidates elected as *nazims* and *naib nazims*, from 16 to 32. Similarly, in Sindh province in 2005 four women became district *nazims* as compared with only two in 2001. It should be noted, however, that Sindh's literacy rate and educational standards are better than those in less advanced provinces like Balochistan and NWFP. Nationally, the candidature for district and town/*taluka nazims* was almost totally a male affair, with only 1.4 per cent women candidates (Pattan 2006).

Determining whether or not social change actually occurred as a result of the DOPP is a complex matter. It requires study not only of the institutions of local government, but also of diverse aspects of Pakistani society including trends in the economy, demography, culture, history, law, politics, education and religion. Two terms of local governments under DOPP, cumulatively eight years, are not sufficient to gauge any definite trends in the political milieu of the country. However, based on the limited data presented above it is possible to identify some early signs of change and to suggest that the direction of the reforms did indeed have the potential to initiate modernisation of the political and administrative system in Pakistan, as envisaged by the military government.

3.4 Recent developments, prospects and conclusions

In a study of five fragile countries Anten et al. (2012) conclude that Pakistan offers the most detailed example of a process of decentralisation that has only partially achieved its objectives. This chapter echoes their concern that decentralisation cannot proceed effectively in a governance system that suffers from a number of dysfunctional factors.

A central characteristic of the polity of Pakistan has been alternating civilian and military rule, with each period of military rule patronising and introducing its own brand of grassroots democracy. Within that context, the Devolution of Power Plan introduced by General Musharraf in 2001 was a radical departure, as it comprised a package of changes to the public sector including decentralisation, electoral, public service and police reforms. In effect, it was an attempt to change the governance paradigm. Although the data is patchy, available evidence suggests that over the period 2001–09 substantial progress was made towards effective decentralisation, in particular a sound system of democratic local government.

However, since 2009 the decentralisation agenda has faltered, at least as far as local government is concerned. After the general elections of 2008, a new civilian government came into power and General Pervez Musharraf stepped down. Based on past experience in Pakistan, there was apprehension that the civilian government would not maintain local government institutions, especially the DOPP system. This is exactly what happened, and at the time of writing the local government elections originally due in 2009 had yet to be held and local governments were being managed by non-elected administrators. It appears that the DOPP, although home-grown, had the tag of a military regime and therefore suffered from negative perceptions, even though decentralisation is still seen as a necessary part of broader governance and public sector reform.

The DOPP had also included a component of devolution from federal to provincial governments, named 'Higher-Level Restructuring'. Despite pressure from the provinces, this did not take place under the Musharraf government, but in 2010 it was implemented through the 18th constitutional amendment. As a result, *inter alia*, the Ministry of Local Government at the federal level has been abolished. Also, at around the same time, the federal government disbanded the National Reconstruction Bureau and replaced it with a Policy Analysis Unit (PAU) headed by an adviser to the president. The PAU operated for only a brief period until it was in turn abolished. Thus from 2008, when a civilian ('political') government returned to power, most of the features of DOPP have been steadily eroded.

Achieving complete devolution of power in Pakistan is clearly a huge undertaking. Such institutional reforms are complex, time-consuming and inevitably opposed by those interest groups that benefit from the existing system. For example, the effective diffusion of economic power is an essential prerequisite of meaningful devolution, and one that has perhaps received insufficient attention. Economic power, notably that derived from ownership of land, gets parlayed into political power which, in collusion with other entrenched interest groups such as the bureaucracy, restricts the empowerment of citizens.

Decentralisation is inherently neither good nor bad. It is a means to an end. Successful decentralisation can improve the efficiency and responsiveness of the public sector, and also contribute to significant social change, which cannot occur without supportive institutional development. At the local level, the DOPP brought about substantially enhanced participation of women in government, involvement of a broader cross-section of society in political life, and more educated, responsive and democratic leadership.

According to Anten et al. (2012), institutional reforms that do not align with the interests and incentives of power-holders are unlikely to lead to robust new arrangements. They argue that the World Bank's recent emphasis on an 'experimental best-fit' route to reform of the state is a sensible acknowledgement of these difficulties.

Political factors are therefore crucial in determining the possibilities for reform and development, especially in a fragile state environment. Strong political will and leadership are needed to create and maintain conducive conditions for a steady process of institutional change and development. In the case of DOPP, once the main architect of reform had departed the scene, progress came to a grinding halt. Meanwhile the current political environment remains uncertain.

We conclude that decentralisation cannot be approached as a stand-alone activity, but must draw on and form part of a country's broader democratic and political culture. Parallel institutional development needs to be ongoing, and for this to occur supportive elements have to be designed and introduced in the constitutional framework and political system. Specifically, local government should be regarded not just as the lowest tier of the government, but as a distinct sphere that is closest to the citizens, with sufficient administrative and financial autonomy to serve its constituents. Unless these elements are institutionalised, the sustainability of decentralisation programmes remains at risk. In Pakistan, it would seem that for various reasons military governments have been more willing to accept this challenge: if civilian governments are shy of nurturing grassroots democracy, it raises significant questions about their democratic values and commitment to empowering citizens. Given the experience of the last five years of 'political' government, the prospects for local government in Pakistan are not encouraging.

Notes

1   The terms 'elected' and 'non-elected' are not used here, as military regimes also installed elected
    governments, albeit of a relatively controlled nature. Within the military, the army typically dominates.
2   'Civilian' martial law, because it was imposed by an elected 'political' government.
3   District authorities are extensions of provincial governments.
4   The concept of subsidiarity is based on the premise that lower levels of government are closer to
    citizens, and can therefore make more 'intelligent' decisions about 'who does what'; that is, it is less
    about politics and more about principles. The Aberdeen Agenda on local democracy, adopted by the
    Commonwealth Local Government Forum, provides that local government should have appropriate
    powers in accordance with the principle of subsidiarity.

References

Ahwoi, K (2010), *Local Government and Decentralisation in Ghana*, Unimax McMillan, Accra, Ghana.

Ali, SR (1980), *Local Government in Pakistan*, The Centre for Research in Local Government, Karachi University, Karachi.

Alam, M (1999), *Local Councils System in Sindh and Elections*, UN Development Programme (UNDP) and Norwegian Agency for Development Cooperation (NORAD), Islamabad.

Alam, M (unpublished), New Local Government Reforms – A way forward towards inducing social change, International Development Department, University of Birmingham, UK. MBA dissertation.

Anten, L (2012), 'The political economy of state-building in situations of fragility and conflict: from analysis to strategy', Conflict Research Unit, Netherlands Institute of International Relations (Clingendael), available at: www.clingendael.nl (accessed 20 January 2013).

Bari, F (2001), *Report of the Local Government Elections*, Pattan Development Organisation, Islamabad.

Bhave, A and C Kingston (2010), 'Military coups and the consequences of durable de facto power: the case of Pakistan', *Economics of Governance*, Vol. 11 No. 1, 51–76.

Briscoe, I (2008), 'The Proliferation of the Parallel State', working paper, Fundación para las Relaciones Internacionales y el Diálogo Exterior (FRIDE), Madrid.

Cheema, A, AI Khawaja and A Qadir (2003), 'Local government reforms in Pakistan: context, content and causes', available at: www.hks.harvard.edu/fs/akhwaja/papers/Chapter8.pdf (accessed 12 December 2012).

Cheema, A, AI Khawaja and A Qadir (2005), 'Decentralization in Pakistan: context, content and causes', Kennedy School of Government Faculty, Research Working Paper series – RWP 05-034, USA, available at: http://dx.doi.org/10.2139/ssrn.739712 (accessed 12 December 2012).

Local Government Alliance (2009), 'Saving local democracy in Pakistan', *LGA Newsletter*, October, available at: www.lga.org.uk (accessed March 2013).

Montiel, L (1988), Institutional development of local government in a developing country: the case of Venezuela, thesis submitted to the Faculty of Commerce and Social Science of the University of Birmingham for the degree of Doctor of Philosophy, International Development Department, University of Birmingham.

Pattan (2006), *Common Grounds, Survey of Candidates, Councillors and Nazims*, Pattan Development Organisation, Islamabad.

Randall, SC and S Hermann (1981), 'Conceptualising social change: problems of definition, empirical reference and explanation', in S Hermann and S Randall (Eds.), *An Introduction to Theories of Social Change*, Routledge and Kegan Paul, London.

Siddiqui, K (1992), *Local Government in South Asia*, University Press Limited, Dhaka.

Sivaramakrishnan, KC (2000), 'Urbanisation and problems of governance', in VA Pai Paqnadikar (Ed.), *Problems of Governance in South Asia*, Konark Publishers, New Delhi, 13–16.

Waseem, M (1994), *Politics and the State in Pakistan*, National Institute of Historical and Cultural Research, Islamabad.

World Bank (1996), *Supporting Fiscal Decentralization in Pakistan*, World Bank, Washington, DC.

World Bank (1998), *A Framework for Civil Service Reform in Pakistan*, World Bank, Washington, DC.

Chapter 4

Decentralisation and Community Budgeting in England

Nigel Keohane

The United Kingdom has been described as the most centralised country in Europe: in 2005, the UK's local authorities raised only 17 per cent of their income from local taxation compared with the Organisation for Economic Co-operation and Development (OECD) average of 55 per cent (Blöchliger and Petzold 2009). While the smaller devolved nations of Scotland, Wales and Northern Ireland have received significant delegated authority over the past 15 years, England has retained its centralised balance of power. This chapter assesses recent reform initiatives designed to redress this imbalance.

Since 2009, English local government have been dominated by the concept of 'Total Place' or 'Community Budgeting': the aim is to bring together all the public money spent in an area by national and local governments, and to commission services locally in a more co-ordinated way in order to make the best use of scarce resources and tailor services to community and individual needs. This chapter reviews how the Labour and subsequently coalition governments have pursued this agenda and the political, practical and philosophical barriers they have faced. It then sets out a series of methods by which the principle could be extended in England, and its implications for public services and governance. The chapter describes and assesses how programmes for decentralisation have been undertaken in England since 2010, considers options for their development in the future, and presents lessons for other countries seeking to localise power.

4.1 'Total Place' and 'Community Budgeting': the genesis of reform

In the final years of its 1997–2010 administration, the Labour government initiated a programme of pilots called 'Total Place'. These built on a number of localist reforms adopted by the government during its previous dozen years in office. The common feature among these programmes was a set of priorities and actions that were agreed between municipal and national governments.

The Total Place pilots aimed to develop this concept further, and make a reality of the government's vision of 'joined-up' government. Not only were national and local governments to agree on what outcomes to pursue, but all public spending in an area was to be brought together as a single pot. Total Place was also the acme of the focus on 'place' or geography as a unifying force in public management and service delivery.

In part at least, the ideas behind Total Place emerged organically from previous reforms. However, they were motivated also by dissatisfaction at the speed and scale of devolution. Reforms under the Labour government from 1997 to 2010 had little impact on the overriding balance of power between the centre and the locality. They compared unfavourably with momentous shifts of power down to the devolved administrations of Northern Ireland, Scotland and Wales. The complexity of the governance of English local government[1] proved difficult to reform. Given the obstacles to major institutional reform, the aim was to encourage councils to adopt a stronger leadership in their area without providing them with legislative powers. Councils, therefore, were to achieve their objectives by influencing partners in the public, private and 'third' sectors.

On the fiscal side, the government ignored the recommendations of a major review that had called for local authorities to raise a significantly higher proportion of their revenue from their own local tax base (Lyons 2007). Total Place theoretically helped resolve this dilemma. In each local area, the objective was for funding from the local authority, health services, criminal justice, the Department for Work and Pensions and other central departments to be pooled. Responsibility for the use of those funds was then to be delegated to local decision-makers and professionals, and for services to be commissioned at the local level using all the available resources. This would reduce council financial dependence on the central Treasury.

Second, the agenda arose from a growing recognition that societal demands were becoming more differentiated. While national-led improvement (through targets and performance management) had resulted in some acknowledged advances, satisfaction with local public services had stagnated, as had the productivity of those services (Office of the Deputy Prime Minister 2006).

Total Place tapped into growing evidence that commissioning of many services – such as family social services – was inefficient and unco-ordinated. Successful councils pointed to the benefits of orchestrating interventions early, which could prevent significant social and economic costs in the future. However, these relied on service commissioners from different parts of government being ready to commission jointly. Additionally the model of network government, which had thus far relied on councils to persuade public service partners in their local area to collaborate voluntarily and commission jointly, had been an inadequate response to these challenges. Although public agencies and local authorities had been allowed – and indeed encouraged – to pool budgets into common pots to spend on shared priorities, progress had been slow. Take for example health and social care services, where in 2009 only 3.4 per cent of funding was formally pooled (HM Treasury 2009). Although the introduction of Local Strategic Partnerships had led to much closer collaboration between public agencies, little pooled budgeting or joint commissioning had emerged, with central prescription often cited as the barrier (Department for Communities and Local Government 2009).

The Conservative opposition welcomed the scrutiny of regional government and evidence of the costs of duplication across tiers of government. This strengthened its case for the abolition of unelected government agencies (such as Regional Assemblies) and the ending of the regional tier of government outside London (Conservative Party 2009).

Finally, these developments coincided with a realisation that major budget cuts would have to be made to assist national fiscal consolidation; reductions that would dwarf the efficiencies that local government had been making in previous years.

4.1.1 New areas of focus

The movement also focused on a number of new areas. The concept of 'co-production' took a central role, with public agencies seeking to act collectively and to encourage citizens to contribute to social outcomes. There was also a growing recognition that frontline professionals had been overlooked in the devolutionary journey (Cabinet Office 2009). New theories of leadership and management informed the pilots – there was growing interest in 'public value theory' and 'whole systems' problem-solving techniques (Benington and Hartley 2009). As the London Borough of Lewisham explained:

> Decisions in relation to how resources are allocated are often taken at different spatial levels and via different Government department or policy silos. However, cost is often borne through the whole system, across a range of different individual agencies working within that system (Lewisham Strategic Partnership 2010).

Understanding which agency was intervening at which points in the lives of citizens, and how service decisions and investments were made, could allow for a much more effective system of government.

4.1.2 The Total Place pilots

While only 13 official Total Place pilots were launched, the concept dominated the sector's thinking and a further 80 areas also ran unofficial programmes concurrently.

Pilots were made up of three activities:

- counting all the public money that went into an area;

- focusing on the needs of citizens and their journey through public services;

- changing the culture of public management and professionalism locally.

Each pilot looked at one or more specific service and/or delivery challenge. These included integrated local approaches to assets; family services; drug and alcohol abuse; offender management; re-employment programmes; and early years and maternity services.

So what did the pilot studies discover? They reported back in March 2010 and suggested that significant financial savings (approximately 10–15 per cent) could be made across a whole range of services if councils and their partners were allowed to centre services around local citizens' needs, cut duplication of services and intervene earlier to prevent rather than cure expensive problems. Reports from the pilots and from independent research organisations called for major reforms to the systems of government to unlock these opportunities and innovations.

The information gathered through the pilots allowed local authorities and their public sector partners to map out customer journeys and understand how public services interacted with the user. Examples from London and Birmingham are presented in Boxes 4.1 and 4.2.

Box 4.1 Reforms to English local government 2000–09

Many of the devolutionary reforms introduced in the decade beginning 2000 can be separated into the following categories:

Central–local relations

The *2007 Central Local Concordat* sought to establish a series of principles that would guide the relationship between national and local government. This was complemented with the *Sustainable Communities Act*, which gave local authorities a right to request additional specific freedoms or new powers from the national government.

Place-shaping

The government led attempts to provide local authorities with a greater role as the primary elected local agencies, so that they could influence programmes outside their direct control. This included the 'General Power of Well-being' – a power to do anything that promoted the economic, social or environmental well-being of an area (*Local Government Act 2000*).

Joined-up government

Local Strategic Partnerships were set up to promote collaboration between all public partners in a locality.[2]

Citizen-centred services

A series of policy changes sought to increase choice in public services, and promote 'double devolution': from central to local government and then to community-based service providers and individuals themselves.

Box 4.2 Total Place case studies

London Councils and commissioning

On behalf of the capital, London Councils (an organisation representing all 33 London boroughs) commissioned a report that set out major financial and public service benefits, if responsibility for commissioning were devolved to lower tiers of governance in London. Particular lessons included the benefits of

(continued)

(*continued*)

early intervention in chronic health and diabetes – savings were estimated at 20 per cent. These would flow from treating people before conditions became so acute that emergency health intervention was required. In anti-social behaviour and youth offending a similar lesson emerged, namely that young people at risk could be identified and supported and young offenders managed so that costly criminal behaviour could be reduced. As the report noted:

London's local authorities end up picking up many of the direct costs and an even greater proportion of the indirect costs of this social problem. At the same time they are the democratic bodies closest to their communities and with the best community knowledge. We therefore propose that councils should have a much stronger role as a unifying organisational link between the other bodies at work in this system (PwC and London Councils 2010: 26).

London Councils' research indicated that, as well as savings of some 23 per cent flowing to local authorities in the capital from any change, the central government's National Health Service would also benefit, though to the lesser degree of 10 per cent. London's report called for integrated 'case management': a flexible, end-to-end management and organisation of the public service support required to meet an individual's needs, overseen by a key worker.

Birmingham City Council and drug abuse

Birmingham City Council has a population of approximately 1 million. The pilot project found that the city had about 11,000 people who had issues with drug use. Each of its 6,400 drug addicts averaged £833,000 of social costs in their lifetime. It was estimated that, for every £1 invested, £10 could be saved if the right intervention were made by the right agency at the right time. However, three quarters of the saving would accrue not to the council itself, but to other public sector partners. Being able to access this money was, therefore, fundamental to being able to make the additional investment in these services.

However, the pilots unearthed a series of barriers and problems that were preventing effective joined-up government:

- National targets, data requirements and processes forced different agencies to follow their own set procedures for delivering services. The rigidity of existing hierarchical reporting and accountability structures from agencies up to their departmental chiefs was seen to undermine collective endeavour at the local level.

- Budgets allocated for specific services and institutional funding left little flexibility to local government in spending decisions. In some instances it was shown that local authorities controlled a mere 15 per cent of the public money spent in an area.

- London Councils' analysis found that 'a significant weakness in existing arrangements is that insufficient attention is given to early interventions that avoid greater and more expensive problems occurring later' (PwC and London Councils 2010: 40). This was replicated across all the pilot areas.

- Independent research illustrated the significant cultural barriers that divorced different professional groups from each other (New Local Government Network 2010).

- Leadership and change experts argued that despite the financial analysis, many of the challenges associated with the agenda were not static and resolvable through conventional solutions (Grint 2010).

- Analysis estimated that in the sphere of economic development it cost national, regional and local organisations some 135 million pounds sterling (£) to spend £176 million on projects in the county, because of the multiple layers of decision-making and bureaucracy (Leicester and Leicestershire Public Service Board 2010).

At the heart of the issue sat the inability of local decision-makers and service commissioners to access funding from across all areas of the public purse to intervene at the right juncture before the costs of services escalated. However, the pilots identified not only that other agencies (such as the health service) spent more money than local authorities, but also that councils had little control over much of their own spending; much bypassed them straight into the hands of citizens (such as through personal budgets and welfare payments).

4.1.3 Implications and suggested reforms

Reports called for major reforms to the systems of government to unlock opportunities. Suggested changes included:

- significant devolution of money from central departments and departmental agencies to local councils or to local public service commissioning boards;

- new methods for pooling budgets locally;

- removal of all national prescriptions about how local budgets should be spent, and abolition of national targets that told councils which policies to pursue; and

- changes to national and local governance so that ministers could delegate accountability to local politicians.

Beyond this, the research had potential implications for the wider governance of England. From 1997 there had been significant devolution to the assemblies in Cardiff (Wales), Stormont (Northern Ireland) and Edinburgh (Scotland). However, England did not have its own parliament. In this regard, the pilot projects suggested an alternative route to delegate power, namely to city regions or subregions. While creating the mayoralty of (Greater) London was assumed to have resolved many of these anomalies in the capital, there remained little fiscal freedom and only limited control over a whole range of public services. What is more, London Councils argued that many services should be commissioned and delivered at more localised levels (PwC and London Councils 2010).

In London this culminated in a *Manifesto for Londoners*, which argued that:

> Each of the [local political] parties ... has a common desire to better integrate services at a local level within a framework of clear democratic accountability. This manifesto explains why London should be in the first wave of change to a less centralised and more joined up form of government ... We show how devolution will allow a newly elected national government to move faster to reduce the national debt (PwC and London Councils 2010).

Recommendations to promote effective commissioning included accountability for non-acute care budgets to reside with the local council; worklessness programmes to be commissioned by councils through a joint board across the economic subregions of London; and that the Metropolitan Police Authority should devolve neighbourhood policing budgets to London boroughs.

Elsewhere, in seeking to resolve public service challenges, the pilots discovered benefits in geographic scale. In cases such as schools policy and drug and alcohol abuse, councils sought to collaborate with neighbours in formal arrangements to commission and regulate effectively. Therefore, the pilot projects presented options for the devolution of significant responsibilities from the Westminster parliament to subnational government across a whole range of public services.

4.2 The coalition government and the 'Big Society'

These significant demands for devolution made the agenda heavily dependent on major decentralisation from national politicians and Whitehall. In March 2010, the early signs were that the Labour government was only ready to make piecemeal rather than radical reforms: reducing some of the regulatory burdens which forced different agencies to compete on priorities and for resources, and giving councils some limited additional freedom over expenditure (HM Treasury 2010). However, Labour's commitment was not fully tested because, following a general election in May 2010, the Conservatives and Liberal Democrats joined to form a new coalition government.

From the outset, the coalition sought to proclaim its localist beliefs. Many national restrictions on council spending have been removed. Central performance management has been reduced, and the national auditor that scrutinised local authorities abolished. A review was set up to explore the case for the localisation of business rates, which previously had been nationalised and then redistributed to councils as grants. The report concluded that, in the future, councils should be able to retain some of the proceeds of business rate growth in their areas. An influential parliamentary committee has subsequently called for additional powers for councils to be codified in law (House of Commons Political and Constitutional Reform Committee 2013).

Three specific strands of decentralisation can be detected in the government's localism strategy: municipalism; decentralisation through market-based public service reforms; and direct democracy. These changes have taken place in the context of major cuts in central grants to local authorities of 28 per cent over four years, part of a wider effort to reduce the government's budget deficit (Table 4.1).

In seeking to boost contestability and competition in public services, there has been a move to diversify provision to include private providers, civil society, public sector mutuals and co-operatives. For instance, parents are being encouraged to set up their own schools independent of local authority control, and general practitioner doctors are being given greater control of commissioning in health. Meanwhile, the prime minister's vision of a 'Big Society' has encompassed a focus on the family as a societal institution; neighbourhoods, communities and networks; and charities and the voluntary sector (HM Government 2010).

Many of the coalition's reforms deliberately bypass municipal government. Therefore, head-teachers of 'free schools' are no longer overseen by the local authority and citizens will have the right to a referendum if the Secretary of State considers that the local authority is introducing an 'excessive' council tax rise.

These reforms have tended to fragment the previous public sector architecture. Theoretically, this may make it harder to join up commissioning and funding across public bodies. However, the coalition has also sought to pursue a policy similar in concept to the Labour government's Total Place initiative. In its October 2010 spending review, the coalition announced a series of 'Community-Based Budgets', under which a neighbourhood would receive a complete pot of public money and be left to decide how to prioritise expenditure and commission services:

> By uprooting the silos, unlocking and relinquishing the spending controls administered by Whitehall we can give towns and places the freedom to direct spending to best meets the needs of the citizens within their boundaries (Department for Communities and Local Government 2010a).

Although the terminology of Total Place was dropped, 16 somewhat similar pilots were identified focusing on family services.

In 2011, the government committed in its *Community Budget Prospectus* to extend the Community-Based Budget pilots through the second half of its resource review. Two localities were allowed to pilot a comprehensive community budget approach. In June 2011, the government announced its desire to roll out the concept of Community-Based Budgets more widely, with a review testing how Community-Based Budgets can be used to 'give communities and local people more power and control over local

Table 4.1 The coalition government's decentralising reforms

Municipalism	General Power of Competence for local government
	Business rate retention by local authorities
	Directly elected mayors
Marketisation	Parents able to set up their own 'free schools'
	Healthcare commissioning delegated to groups of doctors
Citizen control	Referendums
	Neighbourhood control of planning decisions
	Directly elected police commissioners

services and budgets, [and] develop outcomes, service solutions and a single budget, or options for pooling and aligning resources, comprising all spending on public services in an area' (Department of Communities and Local Government 2011a).

A small number of pilots have also been established to explore how Community-Based Budgets could function at the neighbourhood and municipal levels, and how central government could facilitate them (HM Government 2011). As part of these, the government has committed to providing funding to support both the administration of the pilot projects, but also to ensure the involvement of Whitehall departments. Joint teams comprising officials from Whitehall and local service providers have been assembled to support the work locally (HM Government 2011).

The most significant step has been the government's announcement that eight 'City Deals' have been agreed with the biggest cities outside London. Although each of these agreements differs, budgets and responsibilities devolved include transport, rail franchising and workforce skills (Office of the Deputy Prime Minister 2012). The government has pledged to extend this approach to other cities, with 14 additional areas encouraged to participate in the next tranche.

4.3 Models for adopting area-based budgets

These attempts to reform public services through delegated area budgets have resulted in a range of different approaches, described below. Each model offers routes to connect budget decisions and commissioning at the local level, and each requires different action at the centre of government to make them effective.

- **Model 1: Agreement** between national and local government, where commissioning responsibilities and funding are devolved

- **Model 2: Commissioning and contestability,** which draws on the government's changes in the *Localism Act* and seeks to decentralise decisions

- **Model 3: Informal networking,** where service providers and other stakeholders are left to align funding and services in their localities through personal relationships and network governance

4.3.1 Model 1: Agreement

Model 1 draws on the philosophical premise that citizens themselves and each tier of elected government are entitled to have a role in shaping the nature of provision and the priorities within their jurisdiction. It requires significant buy-in from central government departments, who have to be ready to hand over responsibility for funding. The official pilots of both the Labour government and the coalition have been founded on this principle of negotiation: local areas have made requests for budgetary freedoms or public funding streams and, in return, have pledged to deliver a series of agreed outcomes.

The City Deals represent this vision. For instance, in the Greater Manchester City Deal, the authority has been given additional powers to promote the economy and employment, while also receiving a share in the reward (Department of the Deputy Prime Minister 2012) (Box 4.3).

Box 4.3 The Greater Manchester City Deal

Greater Manchester will raise £1.2bn and invest it locally in the economy. The City will be able to retain (or 'earn back') a share of the national tax take created by this growth on a payment-by-results basis, and will reinvest 'earned back' funds into further infrastructure projects.

A 'Greater Manchester Investment Framework' will be set up to channel European, central government, private sector and council investment towards projects that boost Gross Value Added in Manchester.

The City will boost the number of apprenticeships by 10 per cent in return for greater influence over skills commissioning, including through use of incentives for providers. The City Region will also receive responsibility for the Northern rail franchise, and for local transport funding.

Adopting these agreements is likely to lead to a diverse range of devolutionary deals across different localities. Greater local autonomy can be expected in some areas than in others. First, different localities will pursue different outcomes. Second, the central government may only negotiate with councils that it judges to meet specific criteria. In England, initial emphasis was on negotiating only with large city regions, or only with councils that have robust governance frameworks in place (Department of the Deputy Prime Minister 2012). Subsequently, the City Deals have been expanded to include smaller cities (Department of the Deputy Prime Minister 2013), but have continued to exclude some areas from the opportunities. Third, these reforms will rely on each locality being able to build up a strong and persuasive evidence base as to how public money could be used more effectively. This was not always the case under the original Total Place pilots. Fourth, for cautious central authorities negotiated settlements offer a route to trial different approaches while limiting the risk to the national treasury, because they operate as pilots of alternative commissioning arrangements.

There is also significant scope to pursue this model below the municipal authority level. An aim of the last two governments has been to increase the proportion of public expenditure managed directly by communities. Many of the initial Total Place pilots were managerial in content and focus. However, as the London Borough of Croydon acknowledged, 'We [the state] do not have all the answers. Government will need to become more porous: we are convinced that there is power in letting people into the previously closed systems of policy making' (Croydon Council 2010: 14). This strategy appeals particularly to the coalition government, with its desire to rebalance from state to citizens.

Such approaches would require:

- central government to devolve significant portions of national departmental expenditure to local areas;

- a robust and trusted process for negotiating expenditure and the outcomes to be achieved; and

- new governance arrangements to determine how ministers could step back from decision-making, how money voted through parliament would be held accountable and what the democratic decision-making structure across a locality could look like.

Once these requirements were fulfilled, communities could be given spending power in a number of ways, some of which are discussed briefly below.

Neighbourhood community budgets

Already, a number of councils in England operate small community budgets at the electoral ward and parish level. These commonly consist of sums of between £10,000 and £100,000 devolved to decision-making groups at the neighbourhood level, where they can decide how to shape their local environment. Given the specific nature of neighbourhood challenges, authorities such as Birmingham City Council have argued that this approach would allow communities to respond to the specific problems they face through devolving budgets for all parts of state expenditure (Localis 2010).

The government has launched ten pilots to explore how citizens within a neighbourhood can help design public service provision in their area and decide how to spend their area budget. The aim is to understand what range and type of service could be delivered in this way. The pilots are covering the following service areas: family policy; health and well-being; community assets; housing; worklessness; social enterprise; economic growth; anti-social behaviour; and gang violence (Department for Communities and Local Government 2011b).

A number of methods could be employed to help manage risks, increase community involvement and give credibility to community decisions; for instance, auditing expenditure by community groups or decision-making bodies.

Participatory budgeting

Participatory budgeting offers a second option. Although a number of localities have used the method, participatory budgeting is not widespread in England. Where such budgets have been used, they have also tended to be marginal or discretionary sums – an investment in community engagement rather than effective state budgeting for efficiency. However, recent evaluations have shown that participatory budgeting can increase levels of understanding between communities and service deliverers (Department for Communities and Local Government 2010b).

Participatory budgeting could provide a tool to give credibility and strength to Community-Based Budgets. If local communities were permitted to keep a specific proportion of any savings made at the neighbourhood level, this could be added to a community pot to create positive incentives for participation. Direct citizen input would provide clarity and transparency about how decisions on spending revenue from across a range of departments and agencies are prioritised and decided on, giving reassurance to ministers, civil servants and the public that this money was neither being used fraudulently nor captured by bureaucracy.

4.3.2 Model 2: Contestability and commissioning

An alternative model for devolving funding to the local level is on a straightforward commissioning basis. This is in sympathy with the government's reform programme, which is seeking to break up state provision by diversifying and outsourcing supply (Cabinet Office 2011a).

The 'community right to challenge'

As part of its *Localism Act*, the government has introduced a range of 'rights' to local citizens and communities to break the public sector monopoly of provision and give communities greater involvement in service delivery. These new 'rights' include:

- a 'community right to challenge', which gives communities the right to submit an 'expression of interest' in taking over and running a council service;

- a 'community right to bid', which allows communities to bid for ownership of local assets if they are of importance to the community (Department for Communities and Local Government 2012).

Under these initiatives, 'communities' include citizens, social enterprises, public sector workers, charities, lower-tier (parish) councils and other local organisations. However, major questions have been asked about how these rights would be exercised: what would constitute a local asset that citizens could bid to take over? If a community group started to run a service, how would the state ensure that access to the service is not restricted and that quality is sustained?

Under the Localism Act, the government intends that local council services should be opened up to contestability, so that community groups can take over local public services. Any community group, co-operative or parish council can register a challenge to run a service currently run by a local authority. The authority then has to consider the challenge and, if it accepts it, run a tendering process. In the context of budget reductions, initiatives where communities take responsibility for services are already under way across the country, especially in relation to library and environmental services. To encourage other community groups to come forward to use the right, the government has set up a website as well as tailored support to help groups that wish to run services.

A local authority 'right to challenge'?

Subsequently, some have argued that the government should widen the applicability of the right to challenge to include all central government services, as well as those of local authorities (New Local Government Network 2011a). Under this proposal, councils as well as community groups would be able to bid to run services currently delivered by national departments and agencies.

Such an approach would draw on the principle of subsidiarity – all parts of the state apparatus would have to defer to forces at a lower level, a principle that the

Prime Minister, David Cameron, has strongly endorsed (Cameron 2011). From a practical point of view, a local authority right to challenge could allow them to develop economies of scale and scope and to establish pooled budgets across a range of service areas.

As noted earlier, theoretically Model 2 would simply be an alternative commissioning process rather than central government ceding democratic control in any way. While under Model 1 outcomes would be negotiated and agreed between national and local governments, under Model 2 the outcomes would be determined nationally and delivered locally. Central government is able to retain significant control of the budgets released. Because a commissioning arrangement is maintained, lines of financial accountability remain simpler with ministers accountable for spending that is officially voted through by parliament.

4.3.3 Model 3: Informal networking

Without any governance, funding or commissioning reforms, local authorities are left with a series of less transformative options for pursuing integration at the local level and building public services around the needs of citizens and communities. Nevertheless, some of these approaches offer scope for councils to reform public services locally.

Using new powers

Even without additional delegated budgets, the new General Power of Competence may give councils additional leverage to bring public sector partners together. The new power gives councils the right to undertake any activity that is not prohibited expressly in law. As this power is being granted to councils but not to other parts of the public sector, potential partner agencies may be motivated to commit to a joint venture with the local authority to be able to make use of its additional freedoms to trade and develop new services.

There is increased scope to pursue some of the lines of enquiry of joined-up government without approval or authorisation from the centre. For instance, Kent County Council has advanced specific practical policies that bring together local service deliverers. Its 'Kent Card' is a payment, service access and entitlement card that can be used across all public agencies in the county. Meanwhile, the 'Maidstone Gateway' places all public agencies under one roof for the convenience of residents as well as efficient use of assets.

These are worthwhile initiatives. However, while a series of improvements and efficiencies are possible, many parts of state funding (such as health, social security expenditure and education) are likely to remain off-limits.

Market regulator and behaviour shaper

In a world where public service institutions and democratic control are more fragmented, there are strong arguments to suggest that the most meaningful method of building services around the needs of an individual is through market regulation and behavioural change.

The Cabinet Office is taking an increased interest in behaviour change, recently setting up a Behavioural Insight Team. Policies in public health, pensions and climate change have adopted approaches to influence more positive behaviour among citizens (Cabinet Office 2011b). However, two opposing models of behaviour change are emerging, which offer contrasting approaches to connecting decision-making and investment decisions.

On the one hand, deliberative democracy as a collective educational tool is identified as a means of developing community decisions that reflect shared consideration of a problem. This can be powerful as a force for democratic engagement and participation, but also as a method for the population to agree and adopt socially desirable outcomes (John et al. 2011).

Alternatively, more traditional government-led behaviour change schemes may offer more immediate routes forward. If local decision-makers have only limited influence over the spending decisions of other public agencies, there remains scope to shape the paths of citizens and how they interact with public services through 'nudge' approaches. By applying lessons from behavioural science, policy-makers can steer citizens into more socially optimal activities. Carried out well, this approach may allow the state to shape how individuals spend their personal budgets in areas such as adult social care and health.

Social investment opportunities

The government's Big Society agenda is putting significant store in social investment as a means to access additional external finance to fund public services. Social Impact Bonds are currently being piloted in Peterborough, seeking to attract investment from the capital markets to run early intervention and prevention programmes, while the state continues to fund traditional services. To help introduce social investment, the government has established a 'Big Society Bank', which will seek to fund small providers and facilitate social investment. At the same time, a number of innovative local authorities are developing their own local Big Society Banks (New Local Government Network 2011b). If social investment approaches are successful, there may be opportunities to create virtuous pools of funds that can be invested, built and re-invested in local preventative schemes. While these funds would not match the level of investment that could stem from pooling all public sector budgets across an area, they may represent opportunities to work towards area investments. Alternatively, councils may be able to create funding pots which subsidise other commissioning parties that are ready to commit budgets to shared commissioning approaches.

4.4 Conclusion

With the advent of the coalition government, radical decentralisation has raised complex questions about what decentralisation means, about the nature of accountability and about how communities resource and provide for themselves. Localism itself is becoming an increasingly contested concept. The differing concepts of decentralisation and localism put forward through Labour's Total Place pilots, and subsequently by the coalition government in the form of community Budgeting and the Big Society, exhibit similarities as well as differences. Despite the change in government, many local areas can continue to pursue their aspirations for locality-based expenditure programmes and tailoring of services. There remain alternative models for pursuing this objective. Both the coalition and the Labour governments have ultimately sought to reach agreements between national and local commissioners.

Much remains unknown and there are evident risks in pursuing some of the policies and approaches now being contemplated. Are central government departments likely to act as willing partners? What are the implications for the purpose and role of central government? How far will the expected outcomes and savings be delivered? Yet, in times of economic hardship and fiscal constraint, UK governments appear to think that the potential benefits of these new ways of managing, funding and joining up services justify any risk involved.

Notes

1   English local government is made up of a range of single-tier local authorities (unitary authorities, London boroughs and metropolitan boroughs) alongside two-tier structures (counties and districts in rural areas).
2   Local Strategic Partnerships were convened in each local area by the council, with membership comprising major public sector partners such as health and policing, alongside voluntary and private sector partners.

References

Benington, J and J Hartley (2009), 'Whole Systems Go!' Improving Leadership across the Whole Public Service System, National School of Government, Sunningdale.
Blöchliger, H and O Petzold (2009), Taxes of Grants: What Revenue Source for Sub-central Governments? OECD, Paris.
Cabinet Office (2009), Excellence and Fairness, Cabinet Office, London.
Cabinet Office (2011a), Open Public Services White Paper, Cabinet Office, London.
Cabinet Office (2011b), Health and Behavioural Insight, Cabinet Office, London.
Cameron, D (2011), 'How we will release the grip of state control', Daily Telegraph, 20 February 2011.
Conservative Party (2009), Control Shift, Conservative Party, London.
Croydon Council (2010), Child: Family: Place: Radical Efficiency to Improve Outcomes for Young Children, Croydon Council, Croydon.
Department for Communities and Local Government (2009), Long-term Evaluation of Local Area Agreements and Local Strategic Partnerships, Department for Communities and Local Government, London.
Department for Communities and Local Government (2010a), 'Announcement: 16 areas get "community budgets" to help the vulnerable', Department for Communities and Local Government, London.
Department for Communities and Local Government (2010b), National Evaluation of Participatory Budgeting in England Interim Evaluation Report, Department for Communities and Local Government, London.

Department for Communities and Local Government (2011a), '14 Areas to Pioneer Scheme to "Pool and Save" Billions', Press Release, 21 December 2011, Department for Communities and Local Government, London.

Department for Communities and Local Government (2011b), *Second Phase of the Local Government Resource Review: Terms of Reference June 2011*, Department for Communities and Local Government, London.

Department for Communities and Local Government (2012), *Community Right to Challenge: Statutory Guidance*, Department for Communities and Local Government, London.

Department of the Deputy Prime Minister (2012), *Unlocking Growth in Cities: City Deals – Wave 1*, Department of the Deputy Prime Minister, London.

Department of the Deputy Prime Minister (2013), *Announcement Wave 2 – City Deals*, Department of the Deputy Prime Minister, London.

Grint, K (2010), *Problem, Purpose, Power, Knowledge, Time and Space*, Leadership Centre for Local Government, London.

HM Government (2010), *Building the Big Society*, HM Government, London.

HM Government (2011), *Community Budgets Prospectus*, HM Government, London.

HM Treasury (2009), *Smarter Government White Paper*, HM Treasury, London.

HM Treasury (2010), *Total Place: A Whole Area Approach to Public Services*, HM Treasury, London.

House of Commons Political and Constitutional Reform Committee (2013), *Prospects for Codifying the Relationship between Central and Local Government*, The Stationary Office, London.

John, P, G Smith and G Stoker (2011), 'Nudge Nudge, Think Think: Two Strategies for Changing Civic Behaviour', *Political Quarterly*, 80, (3), 361–370.

Leicester and Leicestershire Public Service Board (2010), *Leicester and Leicestershire Total Place Final Report*, Leicester and Leicestershire Public Service Board.

Lewisham Strategic Partnership (2010), *Total Place in Lewisham: Public Services Working Together with Citizens for Better Outcomes*, Lewisham Strategic Partnership, London.

Localis (2010), *Total Neighbourhood* Localis, London.

Lyons, Sir M (2007), *Place-shaping: A Shared Ambition for the Future of Local Government*.

New Local Government Network (2010), *Greater than the Sum of Its Parts: Total Place and Future Public Services*, NLGN, London.

New Local Government Network (2011a), *Local Government Right to Bid*, NLGN, London.

New Local Government Network (2011b), *Realising Community Wealth*, NLGN, London.

Office of the Deputy Prime Minister (2006), *All Our Futures: The Challenges for Local Governance in 2015*, Office of the Deputy Prime Minister, London.

Office of the Deputy Prime Minister (2012), *Unlocking Growth in Cities: City Deals – Wave 1*, Office of the Deputy Prime Minister, London.

PwC and London Councils (2010), *London Councils: Total Place – Towards a New Service Model for Londoners*, London Councils, London.

Chapter 5

Ironic Localism and a Critical History of English 'Reform'

Mike Bennett and Kevin Orr

There are two particular challenges in writing about the outlook for twenty-first century local government in England, and the forces that may come into play, especially with the implication that we are drawing lessons which might benefit local government in the rest of the Commonwealth. The first is to avoid seeking to pre-empt events and foresee trends that stretch into the future, inevitably beyond our own existences. The second is to resist the temptation to describe our own time as somehow historically special; a stage of history at which our successors' destiny will be decided.

The task, therefore, is neither to overestimate our powers of foresight, nor the exceptional nature of the pace of change. This has led to a stance of critical uncertainty. Our foresight may be limited, but that does not excuse us from using the best of our experience to try to prepare the future. We have, therefore, done our best to read the runes of local government's future destiny. In doing so, however, we have not sought to deliver a classic, horizon-scanning survey of the 'big issues' (economic austerity, social unrest, democratic disengagement, rise of political extremism and so on), nor have we gone for a micro review of UK policy trends.[1] Instead we have interpreted our commission quite broadly, by looking backwards rather more than looking forwards. This approach also speaks to our understanding of local government not as a homogenised institution about which there is a single, essential story to be told (of past, present and future), but rather as a mélange of traditions, assumptions and competing voices (local and national) which have jostled with each other over time.

If one theme is consistent, albeit recurring in different ways reflective of time and circumstance, it is the ever-present tension between different levels of government. We therefore begin our analysis with Eric Pickles, Member of Parliament (MP), English Secretary of State for Communities. In doing so we consider how his political interventions can be understood as drawing upon and perpetuating the longstanding to-ing and fro-ing of traditions of centralisation and localism.

5.1 The irony of 'localism, localism, localism'

Whatever happens in the rest of the twenty-first century, it is likely that Eric Pickles MP will be remembered as a controversial politician in English local government. A radical Thatcherite leader of metropolitan Bradford in the late 1980s, Pickles held a number of shadow frontbench posts in opposition before he became Secretary of State for Communities in David Cameron's Conservative-led coalition in May 2010.

Surrounded by his southern and privately educated colleagues, Pickles cuts a distinctive figure on the Conservative frontbench. The 'straight-talking northerner' stereotype is one that he plays on knowingly and to good effect. In a speech to the Conservative party conference in 2007, he prefaced his explanation of Conservative local government policy with a statement of personal credo:

> I used to be a blunt Yorkshireman, but now I am an Essex Boy.[2] There is one thing that unites these two great counties, they like people who mean what they say. So, let me tell you something straight. The long-term success of the next Conservative government depends on giving people more opportunity and power over their lives. We are passionate about transferring power to local authorities and to do it in a way that will make it difficult for central government to ever take those powers back. Councils will help us to dismantle the centrist state, distributing its power to the people. Once that power is in their hands it will be impossible to take away. We have optimism and trust in our councils. We live in a new world where the destructive fringe that existed within some local authorities in the 1980s has long gone. … Conservatives will match this mood by giving ALL Councils greater flexibility both in finance and functions. We are sure that you can trust our Councils with funding without stipulating the way every single penny must be spent. … To do this you need to have a deep trust that communities will set sensible priorities and govern themselves well, and if they don't that the electorate will have the good sense to kick them out (Pickles 2007).

This blunt statement of the party's commitment to 'localism' could not have been clearer. It describes a Conservative commitment to taking power away from the central state, to diffusing power to councils because freedom demands it and, as we will discuss later, it feeds off a long-established tradition of localism in the local government milieu. Pickles' intervention does not suggest that 'localism' would bypass local government in the way that previous Communities Secretary David Miliband's 'double devolution' envisaged devolving beyond councils to neighbourhoods and communities. Furthermore, there is a strong, unqualified statement of belief in local government's competence. They are well run, there are no reasons not to trust them and Pickles is saying that, philosophically speaking, central government has no right to distrust democratic choices made by the electorate. It is not for central government to intervene when the electorate has every right to choose and to change their local leaders. This approach was further distilled into a joke that Pickles used repeatedly in speeches while in opposition. 'I have three priorities,' he used to say, 'my first priority is localism, my second priority is localism and my third priority is … localism'.

Four years after this speech, now in government, having piloted the Localism Bill through parliament and on the day it received Royal Assent, Pickles once again asserted how his government had changed local government for good, and revisited his campaign joke:

> Since ancient times governments and politicians have sought to wield power, which has always been about command and control … [but] this Government is leading the clarion call for more people power. … Localism Localism Localism has been our mantra for some time now. We entered Government listening to the

people and we were clear localising power and information would be a priority. Even as global problems mounted and dominated public attention, we remained steadfast in our pursuit of localism ... And the compulsory imposition of Whitehall knows best decisions have [sic] been shut off at the source. This act of localism is an act of political realism. Gone are the days of top-down command and control over communities – they have ceased – everybody is crossing the Rubicon into a new era of people power and local say so (Pickles 2011).

Here Pickles' claims are if anything even bolder. His thunderous blast reaches back to 'ancient times' to say that until now things had always worked in a certain way. Before the Conservative/Liberal Democrat coalition, governments had held power back from citizens; power had always served that state. The administration to which he belongs, however, has broken free of history, empowered the citizens and changed the way that government works. 'Crossing the Rubicon' is an allusion to Julius Caesar, who led his army over the river (Rubicon) towards Rome, launching an attack on the Empire in full knowledge that, if he did not succeed, he and his army would be condemned to death. What are we to make of such rhetoric? Is Pickles saying that, if his localism policy does not succeed, then he knows he faces certain political death? Is he comparing his own heroic leadership to that of Caesar's? Or is deliberately suggesting a radical break with history, even if he knows the truth is rather more mundane? Either way, Pickles' more literal assertions are uncompromising and his claim to have changed the course of history unambiguous.

Yet, for all his straight talking, there is more than a hint of irony in his claims to have entrenched localism beyond the point of no return. While some in the local government sector appear to take the promise of localism at face value, there are others who are more sceptical that Pickles really has crossed the Rubicon to fight against centralism. At the very least, elements of localism seem to co-exist (uneasily) with strands of centralism.

Some would begin, for example, by pointing to a letter written by Pickles to Nottinghamshire County Council to complain that the council has made 'disproportionate' cuts to its funding of the voluntary and community sector. The secretary of state, who in opposition railed against central interference as a bureaucratic iron cage and who urged councils to 'just say no' to central guidance, now says:

> I would be grateful if you could reconcile your council's decision on funding the voluntary and community sector to the strategic guidance (Pickles, in Butler 2012).

Sceptics may also submit the new stacks of guidance which the government is issuing to local authorities on a wide range of issues including local tax rates, council pay policies, neighbourhood bin collections, street parties and council prayers, and point to the sometimes brutal way in which ministers criticise councils (Keeling 2012; Ross 2012) for choices with which they disagree. Indeed it appears that local government ministers have alienated even the normally loyal Conservative council leaders who have bypassed their secretary of state and written directly to the Prime Minister, David Cameron, to warn that a 'retrograde tendency towards greater centralism' and 'constant criticisms' by ministers have left local activists 'angry' and possibly unwilling to help the party win the next general election (Keeling 2013). Finally, sceptics look, with eyebrows raised, at the way in which the Localism Act centralises power by providing 'unprecedented ability for the Secretary of State to introduce significant measures through secondary regulation' (Local Government Information Unit [LGIU] 2011). Many agree with Sir Merrick Cockell, Conservative Chair of the Local Government Association (LGA), who says that 'this bill actually centralised more powers than it localised' (Cockell 2011), or again with Sir Howard Bernstein, Chief Executive of Manchester City Council, when he says, 'These are fundamentally the same problems that we've had with successive governments over the last 20 years. This current government is probably a little bit smarter because it has managed to develop a headline or narrative around localism, which is meaningless in the context of what it's trying to do' (cited in McCann 2012).

In other words, sceptics would point to a track record of centralising action that provides a stark contrast to the localist talk. It was therefore no surprise to many when the secretary of state began to talk about 'guided localism', notably in evidence to a parliamentary select committee which subsequently labelled the government's approach to localism as incoherent and inconsistent, and its understanding of localism as 'elastic' (Communities and Local Government Select Committee 2011). In response, in September 2011, the Department for Communities and Local Government issued a weighty statement which defended the government's interpretation (Department of Communities and Local Government 2011). Significantly, in that paper we see the clear evolution of Pickles' view. Now the definition of localism has apparently reverted to the previous New Labour view 'that power should belong at the lowest appropriate level ... Whilst the most appropriate level will vary from service to service, it is the Government's clear view that, overall, power has accreted at too high a level over the years and that a process of decentralisation is needed to give power away' (Department of Communities and Local Government 2011: 5). It adds, by way of confirmation, 'the Government believes decentralisation should go beyond transferring power from central government to local government, important though that is. There should be a parallel decentralisation of power from central government to local government and to people and communities' (Department of Communities and Local Government 2011: 7).

While in opposition, Pickles' straight talking made it very clear that localism was about local government. Now the definition is much more qualified: it appears that the focus for reform has moved from campaigning for local government as an insurgent against the incumbents, to seeing local government itself as the incumbents that need to be challenged. Indeed, the disjunction between what ministers say and what they do in the name of localism suggests that the commitment to localism was part of what Stoker and Taylor-Gooby call 'politics as normal' rather than an ideological commitment to 'high Tory romanticism of a more organic social order in which individuals contribute to a common good through their own direct efforts' (Stoker and Taylor-Gooby 2011: 11–12). There is, therefore, a double irony in Pickles' rhetorical commitment to localism.[3] First, that the continuing deployment of localist rhetoric is knowingly out of kilter with his action: we can never know his motives for this approach, but it is worth noting that his strategy has been convincing, and remains popular in many influential non-local government Conservative circles. The second irony is that, given the long history of reform narratives providing principled cover for realist political manoeuvring, Pickles' claims to localist policy while in opposition were taken so uncritically.[4] For both these reasons, we speak of Eric Pickles as an exemplary, contemporary proponent of ironic localism.[5] The next sections consider two antecedents of ironic reform discourse.

5.2 Jump-cutting through the long history of 'reform'

Our first case study is Tudor England in the time of Henry VII, and the second is the Reform Acts of 1832 and 1867. This unusual starting point represents an almost exaggerated gesture designed to disrupt our idea that the 'now' is new. The narrative is intended to perform an unsettling function, unpicking certainties and allowing a fresh vision of present-day issues.

Using this approach, we want to look at the way in which leaders talk about ideas of reform, how they contextualise the challenge of change and how they frame their own responsibilities and those of others. In this way we aim to show that Pickles' use of the language of localism stands in a long pattern of ironic or tactical deployment of commitment to reform.

This analysis, therefore, questions the view that the twenty-first century is a uniquely localist moment and that there is an epoch-changing, paradigm-shifting collection of circumstances that create the conditions for localism to flourish. Rather, the current discourse of localism, when looked at in historical context, can be understood as a government using the talk of change to retain the mantle of insurgents, rather than become the established incumbents. This is, we suggest, a lesson worthy of study by all who argue for local government 'reform'.

5.2.1 The Tudors and central–local relations

Henry VII is well known as the founder of the Tudor dynasty in unifying the warring factions in the Wars of the Roses, and for the way in which he built the foundations of the British monarchy. But Henry's constitutional agenda was much broader than uniting the competing Houses of York and Lancaster. Under the feudal system, the government of localities was dominated by rich landowners who had the resources to resist central interference. However, following the Wars of the Roses the local nobility could not compete with the King's increased influence, and Henry seized this opportunity to centralise power, while at the same time creating elements of a recognisably modern form of local government built on common legal foundations.

The key to this centralisation was the professionalisation of the office of Justice of the Peace, seen as an essential condition for maintaining order in local communities, for executing the King's wishes and being held responsible when things went wrong (Tanner 1951). The main legislative instrument was the 1489 Justices Act, which was directed against the negligence and corruption of some Justices of the Peace in an attempt to heighten their accountability and improve their performance.

The Act proclaimed:

> The King our Sovereign Lord considereth that by the negligence and misdemeaning, favour, and other inordinate causes of the Justice of the Peace in every shire of this his realm, the laws and ordinances made for the politic weal, peace, and good rule …, be not duly executed according to the tenor and effect they were made and ordained for; wherefore his subjects be grievously hurt …; for to him is nothing more joyous than to know his subjects to live peaceably under his laws and to increase in wealth and prosperity (cited in Tanner 1951: 465–8).

Henry's Justices Act sets out a powerful case for reform in the local criminal justice system, but gives us the perhaps ironic case of the Sovereign seemingly rendered impotent by local bureaucracy. He conveyed the will to change the way things work, but was frustrated that local justices did not do his bidding. He may have created the British monarchy, but Henry portrayed his sovereignty as incomplete and divided. Even at the height of his powers he claimed that his writ did not rule in the towns and shires of England.

Faced with these limits to his power, Henry's response is twofold. First, he constructs a new legal framework, nominally for citizens to hold local justices to account. But second, because of his inability to command the justices' obedience, we also see Henry appealing directly to his subjects, over the heads of local officials, mobilising public opinion to place blame and responsibility firmly on others.

While the value system, attitudes and expectations of people in Tudor times towards their 'government' are largely obscure to us at this distance, Henry's renaissance reforms embody a recognisably modern approach to politics. He promises his people that he wants to improve their lives and he empathises with their problems. By demonstrating his zeal for reform he places himself, discursively, outside the establishment that he is criticising. He frames the challenge as one that can be achieved within existing resources. He has done all that he can, he wants things to change and he is putting pressure on others to show he is on the side of the people. As he says, the system 'lacketh nothing but that said laws be put in due execution' (*Justices Act 1489*, cited in Tanner 1951: 466). In other words, where life does not improve as desired for his subjects, where robbery or counterfeiting continues unchecked, it is clear from his declaration that he will blame local officials for inefficiency and ineffectiveness in not executing what he has ordained to be.

5.2.2 The nineteenth-century reform movement

Reform movements in local government ('localism' being an early twenty-first century example) share key features with other narratives of parliamentary or democratic reform, such as the nineteenth-century reform movement. While the so-called 'Great' *Reform Act of 1832* is often looked back upon with nostalgia as one of the landmark points in the growth of British democracy,[6] its architects would have been horrified to think they would be remembered as such. Following the death of its leader, Lord Liverpool, in 1828, factionalism and infighting within the Conservative Party and the rise to the leadership of the hardliner Wellington saw the party suffer heavy electoral defeat in 1831. This dramatic change of political control, combined with increased popular unrest calling for reform, led to a growing will for change. The House of Lords initially resisted the Whig proposals that consisted largely of the reconfiguration of parliamentary boundaries and constituencies, including representation of some large industrial areas such as Birmingham, Leeds and Sheffield for the first time. To persuade the Lords to back his measures, Prime Minister Earl Grey promised that change would go no further:

> If any persons suppose that this Reform will lead to ulterior measures, they are mistaken; for there is no one more decided against annual parliaments, universal suffrage, and the ballot, than I am. My object is not to favour, but to put an end to such hopes and projects (cited in Evans 2000: 24).

But it was Robert Peel, leading the opposition to the bill, whose pessimistic analysis turned out to be more insightful, saying that 'my belief is, that neither the monarchy nor the peerage can resist with effect the decrees of a House of Commons that is immediately obedient to every popular impulse, and that professes to speak the popular will' (cited in Wright 1970: 118–20).

In a related debate, Peel argued that this reform was a slippery slope to democracy:

> It was surely absurd to say, that a man of ten thousand pounds a year should not have more influence over the legislature of the country than a man of ten pounds a year. Yet each was entitled to a single vote. How could this injustice, this glaring inequality, be practically addressed ... How could the government end but in democracy, if the influence were merely accorded to numbers (cited in Machin 2001: 25).

But, while the 1832 Act did somewhat increase the electoral franchise, the 'increase in the electorate had not brought the system much closer to anything resembling democracy' (Wood 1982: 85). As Lynch argued, 'when the concessions were made in the "Great" Reform Act of 1832, they were in the view of those who made them the minimal required to assuage the most powerful groups amongst the disenfranchised and to ensure that power remained in the same hands as before' (1992: 386).

As counterintuitive as it now seems, the reform movement was fundamentally about resisting greater change. Lang argued that 'to modern eyes, what was wrong with the unreformed parliament was that it was undemocratic; it is difficult to grasp that that was, to the eighteenth-century eyes, including those of many reformers, one of the system's greatest assets' (1999: 3), and Whig Thomas Macauley declared that he 'support[s] this measure as a measure of reform; but I support it still more as a measure of conservation. That we may exclude those whom it is necessary to exclude, we must admit those whom it may be safe to admit' (cited in Wright 1970: 117–18).

The irony, therefore, is that those arguing for reform were doing so in order to preserve as far as possible the status quo.

The subsequent 1867 Reform Act was another product of tactical, political manoeuvring (what Stoker and Taylor-Gooby call 'politics as normal' [2011]). The Conservatives were keen to correct the disadvantage that they had suffered since the previous Reform Act, but had to find a way of tying in the more moralistic reformers. The Conservative leader Disraeli judged that, by including proposals for increased suffrage, sufficient radical Whig support could be attracted to carry a bill which he thought would increase electoral advantage for his party.

Thus, far from progressing logically from first principles towards democratic emancipation, the Reform movement was significantly influenced by party manoeuvring, the search for political advantage and a desire to change only so that things could remain largely the same.

> The history of nineteenth century parliamentary reform is not a story of stately progress from the darkness of corrupt manipulation and highly restricted voting rights to the broad sunlit uplands of open, participatory democracy. Britain had its democrats in the late eighteenth and early nineteenth centuries, but the overwhelming majority of reformers in parliament wanted change in order to frustrate democracy and preserve what they saw as the essentials of good government (Evans 2000: 92).

As with Pickles and Henry, here we see a telling example of ironic reform: politics carried out in the name of change for the purposes of consolidation; politicians assuming the mantle of the radical in order to preserve the status quo; and the language of reform being used to play to an array of interest groups and constituencies to bolster personal and political advantage.

5.3 Localism: the eternal return of the same?

So what does this analysis tell us about local government and where its future may lie in the twenty-first century? One way of exploring the apparently eternal antagonism within central–local relations is through the co-existence of interacting traditions of governing. Local government is more than a collection of institutions and statutory responsibilities. It is also a space for political sense-making and storytelling, in which competing versions of its purpose are played out. Two of the most prominent of these contested traditions can be described as localism and centralism, each of which represents distinctive values and assumptions about what ought to be the proper domain of local and central actors and institutions.

In this way, the localism tradition might be said to position local government as a key vehicle for forming a sense of identity and direction for communities. This view incorporates the notion of civic pride, or what Joseph Chamberlain (1885) called 'local spirit' or 'municipal patriotism'. The localism tradition in the UK draws on neo-Victorian narratives of trusted guardians and 'city fathers' who do the public good in the locality. Those who have felt a sense of loss or perceived the diminution of the institution have often spoken in terms of the erosion of localism, and such anxieties are age-old. A long line of commentators has offered normative rationales for the importance of the institution of local government based on the idea that such 'community-based' organisations are better placed to assess and respond to the needs of local people than are more remote central government ministries (Jones and Stewart 1983; Stewart 2001).

Aspects of New Labour's 'modernisation' narrative carried echoes of this tradition in calling for the 'revitalisation' of local government and communities (Blears 2007). The tradition also surfaced in the debate about the concept of 'new localism', advocates of which have emphasised community leadership rather than a service-delivery role for local government (Stoker and Wilson 2004; Bennett 2006). The priorities for action that this tradition highlights are the need to nurture the local economy, environment, culture and communities. It implies a correspondence of interest between the institution and the locality, and emphasises councils' roles in shaping identity, protecting local interests and expressing local values. It creates a sense of difference by defining places in relation to 'the local' and the 'non-local'.

The centralism tradition portrays local government as subject to a central state which tends to act in ways that delimit council autonomy (Keith-Lucas 1977; Burgess and Travers 1980; Duncan and Goodwin 1988; Wilson and Game 1994; Rao and Young 1997). It emphasises the ways in which central control is exercised by, and power is concentrated in, central government. Its antecedents appear to have existed as long as local government itself. Alexander cited a frustrated local alderman as saying in the 1850s that 'it was much to be regretted that Parliament, in passing measures urging on public improvements, did not at the same time decrease the difficulty and expense of carrying them out' (Alexander 1985: 48). Jennings' (1935) account of 'Central Control' quoted Sydney and Beatrice Webb's observation of Sir Robert Peel's 1815 legislation requiring prison authorities to provide statistical reports of their gaols as:

> the first that dictated to local authorities the detailed plan on which they were to exercise a branch of their own local administration; the first that made it obligatory to report, quarter by quarter, how their administration was actually being conducted; and the first that definitely asserted the duty of a Central Department to maintain a continuous supervision of the action of the local authorities in their current administration (Webb and Webb 1922: 462).

Similarly, Joseph Chamberlain (1885) complained that Home Secretary Sir William Harcourt's 1885 bill for local government reform involved 'immense centralisation'.

Almost a century later, the discourse of centralisation was just as pronounced, as one councillor complained apocalyptically that:

> Local government, I am saying quite frankly, has already declined in significance since 1970. The reorganisation of local government has been the biggest con trick ever played ... Housing has already been effectively taken over by national government. Now we have got water and sewage disposal, which will be taken away very soon. Before long, we will be able to see that the police, the fire brigades and even education will follow suit ... I am telling you now – I am forecasting – that before the end of this century local government will have effectively disappeared and we shall have Government directives and appointed boards (Phillips 1973: 51).[7]

Under the Blair government, the chair of the Local Government Association described a wish to 'achieve a dramatic reduction in the imposition of national targets, standards and performance indicators on local government, a radical overhaul of the burdensome system of inspection and regulation, and to build a new way of managing the central–local relationship' (Bruce-Lockhart 2006: 22).

What emerges from this picture is a sense that localism and centralism have long been co-existing concepts through which the lived experience of local government has been interpreted. At different times in the twentieth century, we have had governments elected with more or less localist manifestos or more or less centralist commitments. We also see a litter of Royal Commissions and other inquiries looking at the proper relation between central and local government. It is eye-opening to look back and see that almost each decade seems to have undertaken a serious examination of reform. The Royal Commission of 1925–28, the Local Government Boundary Commission of 1945, a Royal Commission of 1966–69, the 1972 Bains Report, the Local Government Commission of 1992 and the Lyons Report of 2007, all wrestled with the 'more strategic, but more engaged with communities conundrum' (Bennett 2006: 6); yet none produced reforms which created an enduringly popular political settlement.

Seeing the eternal return of the same issues in central–local relations, the irony is that the latest simulation of reform-as-localism under Eric Pickles has been taken so uncritically by a range of local government leaders, central local government actors and local government think tanks (Cox 2007; Coen and Raynes 2007; Keohane and Scott-Smith 2010; NLGN 2011).

5.4 Local government and the internalisation of reform

Local government actors have developed new skills of camouflage as a form of evolutionary survival. Following near extinction under Prime Minister Margaret Thatcher in the 1980s, leading local government storytellers generated a new capacity to tell tales which were more or less pleasing (or at least inoffensive) to new ministers. By mimicking each new language and reproducing the narrative of reform produced by successive governments, local strategists have enabled their councils to blend into the new landscape, ensuring they cannot be charged with being beyond the government's pale (see Table 5.1).

The Conservative government of Margaret Thatcher is often said to have had a radical reforming view of local authorities, seeing local government as 'wasteful, unaccountable and ultimately undesirable' (Seldon and Collings 2000: 76). The attempted introduction of outsourced contracts into a range of white- and blue-collar services sought to take politics out of services and promoted a new vision of local government purpose. Local government's controversial behaviour, the 'Looney-Left' and its commitment to disputed international causes, framed a critique of local authorities as being too political, using local taxes to pursue non-local issues ('South Africa and nuclear policy' [Ridley 1988: 35]) when really they existed in order to secure value-for-money services for local people (Orr 2005). While the then Secretary of State Nicholas Ridley's objective that 'enabling' councils delegate 'as much as possible to the private sector' (Ridley 1988: 29) did not come to pass in his lifetime, the narrative of local government's purpose did change as result of the Thatcher years, and outsourcing has been widely embraced in some local government services (Seymour Pierce 2013).

Table 5.1 Interplay of central–local discourses

Government	Government discourses	Local government discourses
Thatcher (1979–1990)	Market reforms, public sector crisis, towards a residual role for local government	Resistance, collectivism – followed by New Public Management, enabling
Major (1992–1997)	Consensus through 'consultation', value for money, top-down re-organisation and choice through citizen's charter	Consolidation of mainstream, reform of central bodies, desire for consensus
Early Blair (1997–2005)	Earned autonomy, performance and regulation, Best Value, political leadership reforms	Improvement and development, self-criticism, partnership, commissioning for outcomes
Late Blair/Brown (2005–2010)	Double devolution, communities and neighbourhoods	Localism, place-shaping, rejection of regulation
Cameron (2010–present)	'Localism, localism, localism', guided localism, transparency, the Big Society, open public services, anti-officer	Open access, open source, localgov2.0, the Big Society, sharing, austerity

Although councils opposed much of the government's policy agenda, local government rationalised many of the government's objectives and integrated the principles of contracting-out into their new ways of working. While resisting Ridley's vision of a 'residual role', councils did adopt (and adapt) the government's 'enabling' vocabulary.[8] Management by objectives, and the New Public Management, refreshed local government's narrative by providing a new focus on customers and users of services.[9] Now councils talked about better management, about a mixed economy of provision, about performance measurement and efficiency. The rise of managerialism saw a decline of deference towards dominant professional groups in local government, and opened up services to external scrutiny and challenge. This evolution involved changing the relationship with service users, absorbing the language of customers and consumers, introducing charters and choices.

Subsequently, under John Major, the next Conservative government pursued a more emollient policy towards local government. Thatcher's controversial 'poll tax' was replaced and in came a concern with a more consensual approach. Indeed, as Wilson and Game report, 'In October 1992 Michael Howard, then Secretary of State at the Department of the Environment, argued that "the old image of eternal central-local conflict is out of date". He maintained that ministers "have taken an entirely fresh look at the way in which we bring local authorities into the Whitehall decision making process"'.[10] In future, local authorities and their representatives could expect to be consulted when government departments developed policies that put additional burdens on councils. Indeed Wilson and Game go on to quote the Association of County Councils' Secretary Robin Wendt, who welcomed 'a sign of a new partnership which in government is indicative of an advance on where we were a year ago' (Wilson and Game 1994: 115). Clearly this optimistic assessment did not hold for long, but it shows the new minister's wish to signal a move towards a softer stance, and the desire of the corporate face of local government (by which we mean central bodies, umbrella groups etc.) to speak positively and to act co-operatively.

The Major government pursued a policy of reorganisation, introducing unitary authorities[11] in Scotland and Wales, as well as in parts of England. The 1992 Local Government Act also gave significant new powers to the Audit Commission to 'give such directions as it thinks fit for requiring relevant bodies to publish such information relating to their activities in any financial year as will, in that Commission's opinion, facilitate the making of appropriate comparisons (by reference to the criteria of cost, economy, efficiency and effectiveness)' (Local Government Act, 1992, Part 1, Section 1).

These powers were later used by the Audit Commission under Blair's governments to put in place a powerful framework of public audit and inspection, which would become one of the hallmarks of his government. Through this web of performance information and public reporting, and along with a new duty to provide 'Best Value', councils were graded in various ways and the results published. Such disciplines formed part of a new narrative that local authorities could knuckle down and show themselves responsible enough to be conceded further powers and responsibilities. This formula evolved over time and went through different incarnations from 'earned autonomy' to 'pathfinder councils' to 'trailblazer councils', and was supported in turn by local government through the Improvement and Development Agency (IDeA). While the criticism of councils from Blair's hardline reformist message could be tough, it seemed that many in local government agreed with it, and that the promise of freedom to come motivated much of the sector to engage with the new approach.

Under the later Blair governments, and the short Brown administration, the energy associated with early reforms seemed to drain away and was replaced by narratives on community engagement and building social capital which, as objectives that no-one could oppose, were easily adopted by local government. The key concept in Sir Michael Lyons' long-awaited report (2007) was 'place-shaping'. This was a development of the idea that local government politicians should be leaders of community, rather than simply leaders of an organisation or deliverers of services. Place-shaping local authorities exerted leadership to mobilise all the resources in their territory to deliver outcomes for citizens. Lyons' report was warmly welcomed in local government and its language became fully integrated for a number of years.

On becoming shadow Secretary of State of Communities and Local Government in David Cameron's frontbench team, Eric Pickles purged 'New Labour talk' and the Conservatives began to develop a new political language for local government: out went efficiency, in came austerity (Laws 2010); out went social capital, in came the 'Big Society' (HM Government 2010); out went 'Best Value', in came 'Open Public Services' (HM Government 2011). On coming to power he announced the abolition of the Audit Commission – which, though a Tory creation, had become, ironically, a symbol of Blairite centralism (Phillips 2011) – and put his focus on transparency, basic services such as bins and tax collection, and reducing the pay and power of local government senior officers. His measures on transparency seem to be the most far-reaching. Councils are now required to publish large amounts of spending data (every transaction over £500), pay levels for senior staff are also published and pay deals must be voted on by full council. The Localism Act also requires local authorities to hold a referendum for any council tax increase over an amount deemed reasonable by the secretary of state. The theme of many of these moves is (rather like Henry) to appeal to public opinion to mediate professional judgement or political choice.

5.5 Local government into the twenty-first century: stories of reform

Before the Conservatives came to power it was entirely possible to question whether their commitment to 'localism' represented a commitment to local government (Bennett 2009), but no one should have been surprised by Eric Pickles' choice to wrap himself in the localism flag. It has been for some time the reformist flag of choice. Localism was Pickles' cry for change in opposition, and he was determined to hold on to its cutting edge in government.

It was Peter Mandelson who exhorted the Labour Party in 2009, at the end of its period in office, to think like 'insurgents, not incumbents' (Mandelson 2009). This is perhaps a lesson that some of David Cameron's government, and certainly Eric Pickles, have learned.

The journalist John Rentoul writes about the current government's similarities to, and differences from, the Blair governments. He has written that one of the strengths of David Cameron is that 'he understands the politics of impossible promises' (2011). Rentoul sees the Prime Minister's 'populism' as more democratic than the 'realism' of other politicians. His promises may be empty (in the sense of unachievable) 'but it doesn't seem to matter, because the Prime Minister's impossible promise gives an impression of what he wants to do' (Rentoul 2011). Rentoul is suggesting that it is not enough for a politician to have an analysis of what it is possible to do. Politicians need to be able to empathise with what voters want to be done, whether that is possible or not.

The ironic, tactical use of the language of reform is one such manoeuvre, and in deploying it so forcefully Eric Pickles has, we argue, joined an illustrious political tradition.

So what will this mean for the next century of English local government? Our interpretation of the past suggests that local government is a robust, if contested, set of institutions and ideas that has developed remarkable endurance over many years.

In our King Henry case study we see the King as a central authority reliant on local government, which effectively limits his own power to rule. He ordains, but he cannot execute. We see the sovereign who appears at the top of the hierarchy, but finds that, when he legislates and makes his decrees, his policy can be subverted for one reason or another. The sovereign is absolute perhaps in matters of war, but not in people's heads, their souls, their intimate lives. The sovereign's power to influence the population, people's behaviour in society – that which is necessary to produce well-being, peace and good rule – is so limited that he is reduced to issuing decrees to influence public opinion and to direct blame elsewhere. While the power of a Sovereign Lord to punish may be absolute, his power to discipline, to influence a population's behaviour, is weak.

More recently, with Eric Pickles, we see how much he too is reliant on local authorities to deliver basic services, and how much he and his team concentrate on influencing the public, forcing local government into the sunlight of immediate public opinion.

In turn, twenty-first century local government will continue to adopt and adapt these new discourses. Some of this is intellectual, not just embracing the argument for transparency but also moving to spread the open data and open government philosophy (localgov2.0); some will be economic, as reduced budgets lead to reduced or reshaped services; some will be influenced by wider social and environmental trends such as immigration, climate change, food security; some will be discursive, for example, re-branding purged languages such as community cohesion and writing new narratives such as the Big Society. We will see the durability of some traditions and perhaps the fragility of others.

We can be sure that, in the course of the century to come, other narratives will develop and other structural forms will be devised. What is unlikely is that local government will cease to exist or that the struggle between central and local authority will become any less fraught with tension, freighted with irony or laden with tradition. What is likely is that politics as usual will continue between central and local actors and institutions in their ongoing struggle to promote their own ideas and interests.

Notes

1 For roundups of this kind see O'Leary and Van Slyke (2010); Stoker and Wilson (2004); 20/20 Public Services Commission (2010).
2 Before becoming MP for Brentwood and Ongar in Essex, Eric Pickles was leader of Bradford Council in Yorkshire, 1988–1990.
3 By this first use of 'irony', we mean that Pickles deploys a rhetorical commitment to localism at times knowingly out of kilter with his actions.
4 We have focused on Eric Pickles as the secretary of state in power today and of most relevance and interest to readers. However, we could equally have written about Tony Blair's New Labour party, which was elected to govern in 1997 on a manifesto that criticised the British state as 'centralised, inefficient and bureaucratic' and promised more 'independent' local government. Once in power, he turned this discourse of reform from the central state he had criticised in opposition towards the councils he had supported. Introducing the principle of 'earned autonomy' Blair wrote, 'If you are unwilling or unable to work to the modern agenda then the government will have to look to other partners to take on your role' (Tony Blair [1998], *Leading the Way: A New Vision for Local Government*, Institute for Public Policy Research, London). However, as the government's authority declined and the Labour party lost power in local government, later Labour secretaries of state adopted far more conciliatory language towards councils in order to try to regain their support.
5 The term 'ironic localism' has been used previously here: http://publicintelligence.co.uk/2011/08/26/shapps-punch-and-judy-localism/ (accessed 15 May 2013).
6 See this celebration as part of Parliament Week, available at: www.parliamentweek.org/stories-of-democracy/stories/from-the-archives-the-representation-of-the-people-act-1832/ (accessed 15 May 2013).
7 For further actor accounts, see Alexander (1982); Broadhead (1989); Campbell (1988); Beecham (1986); Walton (1988).

8 See Leach et al. (1994: 235) for discussion of good and bad enabling.
9 See Orr and Vince (2009) for a discussion of the 'management tradition' in local government.
10 Wilson and Game (1994: 115) quoting from *Local Government Chronicle*, 13 November 1992.
11 Single-tier local authorities that replaced separate regional/county and district councils.

References

20/20 Public Services Commission (2010), *From Social Security to Social Productivity: A Vision for 2020 Public Services*, 2020 Public Services Trust and the RSA, London

Alexander, A (1982), *Local Government in Britain since Reorganisation*, George Allen & Unwin, London.

Alexander, A (1985), *Borough Government and Politics, Reading 1835–1985*, George Allen & Unwin, London.

Beecham, J (1986), 'Widdicombe: three political views. A labour view', *Local Government Studies*, Vol. 12 No. 6, 33–39.

Bennett, M (2006), 'Where now for central and local governance?', in M Bennett (Ed.), *Localopolis Governance and Citizenship in the 21st Century*, Society of Local Authority Chief Executives and Senior Managers (SOLACE) Foundation Imprint, London.

Bennett, M (2009), 'Introduction', in M Bennett and C Dykes (Eds.), *Would a Conservative Government Need Local Government?*, SOLACE Foundation Imprint, London.

Blears, H (2007), 'Confident communities', speech by the Secretary of State for Communities and Local Government to the Development Trusts Association Annual Conference, Oxford Town Hall, 17 September.

Broadhead, J (1989), 'Wrekin's response to the current housing situation', *Local Government Policy Making*, Vol. 15 No. 4.

Bruce-Lockhart, S (2006), 'Real localism needs devolution of power', in Bichard, M (ed), *A Word in Your Ear … Advice to Sir Gus from a Friendly Source*, SOLACE Foundation Imprint, London.

Burgess, T and T Travers (1980),*Ten Billion Pounds: Whitehall's Take-over of the Town Halls*, Grant McIntyre, London.

Butler, P (2012), 'Pickles slams Tory council over "disproportionate" charity cuts', *Guardian*, available at: www.guardian.co.uk/society/patrick-butler-cuts-blog/2012/feb/23/eric-pickles-slams-disproportionate-charity-cuts?newsfeed=true (accessed 27 January 2012).

Campbell, M (1988), 'Revitalizing the inner cities', *Local Government Studies*, Vol. 14, Issue 3: 1–9.

Chamberlain, J (1885), 'The Chamberlain Papers, JC/38/132', cited in K Young and PL Garside (1982), *Metropolitan Politics and Urban Change 1837–1981*, Arnold, London.

Cockell, M (2011), 'Making the Localism Bill work for councils', *Local Government Chronicle*, available at: www.lgcplus.com/briefings/corporate-core/governance/making-the-localism-bill-work-for-councils/5037620.article (accessed 9 November 2011).

Coen, P and P Raynes (2007), 'Making it happen', in D Walker (Ed.), *Real Localism*, The Smith Institute, London.

Communities and Local Government Select Committee (2011), *Third Report*, 9 June, House of Commons, London.

Cox, D (2007), 'Our society, your life', in M Bennett and C Dykes (Eds.), *Norfolk, in Conservatism, Change and Local Government*, SOLACE Foundation Imprint, London.

Department of Communities and Local Government (2011), *Government Response to the Communities and Local Government Select Committee's Report: Localism*, Cm 8183, TSO, London.

Duncan, S and M Goodwin (1988), *The Local State and Uneven Development: Behind the Local Government Crisis*, Polity Press, Cambridge.

Evans, EJ (2000), *Parliamentary Reform, c. 1770–1918*, Longman, Harlow.

HM Government (2010), *The Coalition: Our Programme for Government*, May 2010, Cabinet Office, London.

HM Government (2011), *Open Public Services White Paper*, Cm 8145, July.

Jennings, I (1935), 'Central Control', in HJ Laski (Ed.), *A Century of Municipal Progress: 1835–1935*, George Allen & Unwin, London.

Jones, G and J Stewart (1983), *The Case for Local Government*, George Allen & Unwin, London.

Keeling, R (2012), 'Tory leaders criticise ministerial attacks over council tax', *Local Government Chronicle*, 25 April.

Keeling, R (2013), 'Tory leaders warn PM of "fractious" relationship', *Local Government Chronicle*, 24 January.

Keith-Lucas, B (1977), *English Local Government in the 19th and 20th Centuries*, Historical Association, London.

Keohane, N and L Scott-Smith (2010), 'What localism will mean', ConservativeHome. com, available at: http://conservativehome.blogs.com/localgovernment/2010/12/ what-the-localism-bill-will-mean.html (accessed 9 December 2010).

Lang, S (1999), *Parliamentary Reform, 1785–1928*, Routledge, London.

Laws, D (2010), 'Speech by the Chief Secretary to the Treasury, Rt. Hon. David Laws MP, announcing £6.2billion savings', 24 May, HM Treasury, London.

Leach, S, J Stewart and K Walsh (1994), *The Changing Organisation and Management of Local Government*, Macmillan, London.

Local Government Act (1992), Cm1599, London.

Local Government Information Unit (LGIU) (2011), 'Localism Bill briefing 18 January 2011', Local Government Information Unit, London.

Lynch, M (1992), *Scotland: A New History*, Pimlico, London.

Lyons, M (2007), *Place-shaping: A Shared Ambition for the Future of Local Government*, TSO, London.

Machin, I (2001), *The Rise of Democracy in Britain, 1830–1918*, Macmillan, London.

Mandelson, P (2009), 'Speech to 2009 Labour Party Annual Conference as Secretary of State for Business, Innovation and Skills', Labour Party, London.

McCann, K (2012), 'Whitehall's localism is "meaningless" for local government', *Guardian*, available at: www.guardian.co.uk/local-government-network/ 2012/oct/30/local-government-leaders-manchester-round-up (accessed 30 October 2012).

New Local Government Network (NLGN) (2011), 'Commission on Next Localism', available at: www.nlgn.org.uk/public/commission-next-localism/ (accessed 15 May 2013).

O'Leary, R and DM Van Slyke (2010), 'Special issue on the future of public administration in 2020', *Public Administration Review*, Vol 70, Issue Supplement s1: s5–s11, December.

Orr, K (2005), 'Interpreting narratives of local government change under the conservatives and new labour', *British Journal of Politics and International Relations*, Vol. 7 No. 3, 1–35.

Orr, K and R Vince (2009), 'Traditions of local government', *Public Administration*, Vol. 87 No. 3, 655–77.

Phillips, CF (1973), *Association of Municipal Corporations Annual Conference Proceedings*, 19 September, Association of Municipal Corporations (AMC), London.

Phillips, L (2011) 'Audit Commission had to go, Pickles tells PF', *Public Finance*, 30 June, available at: www.publicfinance.co.uk/news/2011/06/audit-commission-had-to-go-pickles-tells-pf/ (accessed 15 May 2013).

Pickles, E (2007), 'Speech to Conservative Party Conference', 30 September, available at: www.conservatives.com/News/Speeches/2012/10/Eric_Pickles_Conference_2012.aspx (accessed 15 May 2013).

Pickles, E (2011), 'The Localism Bill reverses a century of centralisation', available at: http://conservativehome.blogs.com/localgovernment/2011/11/in-pursuit-of-localism-restoring-a-100-year-democratic-deficit.html (accessed 15 May 2013).

Rao, N and K Young (1997), *Local Government since 1945*, Blackwell, Oxford.

Rentoul, J (2011), 'Coalition doesn't work for Clegg', *Independent on Sunday*, available at: www.independent.co.uk/opinion/commentators/john-rentoul/john-rentoul-coalition-doesnt-work-for-clegg-2345088.html (accessed 28 August 2011).

Ridley, N (1988), 'The local right: Enabling not providing', *Policy Study No. 92*, Centre for Policy Studies, London.

Ross, T (2012) 'England's local government system must be fundamentally reformed, says MP', *Daily Telegraph*, 31 December.

Seldon, A and D Collings (2000), *Britain under Thatcher*, Longman, Harlow.

Seymour Pierce, (2013) *Support Services Annual Review*, London, January.

Stewart, J (2001),*The Nature of British Local Government*, Palgrave, London.

Stoker, G and D Wilson (Eds.) (2004), *British Local Government into the 21st Century*, Palgrave, London.

Stoker, G and P Taylor-Gooby (2011), 'The coalition programme: a new vision for Britain or politics as usual?', *Political Quarterly*, Vol. 82 No. 1, 4–15.

Tanner, JR (1951), *Tudor Constitutional Documents*, A.D. 1485–1603, 2nd ed., Cambridge University Press.

Walton, B (1988), 'The impact of the government's educational legislation on local government', *Local Government Studies*, Vol. 14 No. 1, 83–191.

Webb, S and B Webb (1922), *English Local Government: Statutory Authorities for Special Purposes*, Longman, London.

Wilson, D and C Game (1994), *Local Government in the United Kingdom*, Macmillan, Basingstoke.

Wood, A (1982), *Nineteenth Century Britain, 1815–1914*, 2nd ed., Longman, Harlow.

Wright, DG (1970), *Democracy and reform, 1815–1885*, Longman, Harlow.

PART II. LOCAL GOVERNMENT FINANCE AND ECONOMIC DEVELOPMENT

Chapter 6

Toward a System of Municipal Finance for Twenty-first Century India

Om Prakash Mathur

This chapter is set in the context of two major initiatives to strengthen local government in India: the *74th Constitution Amendment Act 1992*, part of an overall decentralisation strategy which aims at empowering municipalities; and the Jawaharlal Nehru National Urban Renewal Mission (JNNURM), a central government initiative designed to impart greater efficiency and transparency in the functioning of urban local governments. The two initiatives mark a step forward for municipalities to meet the contemporary challenges of growth, urbanisation and improved service delivery. Positioned in this context, the chapter:

- discusses the challenges facing India's municipal finance system;

- sets out the constitutional and legislative boundaries within which the municipal finance system functions, including the changes that have been made therein in recent years;

- provides a brief account of the state of the finances of municipalities; and

- presents a framework of suggestions that might prepare municipalities to address future challenges.

6.1 Challenges for municipal finance

The central theme of this chapter is making municipal finance work for growth, management of the urban agenda and improved service delivery. This theme represents a key public policy challenge for India, and is discussed under three major subthemes.

6.1.1 Improving municipal finance is central to the achievement of India's economic growth objectives

Over the past 20 years, India has registered annual gross domestic product (GDP) growth rates of more than 6.5 per cent – a major achievement in macroeconomic policy management. The same period has witnessed a dramatic shift in India's economic structure, moving to create growth through knowledge-based, financial and other services. As a result, urban areas have come to account for 52 per cent of the net domestic product (NDP, 2004–05), having risen from 45.7 per cent in 1993–94 (Tables 6.1 and 6.2).

Table 6.1 GDP growth rates

Year	Annual growth rate (%)
1971–1981	3.2
1981–1991	5.4
1991–2001	5.6
2001–2010	7.5

Source: Central Statistical Organisation, New Delhi, www.mospi.nic.in

Table 6.2 Urban share of net domestic product

Year	Share (%)
1980–81	41.1
1993–94	45.7
1999–2000	51.9
2004–05	52.0

Source: Central Statistical Organisation, New Delhi, www.mospi.nic.in

While the economic base has shifted inexorably to cities, India's recognition of the role of cities in promoting and accelerating economic development, and subsequent prioritisation of the municipal sector to manage the process of growth and urbanisation, has proceeded slowly. As this chapter will demonstrate, municipal governments have been at best a passive participant in the process of economic growth. Moreover, they have experienced little success in consolidating reform measures to manage the complex and interdependent dimensions of urbanisation. Municipalities have been unable to capture the benefits of urban-based economic growth of recent decades, be that its contribution to national and private incomes, or to government tax revenues. There are questions about the sustainability of the existing system and its capacity to achieve expected development outcomes, such as the maintenance of high economic growth and poverty reduction. There exists a strong perception that the level of urban-based growth in India is held back because of inadequate municipal infrastructure, high regulatory costs and weak municipal institutions.

While there are no India-specific studies on the economy-wide effects of inadequate municipal infrastructure, studies in other countries estimate such costs to be extremely high, reducing both urban productivity and competitiveness, and resulting in increased financial, economic and institutional pressures on the private sector (Anas, Lee and Oh 1996).[1] These studies also show that poor municipal policy and institutional performance in the provision of infrastructure and services contribute to the growth of urban poverty and not to its alleviation. Reforming the system of municipal finance is therefore a priority for both the central and state governments, which as the trends indicate will increasingly depend on cities for accelerated growth and poverty reduction.

6.1.2 A robust municipal finance system is necessary for effective implementation and management of India's urban policy agenda

Over the past two decades, several initiatives have been taken to open up India's urban sector, strengthen municipal institutions to face changing socio-economic realities, and put in place fresh governance structures for deepening local-level decision-making. These initiatives include the *74th Constitution Amendment Act 1992*; an amendment to the *Income Tax Act 1961*, allowing municipalities to issue tax-free bonds; and the Jawaharlal Nehru National Urban Renewal Mission (JNNURM). The initiatives, which collectively constitute the broad parameters of the urban-municipal reform agenda in India, comprise:

- a constitutional status for municipalities;

- functional reform aimed at an enlarged role for municipalities;

- an institutional framework for redesigning central–state–municipal fiscal relations;

- inter-local government linkages and co-ordination;

- market-based financing of municipal services;

- incentives for municipalities to undertake reform of property taxation and the system of user charges;

- public–private partnerships in the provision of municipal services;

- tenural security for slum dwellers;

- reform of the urban land and property market; and

- disclosure and transparency in municipal functioning.

Such changes amount to a prescription for a fundamental realignment of the functions, finances and powers of municipal governments, primarily through the state governments and to an extent via the central government. The notable example of the latter has been the long-standing demand for formal constitutional recognition of municipal governments as a full-fledged order of government, which would be tantamount to a form of home-rule or 'natural person powers', giving them greater autonomy in their relations with both central and state governments.[2]

The process of municipal sector and finance reform has been set in motion. However, progress on key aspects of the reform process has been tardy and uneven. The passage of the 74th Constitution Amendment Act 1992, for instance, was intended to formally recognise municipalities and delineate a space for them to play a larger role in the Indian economy and deepen the process of decentralisation. In reality, however, there is a motley array of institutional arrangements for undertaking several of the functions envisioned for municipalities, resulting in ad hoc responses to the unprecedented demand for urban infrastructure and services. Consequently, low-quality urbanisation is observed in most parts of the country.

The municipal revenue base (property taxes and user charges) continues to suffer from substantial inefficiencies and under-utilisation. Incentives for initiating reforms that have a direct bearing on property taxes – such as the abolition of rent controls – either have not worked or are clearly inadequate. Consequently, the municipal finance system in India remains vulnerable to a broad range of both endogenous and exogenous conditions, which result in poor performance and efficiency in the provision of local public goods. The entire process of reform needs to be deepened and made more broadly based, in order to bring about long-run improvement in the finances of municipalities and thus contribute to the achievement of India's urban policy agenda.

6.1.3 A sound municipal finance system is a pre-requisite for improved service delivery

Most studies on Indian municipal finance point to the insufficiency of municipal spending levels for providing and maintaining infrastructural services at normative levels (Mathur et al. 2002; Mohanty et al. 2007). In 2007/08, municipal government spending (both capital and revenue expenditure) on infrastructure and services such as water supply, sewerage, solid waste treatment and disposal, storm water drainage, city-wide roads and street lighting was placed at 470 billion Indian rupees (Rs; approximately US$10.5 billion[3]) or 1.09 per cent of India's GDP. It comprised Rs186 billion of expenditure to create new infrastructural assets (0.43 per cent of GDP) and Rs284 billion for infrastructure maintenance, establishment charges and salaries (0.66 per cent of GDP). A comparison of these spending levels with the norms recently established by the High-Powered Expert Committee (HPEC) on estimating urban infrastructure investment requirements indicates that municipalities in India underspent to the tune of 1.04 per cent of GDP on infrastructure maintenance.[4] In cash terms, this underspending amounted to Rs226 billion, or Rs731 per capita (~US$16.5) – a phenomenal deficit by any measure. Further, the current level of investment for creating infrastructural assets is a fraction of the amount needed, both to wipe out an accumulated deficit placed at Rs12,376 billion and to meet the infrastructural needs of urban population growth for the period 2012–2031 (Rs18,605 billion).[5]

Other estimates focusing on the aggregate demand for basic standards of infrastructure and service provision also point to significant financing gaps. In their recent report, *India's Urban Awakening: Building Inclusive Cities, Sustaining Economic Growth*, the McKinsey Global Institute (2010) estimated that India needed to invest US$1.2 trillion in capital expenditure in its cities and towns over the next 20 years, equivalent to US$134 per capita per year. This is almost eight times the level of current spending. They further estimate that more than half of this capital investment is necessary to erase India's infrastructure backlog and the balance to fund the future needs of cities. Reforming the municipal finance system is thus a first requirement for mobilising the scale of investment needed to improve infrastructure.

Currently, the capacity of municipalities to generate resources from their tax and non-tax revenue bases is seriously limited. As noted previously, in 2007–08 municipal own-source revenues accounted for a mere 0.54 per cent of GDP. In several states – the majority of these being low income and mainly rural – municipal own-source revenue was only half the national average. The municipal share of national tax revenues continued to stagnate at 1.7 per cent, despite a country-wide trend towards an improved tax to GDP ratio. Decentralisation, as embodied in the 74th Amendment, has made little difference to the tax-raising efforts of municipalities; their tax base

Table 6.3 Shares of tax revenues

Year	Central government (%)	States (%)	Municipalities (%)	Panchayats (%)
(Rural local governments)				
2002–03	44.1	53.2	2.5	0.2
2007–08	50.0	48.1	1.7	0.2

Sources: Government of India, Ministry of Finance, Indian Public Statistics; Thirteenth Finance Commission (2009)

continues to be narrow and marked by low buoyancy. On the other hand, it has been estimated (Mathur 2011) that municipalities have the potential to increase revenues significantly (by about 110 per cent) without any fundamental change in the system of property valuation or the structure of tax rates (Table 6.3).

With the increasing recognition of the contribution of urbanisation to economic growth, the strengthening of the fiscal position of municipalities through finance reforms has become a key component in the Government of India's development agenda. The Indian economy stands to benefit enormously from increases in the rate of urbanisation over the next 50 years. While the overall urbanisation rate in India has been comparatively low in relation to the economic growth patterns of the past two decades, accelerations in the rate of internal migration and natural urban population growth are predicted to increase the urban population from 364 million to about 590 million within the next 20 years (United Nations 2009).[6] The country is projected to have nearly 85 cities with populations of more than 1 million by 2030, and will witness conversion of at least 1,000 villages into new towns if past trends are any guide to the future (Table 6.4).

In summary, the challenges of urbanisation, of higher rates of economic growth, of a shift in the composition of growth towards increasingly urban-based economic activities, and of increasing global competition are unprecedented in their scale and complexity, with enormous implications for municipal governments.[7] As the country urbanises, cities will be required to respond more effectively to the needs and preferences of citizens, business and industry. An effective response to these challenges requires a municipal fiscal policy and strategy that can ensure and balance long-term economic growth and welfare, delineating the respective roles of the three

Table 6.4 The scale of India's future urbanisation

Year	Urban population (million)
2010	364
2015	410
2020	463
2025	532
2030	590

Source: United Nations 2009

tiers of government in financing urban development and services, and establishing fiscal rules that are consistent with the changing socio-economic realities.

Existing fiscal arrangements are inadequate for this purpose, even if current municipal tax powers are utilised to their optimum level.[8] Municipal finance in the context of open economies, decentralisation and globalisation is vastly different from that envisaged in the past, when municipalities functioned in accordance with Dillon's Rule[9] or within the framework of John Stuart Mill's initial formulation of the responsibilities of local governments.[10] International scholars have begun to emphasise that, 'if fiscal decentralisation is to produce sustainable net benefits in developing countries, subnational governments require much more real taxing power than they now have' (Bahl and Bird 2008: 1). In a country where reforms have barely touched this complex subject, questions such as what is a local tax, what constitutes own-source revenue, whether India follows the widely held principle that finance follows functions and what explains current tax assignment choices have surfaced more pointedly than ever before, raising doubts as to how far the principles that should guide municipal finance have been translated into contemporary practice. As Bahl and Cyan (2010) write, 'the story (about practice matching the theory) is more complicated and there is much still to be learned about why governments (or constitutions) make the revenue assignment decisions they do'. This chapter raises these questions in order to initiate a larger debate on the municipal sector and municipal finance.

6.2 India's municipal finance system: basic features

India is a union of 28 states and seven centrally administered territories. In this union, the functions, finances and powers of the central government and state governments are laid out in the seventh schedule of the *Constitution of India*, in what are known as the Union List, State List and Concurrent List. While the constitution now recognises municipalities as a tier of government and provides for their establishment and continued existence, they remain subject to state governments in matters relating to their powers, functions and responsibilities, and also the degree of autonomy that they can exercise. Thus, from their own powers specified in the State List, state governments assign certain functions and duties to municipalities. A municipality has no inherent powers in the Indian set-up.[11]

There have been periodic shifts and changes in the functional domain of municipalities, due to the withdrawal of functions (such as water supply and sewerage) in some states, and the assignment of new responsibilities (such as poverty alleviation and planning for economic and social development) in others. The 74th Amendment offered a different vision for municipalities by incorporating a new Schedule 12, which provides a list of functions that is considered appropriate for municipal governments. Although the list is illustrative rather than binding, it makes a strong commitment to decentralisation. The significance of these Schedule 12 functions for municipalities lies not so much in enlarging the scope of municipal operations as in the fact that many of the functions have been drawn from the Concurrent List of the constitution. At the minimum, it suggests that there is a group of functions where there exists a concurrency of interests across all three tiers of government, including municipal governments. Also, many of the functions listed in Schedule 12 have distributional and developmental attributes: thus their inclusion on the one hand represents an important departure from the past, and on the other hand signals a deviation from the typical Musgrave–Oates model (Oates 1972) of fiscal federalism, under which redistribution is a function best performed at the higher tiers of government.

However, the 74th Amendment failed to spell out how these new functions might be financed. Instead of providing an illustrative list of taxes considered appropriate for municipalities, it mandates the states to constitute, once in every five years, a State Finance Commission (SFC) for making recommendations on:

- the taxes, levies and duties that should be assigned to municipalities;
- the taxes, duties and levies that should be shared between the states and municipalities;
- grants-in-aid to be provided to municipalities; and
- other measures that would augment the finances of municipalities.

In addition, recognising that this process may still leave unmet revenue needs, the amendment requires the Central Finance Commission (CFC) to make supplementary grants to municipalities.[12] The evidence to date is that the SFCs have not been able to bring about any noticeable change in the fiscal domain of municipalities, with the result that municipal taxing authority remains limited to property taxation and a few minor taxes such as advertisement taxes and a tax on non-motorised vehicles. The fiscal base of municipalities is thus dominated by intergovernmental transfers, which account for nearly 50 per cent of their revenues.

Thus the municipal fiscal framework that supports urban services in India has remained largely unchanged, notwithstanding the fact that the macroeconomic context has been transformed and the relationship between municipalities and other tiers of government is in a phase of significant transformation whose implications are still to be fully grasped. Many local taxes and the supporting user-charge system were designed in the nineteenth- or early twentieth-century, and therefore for a different time and a different context. Now they have lost their relevance and can hardly be considered sufficient for meeting the needs of the new environment (United Cities and Local Governments 2010).

6.3 Municipal finances: ground-level realities

Table 6.5 provides an overview of the finances of India's 3,667 municipalities aggregated across the 28 states. In 2007–08, total municipal revenue amounted to Rs444 billion and total municipal expenditure to Rs470 billion. In per capita terms, revenue was placed at Rs1,430 (approximately US$32) and expenditure at Rs1,513 (US$34). Own-source revenues provided 53 per cent of the total, with the balance contributed by assignment, devolution and grants-in-aid from states (33.4 per cent), central government grants (5.3 per cent) and grants from the finance commissions (2.0 per cent). Operating expenditure accounted for 60.5 per cent of the total. Municipalities recorded an operating surplus of approximately 37 per cent, but an overall deficit of about 6 per cent once capital expenditure was included.[13]

Table 6.5 The finances of municipalities (all states)

	2002–03		2007–08		CAGR (%)
	Amount (Rs billion)	Rs per capita	Amount (Rs billion)	Rs per capita	
Revenue					
Own-tax revenue	88.38	311	152.78	492	11.57
Own non-tax revenue	44.42	156	82.44	265	13.16
Total own revenue	132.80	466	235.21	757	12.11
Assignment and devolution	36.57	128	91.71	295	20.19
Grants-in-aid	22.60	79	56.76	183	20.23
Other grants	11.38	40	28.18	91	19.90
Transfers from central government	3.09	11	23.73	76	50.35
Finance Commission transfers	2.77	10	8.69	28	25.74
Total expenditure	**209.20**	**733**	**444.29**	**1430**	**16.26**
Revenue expenditure	156.91	550	284.31	915	12.62
Capital expenditure	59.38	208	185.94	598	25.64
Total	**216.30**	**758**	**470.26**	**1,513**	**16.80**
GDP India	**22,614.15**	**21,415**	**43,208.92**	**37,969**	**13.83**
Own tax as % of GDP	0.39%		0.35%		
Own revenue as % of GDP	0.59%		0.54%		
Municipal expenditure as % of GDP	0.96%		1.09%		

Note: GDP at factor cost (current prices); CAGR=compound average growth rate
Source: Thirteenth Finance Commission (2009)

Important changes took place in the structure of revenues and patterns of expenditure over the period 2002–03 to 2007–08. First, the ratio of own-tax revenues to total revenues declined from 42 per cent to 34 per cent, and the share of own non-tax revenues also fell, from 21 per cent to 18 per cent, meaning that municipalities were raising only a little over half of their total revenues. As a proportion of GDP, own-tax yields dipped from 0.39 per cent to 0.35 per cent, and total own-source revenues from 0.59 per cent to 0.54 per cent.

This decline is a significant development. It is attributable in part to the widespread abolition of *Octroi*,[14] which was an important source of revenue for municipalities (and still is in the municipal corporations in the state of Maharashtra), and in part to the dilution of the property tax regime in several states, such as Haryana, Punjab and Rajasthan, where large numbers of properties have been exempted from paying property tax. It indicates that, unlike the reform of central and state taxes undertaken in India in the mid-1990s, there has been no comprehensive effort to modernise municipal taxes. It also speaks of the low level of buoyancy of municipal tax instruments. While state municipal statutes enumerate close to 50 different kinds of revenue instruments, most of them either are not in use or have extremely low levels of productivity. Several are obsolete, with no relevance to modern socio-economic realities and the changing economy of cities. At the same time, several municipal taxes have been transferred to or appropriated by higher tiers of government. Additionally, as municipalities face greater responsibilities, the issue of their access to central and state government taxes, such as the goods and services tax (GST), needs deeper examination.[15]

Second, despite the relatively slow growth of own-source revenues, total municipal expenditure grew at a compound annual rate of 16.8 per cent, increasing on aggregate from Rs216.29 billion to Rs470.26 billion. Moreover, capital expenditure rose at twice the rate of revenue expenditure from 2002–03 to 2007–08. Thus, despite a decline in own-source revenue as a proportion of GDP, total expenditure registered an increase from 0.96 per cent of GDP in 2002–03 to 1.09 per cent in 2007–08. Nevertheless, this figure remains low compared with other federal Commonwealth countries: for example, an increase in total municipal expenditure of 2.3 per cent in Australia and 7.2 per cent in Canada (International Monetary Fund 2008).

The third important change that took place in the structure of revenues and patterns of expenditure was that, in order to fill the local revenue gap and boost capital expenditure, fiscal transfers from central and state governments rose from 36.5 per cent of municipal revenues in 2002–03 to 47.1 per cent in 2007–08. At the state level, grants-in-aid made to municipalities are used to correct imbalances in fiscal capacity. Municipalities also have access to assignment and devolution grants, which represent a share of state tax revenues. Transfers from the central government come in the form of grants linked to performance and reforms, designated specifically for asset creation and capital works. Intervention by the central government in the municipal sector has, within a short span of time, altered the intergovernmental fiscal framework. The Central Finance Commission determines grants-in-aid at five-yearly intervals, which are allocated through the states to municipalities. These are used to fill the revenue account gaps at local levels and are allocated according to a set of weighted criteria that take into account factors such as urban population, geographic area, level of development, local revenue effort, an index of decentralisation, an index of deprivation and the extent to which states have devolved functions to local government in accordance with the 74th Amendment. However, these criteria may change with every Commission, and the Thirteenth Finance Commission put forward some new ideas for funding municipalities that are outlined later in this chapter.

As Table 6.5 shows, the period 2002–03 to 2007–08 witnessed an extraordinarily large increase in transfers from the central government, which grew at an annual compound rate of more than 50 per cent due to grants under the JNNURM, launched in 2005.[16] Significantly, the JNNURM requires state governments and municipalities to match the central government grants, and the procedure so established is likely to have a long-term impact in leveraging market funds for municipal infrastructure.[17]

This growth in transfers demonstrates that the central government has begun to appreciate the key role of cities in the Indian economy, recognising that investment in urban infrastructure is as much a central government responsibility as a municipal one. It further recognises that macroeconomic trends have important implications for municipal governments, warranting interventions by central government. Urban growth management is thus beginning to be seen as a multilevel developmental activity (Table 6.6).

Table 6.6 Central government grants to municipalities

Year	Amount (Rs billion)	Year	Amount (Rs billion)
2002–03	3.09	2005–06	33.69
2003–04	4.07	2006–07	122.19
2004–05	54.53	2007–08	237.29

Source: Thirteenth Finance Commission (2009)

However, notwithstanding the increased role of the central government, state policies continue to shape and determine the fiscal space of municipalities. There is, therefore, an enormous heterogeneity in revenue structures and arrangements, institutional systems and economic conditions that affect municipal financial performance across different states. Table 6.7 gives the state-level structure of municipal revenues and expenditure.

Table 6.7 State-level structure of municipal revenues and expenditures, 2007–08

States	Per capita own-source revenue (Rs)	CAGR of own-source revenue 2002–07 (%)	Own-source share of total revenue (%)	Per capita revenue expenditure (Rs)	CAGR of revenue expenditure, 2002–07 (%)
Andhra Pradesh	748	13.0	58.5	1,060	18.5
Assam	143	4.8	38.2	205	10.8
Bihar	105	4.8	14.6	711	48.8
Chattisgarh	376	11.6	14.1	1,449	34.1
Goa	282	3.9	57.8	400	8.2
Gujarat	1,079	7.7	61.5	1,135	10.2
Haryana	281	3.6	33.5	328	2.9
Himachal Pradesh[a]	595	14.9	47.8	–	–
Jammu & Kashmir	90	21.2	9.9	452	20.1
Jharkhand	86	12.6	20.2	134	15.5
Karnataka	545	6.4	34.2	750	10.5
Kerala	329	3.6	39.5	517	14.4
Madhya Pradesh	121	6.8	11.6	998	16.9
Maharashtra	2,600	11.7	76.1	2,237	13.8
Orissa	38	14.7	4.5	405	17.6
Punjab	1,049	7.2	89.1	925	10.6
Rajasthan	387	16.6	39.5	447	11.0
Tamil Nadu	396	7.4	38.4	665	8.1
Uttar Pradesh	94	2.1	14.8	245	2.1
Uttarakhand	116	0.6	21.8	330	8.6
West Bengal	394	10.4	51.7	574	6.3

[a]Data relates to 2006–07; CAGR=compound annual growth rate
Note: This and subsequent tables in this section provide finance data for only 21 states
Sources: Statistics of India, 2003–04 and 2008–09; Thirteenth Finance Commission (2009) (calculations made by the author)

The data in Table 6.7 reveal high and rising inter-state disparities in the management of municipal finance. Although the coefficient of variation between states differs with the different constituents of municipal revenues and expenditures, it is large and has risen for all constituents except the state government grants-in-aid to municipalities (see Table 6.8). Some states have evidently paid far greater attention to the municipal tier than others: state policies hold the key to the reform of the municipal finance system.

Of particular concern is the slow growth in own-source revenues in lower-income states, and the fact that the own-source share of total revenue is often low and declining. Increasing locally raised revenues should be seen as a prerequisite for the future growth of municipalities in India. However, as the share of own-source revenues declines, municipalities in several states are at a high risk of losing their fiscal identity as the third tier of government.

While the abolition of *octroi* can be seen as a positive step,[18] it and the dilution of property tax regimes have caused severe erosion of the tax base of municipalities in several states and have resulted in increasing dependence on state government transfers and grants-in-aid. This is a matter of vital concern, touching upon the very nature of the relationship between municipalities and state governments. In response, the High Powered Expert Committee (2011) proposed the creation of an exclusive list of taxes for municipalities, evidently to provide protection to their fiscal domain. In addition, the Thirteenth Finance Commission (2009) proposed that each state should set up a Property Tax Board, which in part will ensure that state governments maintain property tax as the core revenue source for municipal governments and put in place appropriate methods of property valuation and assessment.

This analysis adds up to five major conclusions:

- India's municipal sector is small in relation to the position in other countries and what is required to address urban challenges. With own-source revenues equivalent to only 0.54 per cent of GDP and expenditures only 1.09 per cent, a

Table 6.8 Coefficient of variation in municipal revenues and expenditure

	Per capita average (Rs)		Coefficient of variation (CV)	
	2002–03	2007–08	2002–03	2007–08
Own-tax revenue	311	492	125	154
Own non-tax revenue	156	265	89	97
Assignment and devolution	128	295	86	99
State grants-in-aid	79	183	104	83
Transfers from the central government	11	76	109	123
Finance Commission dispensation	10	28	57	61
Revenue expenditure	550	915	69	77
Total expenditure (includes capital)	758	1,513	64	76

Source: Thirteenth Finance Commission (2009) (calculations made by the author)

sector of this size cannot be expected to deliver services at adequate, standardised levels.

- There are large-scale differences between states. These are partly attributable to state policies – what fiscal powers they assign or devolve to municipalities – as well as the efficacy with which municipalities exercise those powers. However, inter-state differences have also arisen on account of factors over which municipalities have little control; it is these exogenous economy-wide factors that have put municipalities in several states at high risk.

- Smaller municipalities in much of the country have cost disabilities and are characterised by a poor resource base, raising the vital issue of developing a revenue model that will be able to address their fiscal problems.

- Decentralisation as embodied in the 74th Constitution Amendment, when measured in terms of either resource generation or municipal expenditure, has made little progress over the past two decades. There is a need for a fiscal architecture that is consistent with the new functions of municipalities proposed in the 12th Schedule.

- The financing of urban infrastructure and services has to be a multi-tier responsibility.

It should also be noted that financial problems may be exacerbated by the limited management capacity and skills of many municipalities. There are no performance standards to be enforced – a major lacuna in the management structure. However, such issues extend beyond the scope of this chapter.

6.4 A system of municipal finance for the twenty-first century

Municipal finance reforms are currently under way in a number of developing and developed countries.[19] Several countries have undertaken to reform the municipal system in order to pursue and deepen decentralisation goals and objectives or put in place the principle of subsidiarity; in others, reforms are being introduced to institute a new system of local government. In some cases, reforms have resulted in devolution of functions from the higher tiers to municipalities. In Central and Eastern Europe, reforms have focused on local taxation, municipal property management, budget formulation and budget implementation. Reforms in Canada have been designed to advance several overarching goals, such as enhancing governance capacity, improved intergovernmental relations between municipal governments and their respective provincial governments, and improved relations between municipal governments and local communities. However, these goals have not always been shared by all provinces (Garcea and Le Sage 2005).

The Brazilian Constitution of 1988 is often cited as upgrading the political and financial role of municipalities in the country. As Souza notes, 'no Constitution prior to 1988 has provided local governments with the amount of resources they now enjoy – there is a consensus that Brazil is one of the most decentralised countries in the developing world and that financial decentralisation has favoured the municipalities to a greater extent than the states' (Souza 2003). However, Brazil has also put in place a Fiscal Responsibility Law, which prohibits the bailing out by the federal government of new debts contracted by local governments (Brazil Ministry of Planning, Budget and Management 2000).

Beginning with the 74th Constitutional Amendment, India too has entered into an important phase of municipal reform. The rationale for the amendment as embodied in the Statement of Objects and Reasons is as follows:

> In many states, local bodies have become weak and ineffective on account of a variety of reasons, including the failure to hold regular elections, prolonged supersession and inadequate devolution of powers and functions. As a result, urban local bodies are not able to perform effectively as democratic units of self-government. Having regard to these inadequacies it is considered necessary that provisions relating to urban local bodies are incorporated in the Constitution particularly for (i) putting on a firmer footing the relationship between the state government and urban local bodies with respect to (a) the functions and taxation powers, (b) arrangements for revenue sharing, (c) ensuring regular conduct of elections, and (d) providing adequate representation to the weaker sections.

Underlying the statement is the argument that only with such wide-ranging initiatives, in the form of constitutional support and enhanced financial jurisdiction and increased access to financial resources, would municipal governments be able to perform their governance and service delivery functions efficiently and effectively, and play the role expected of them in the twenty-first century. With this, the constitution has laid the foundation for reform of the municipal financial structure. Since the passage of the 74th Amendment, this objective has been advanced in several ways. The *Income Tax Act* has been amended to provide for issuance of tax-free bonds by municipalities. In 2002, the Government of India established a fund called the Urban Reform Incentive Fund (URIF), and the JNNURM established in 2005 now constitutes one of the largest initiatives to reform, among other things, the finances and functioning of municipalities.

But what do these initiatives bring in by way of a municipal finance system that addresses issues of growth, decentralisation and improved service delivery? Are they adequate in relation to India's changing socio-economic realities? What roles will be required of the central and state governments in reinforcing the existing system? This chapter cannot provide a comprehensive response to these questions – that requires further primary research. What it can do, however, is to provide a framework of suggestions to advance the existing reform agenda. This framework is in three parts: broadening the fiscal domain of municipalities; institutional re-engineering for improved municipal finance; and the role and participation of the central government in municipal affairs.

6.4.1 Broadening the fiscal domain of municipalities

Broadening the current municipal fiscal domain is a key imperative for addressing the challenges of growth, urbanisation and improved service delivery. This involves first making the property tax system – the main tax instrument for municipalities – comprehensive, and restoring to municipalities those taxes that meet the criterion of immobility. Several suggestions have been made from time to time to reform the property tax system, the most recent being the Thirteenth Finance Commission's (TFC) proposal for state-level Property Tax Boards. As mentioned previously, these boards are expected to assist municipalities in putting in place independent and transparent procedures for assessing property tax.

Looking beyond property tax, it was shown earlier in this chapter that the fiscal domain of municipalities is too narrow and has a low level of buoyancy. It has also been stated that a key impediment to the devolution of 12th Schedule functions is the lack of an appropriate revenue model. Several states currently share a pool of their taxes with municipalities, albeit erratically. The TFC also suggested that the proposed goods and services tax (GST) be shared with local governments. Its recommendation is grounded in the fact that, since municipal governments now have several redistributional functions within their fold, they should have access to taxes that have greater buoyancy. This proposal warrants support.

6.4.2 Institutional re-engineering for improved municipal finance

Legislative and institutional changes are needed to ensure adoption of prudent financial management practices in carrying out municipal functions. This is critical, as unsustainable and populist fiscal policies often adopted by municipalities jeopardise public service delivery and safety, as well as the viability of the financial system.

Given the reluctance or inability of municipalities to adjust tax rates and other charges to the rising cost of delivering services, it may be necessary to establish a municipal regulator with the responsibility of indexing taxes and charges against costs, to ensure that the value of municipal revenue yields is maintained. Such a body might, for example, be given the power to frame rules in respect of necessary adjustments in tax rates and charges, as well as to penalise municipalities for not adhering to those rules.

6.4.3 The role and participation of the central government in municipal affairs

Thus far the central government has intervened in municipal affairs cautiously, on the grounds that urban development is the domain of the states. The JNNURM, however, brings home the crucial point that cities make a significant contribution to the national economy, and that their growth (or lack of it) has important macroeconomic implications. It thus appears necessary to introduce more proactive policies that involve the central government in urban development matters. Like municipal finance, urban development is emerging as a multilevel responsibility.

Municipal governments in India have in recent years changed phenomenally in terms of the roles and functions they perform. The prognosis is that the next 20 years will see changes of extraordinary significance in the way municipal governments are organised, in their functions and responsibilities, as also in their fiscal and financial architecture. The global evidence attests to the likelihood of such changes. This fact alone requires that the municipal system be continually monitored and adjusted in order to be able to respond to the changes that are occurring both domestically and worldwide, and to prepare municipalities to address the new situations and realities. It places enormous responsibility on the Indian polity to begin to build far more trust and accountability in the functioning of municipal governments.

Notes

1 According to a recent paper on 'Infrastructure and city competitiveness in India', the supply of local infrastructural services such as municipal roads, street lighting, water supply and drainage has a positive and significant effect on city-level attractiveness to investment. According to the paper these effects are robust across econometric specifications and estimation procedures (Lall et al. 2010).

2 This is an elegant device for municipalities to conduct a wide range of activities with less encumbrance from legislations and other statutory regulations.

3 US$1 equals approximately Rs45 (2009 conversion rate).

4 In 2008, the Government of India constituted a High-Powered Expert Committee and tasked it to estimate the investment requirements for urban infrastructure. The norms of expenditure as set by the HPEC are at 2009–10 prices. These have been adjusted to 2007–08 level.

5 See High-Powered Expert Committee (2011). The estimates include the proposed investment needs for water supply, sewerage, solid waste management, urban roads, storm water drains, urban transport, traffic support infrastructure and street lighting.

6 The 2011 Census of India places India's urban population at 377 million. A distinguishing feature of the 2011 Census results is that, for the first time, the net increase in urban population was marginally higher than the net increase in rural population during the decade of 2001–2011.

7 Recent literature on local government finance dwells on the impact of the global crises on subnational government finance and subnational dimension of stimulus packages. See Barcelona Economics Institute (2009).

8 Richard Bird's observations in this regard are pertinent. He writes: 'If the appropriate expenditure role for subnational governments is simply to provide a few minor local services and perhaps to act as delivery agents for nationally determined public expenditures, the revenue assignment questions turn out to be relatively simple. However, if subnational governments are expected to deliver important (and costly) public services and have some discretion in deciding how and to what extent they do so, determining the appropriate revenue assignment is much more difficult' (2010: 1).

9 Dillon's Rule is a judicial interpretation derived from a written decision by Judge John F Dillon of Iowa in 1868, and states that a municipality may only exercise powers conferred explicitly by the statutes of a superior level or order of government (Dillon 1911).

10 Dealing with the question regarding the powers of local authorities, Mill expounded: 'It is obvious to begin with, that all business purely local, all which concerns a single locality, should devolve upon the local authorities. The paving, lighting, and cleaning of the streets of a town, and in ordinary circumstances the draining of its houses, are of little consequence to any but to its inhabitants. But among the duties classed as local or performed by local functionaries, there are many which might with equal propriety be termed national, being the share, belonging to the locality, of some branch of the public administration in the efficiency of which the whole nation is alike interested: the gaols, for instance – the local police – the local administration of justice' (Mill 1910: 354).

11 Most federal countries give the control over municipalities to provinces or states. Therefore, the powers a municipality possesses depend almost entirely on the powers the province wishes to grant. In Canada, for example, municipalities in some provinces operate legislation that spells out every power. By contrast, Alberta gives 'natural person powers' to its municipalities, and British Columbia has created what amounts to a 'bill of rights' for municipalities. In other cases, major urban areas are recognised in various ways as being different from other municipalities. For example, Toronto has been given additional powers under the *City of Toronto Act 2006*.

12 Article 280(3)(c) of the Constitution of India requires the Finance Commission to make recommendations on the measures needed to augment the Consolidated Fund of a state to

supplement the resources of the municipalities on the basis of the recommendations made by the Finance Commission of the State.

13 Surplus of municipal revenue over expenditure should be read with caution: first, revenue income, according to the classification in which the finance data have been compiled, includes central government transfers which are meant for asset creation; and, second, most state governments require municipalities to either maintain a balanced budget or post a budget surplus.

14 *Octroi* is a tax on the entry of goods into a local area for consumption, use or sale. It has been abolished in all states excepting the municipal corporations in Maharashtra.

15 In Belgium, Germany and Switzerland, more than 80 per cent of local tax revenues are derived from personal and corporate income taxes. More than 80 per cent of local government tax revenues in Australia, Canada and the USA are derived from property taxation. Sales taxes are levied mainly by cities in the USA, and there is a mix of local taxes in Austria (30 per cent revenue from sales tax) and Spain (40 per cent revenues from sales tax). See Slack (2010).

16 Reference to the JNNURM grants here includes central government support under the submissions of Urban Infrastructure and Governance (UIG), Basic Services to the Urban Poor (BSUP), Urban Infrastructure Development Scheme for Small and Medium Towns (UIDSSMT) and Integrated Housing and Slum Development Programme (IHSDP).

17 Municipalities can raise resources in the capital market to finance infrastructure. Their powers to borrow are laid down in the *Local Authorities Loans Act 1914*, provisions of which have been incorporated in the respective state-level statutes. Further, taking note of developments in the country's capital market, the Government of India has issued regulations for issuance of tax-free municipal bonds. Fourteen municipal corporations and local authorities have issued such bonds. They are not supported by sovereign guarantees, and municipalities must set aside funds for their redemption.

18 *Octroi* tended to inhibit free internal mobility of goods and services, with adverse effects on the economy. See Rao et al. 1985.

19 Guess (2003); Celina (2003).

References

Anas, A, KS Lee and G Oh (1996), 'Costs of infrastructure deficiencies in manufacturing in Indonesia, Nigeria, and Thailand', World Bank Policy Research Working Paper No. 1604, World Bank, Washington, DC.

Bahl, R and R Bird (2008), 'Sub-national taxes in developing countries: the way forward', *Public Budgeting and Finances*, Vol. 28 No. 4, 1.

Bahl, R and M Cyan (2010), 'Tax assignment: does the practice match the theory?', *Environment and Planning C Government and Policy*, Vol. 29 No. 2, 264–80.

Barcelona Economics Institute (2009), *World Report on Fiscal Federalism*, Barcelona, Spain.

Bird, R (2010), 'Subnational taxation in developing countries: a review of the literature', World Bank Policy Research Working Paper 5450, October, World Bank, Washington, DC.

Brazil Ministry of Planning, Budget and Management (2000), *Brazilian Fiscal Responsibility Law 2000*, Brazil.

Dillon, JF (1911), *Commentaries on the Law of Municipal Corporations*, Little Brown & Co., Boston.

Garcea, J and EC Le Sage Jr (2005), *Municipal Reforms in Canada*, Oxford University Press, London.

Guess, GM (Ed.), (2003), *Fast Track Municipal Fiscal Reform in Central and Eastern Europe and the Former Soviet Union*, Open Society Institute, Budapest, Hungary.

High Powered Expert Committee (2011), *Report on Indian Urban Infrastructure and Services*, Ministry of Urban Development, New Delhi, India.

International Monetary Fund (2008), Government Finance Statistics, IMF, Washington, DC.

Lall, S, H Wang and U Deichmann (2010), 'Infrastructure and city competitiveness in India', in B Jo, B Guha-Khasnobis and R Kanbur (Eds.), *Urbanisation and Development: Multidisciplinary Perspectives*, Oxford University Press, New York.

Mathur, OP, S Pratishtha and A Bhaduri (2002), *Options for Closing the Revenue Gap of Municipalities*, National Institute of Public Finance and Policy, New Delhi, India.

Mathur, OP (2011), *Municipal Finance Matters: India Municipal Finance Study*, National Institute of Public Finance and Policy, New Delhi, India.

McKinsey Global Institute (2010), *India's Urban Awakening: Building Inclusive Cities, Sustaining Economic Growth*, McKinsey Global Institute, New Delhi, India.

Mill, JS (1848), *Principles of Political Economy*, John W. Parker, London.

Mill, JS (1910), 'Representative governments', in *Utilitarianism, Liberty and Representative Government*, Everyman Edition, Dent, London.

Mohanty, PK, BM Misra, G Rajan and PD Jeromi (2007), *Municipal Finance in India: An Assessment*, Development Research Group, Reserve Bank of India, Mumbai.

Oates, WE (1972), *Fiscal Federalism*, Harcourt, Brace and Jovanovich, New York.

Rao, M Govinda, G Pradhan and OP Bohra (1985), *Alternative to Octroi in Rajasthan*, National Institute of Public Finance and Policy, New Delhi, India.

Slack, E (2010), 'Municipal finance in federal OECD countries', background paper prepared for the India Municipal Finance Report, National Institute of Public Finance and Policy, New Delhi, India.

Souza, C (2003), *Brazil's System of Local Government, Local Finance, and Inter-governmental Relations*, School of Public Policy, University of Birmingham, UK.

Thirteenth Finance Commission (2009) *Report of the Thirteenth Finance Commission, 2009*, Government of India, Ministry of Finance, New Delhi.

United Cities and Local Governments (2010), *Local Government Finance: The Challenges of the 21st Century*, Second Global Report on Decentralisation and Local Democracy, Barcelona.

United Nations (2009), *World Urbanization Prospects*, UN, New York.

Chapter 7

Property Rates as an Instrument for Development: An Analysis of South African Policy, Law and Practice

Jaap de Visser[1]

When local governments impose property taxes, their primary objective is to fund their expenditure. However, the role of local government can be seen as far more than simply the provision of local public services. Local government can be an agent of its community, responsible for using its authority in a manner that creatively responds to local needs and thereby enhances the well-being of its area. This chapter asks if this interpretation of the role of municipalities has consequences for the manner in which they tax properties.

South African municipalities have recently been equipped with a new property rates framework, which permits them to differentiate between categories of properties and to legislate for various kinds of property rates discounts. This framework presents a new approach to the use of property rating, by positioning it as an instrument with a stated developmental objective in addition to its revenue-raising function.

This chapter therefore examines to what extent and how South African municipalities actually use their power to levy property rates as a developmental instrument. Do they use property rates as an instrument to reduce poverty, facilitate access to economic opportunities and encourage sustainable use of resources? Or does property tax remain an instrument primarily deployed to raise revenue that funds service delivery? In attempting to answer these questions, the author was limited by the lack of independent research on this topic, and draws primarily from official reports.

First, a brief introduction to local government in South Africa is given. An overview of the legal and policy framework for the levying of property rates then follows, including the expectation implicit in that framework that municipalities should use property rating in a developmental manner. The chapter then proceeds with a discussion of some of the limits and concerns with respect to such use of property taxation. Finally, it canvasses some of the policy innovations in municipal property rating.

7.1 Local government in South Africa

Before 1994, local government in South Africa was designed to implement apartheid. Local government institutions were racially determined and the black majority was denied democratic rights. White municipalities were self-serving entities; they were given exclusive power to tax properties in well-resourced and viable commercial centres, without any obligation to use the revenue to improve the lives of township dwellers. Black municipalities were undemocratic and starved of income and authority. They became the subject of large-scale service boycotts in the 1980s.[2]

The 1993 constitution introduced major reforms: local government was given constitutional recognition and various local government institutions were merged (Steytler and De Visser 2007). Even more fundamental change came with the 1996 constitution, which further entrenched the role of local government. The new system was put into operation in 2000, and now comprises a democratically elected political leadership (section 157 of the constitution) with constitutionally guaranteed authority over listed functional areas (section 156). The constitution also secures local government's authority with regard to certain important financial matters. It empowers municipalities to impose surcharges on fees for services provided and to impose property rates (section 229), and entitles local government to an 'equitable' share of nationally generated revenue (section 214).

7.1.1 Developmental local government

As an unequivocal response to the destructive role played by local government in the past, the constitution posits local government as a sphere of government that is responsible for important developmental matters. The constitutional 'objects of local government':

- provide democratic and accountable government for local communities;

- ensure provision of services to communities in a sustainable manner;

- promote social and economic development;

- promote a safe and healthy environment; and

- encourage the involvement of communities and community organisations in the matters of local government (section 152).

Municipalities are furthermore instructed to give priority to the basic needs of the community (section 153). The 1998 White Paper on Local Government defined this developmental mandate as 'local government committed to working with citizens and groups within the community to find sustainable ways to meet their social, economic and material needs and improve the quality of their lives' (Department of Constitutional Development 1998: 17). According to the White Paper, the main characteristics of developmental local government are:

- maximising social development and economic growth – stimulating local economies and job creation;

- integrating and co-ordinating the efforts of all developmental actors – mainly through integrated development planning;

- democratising development – harnessing the input and energy of local citizens; and

- leading and learning – building social capital at the local level to enable local solutions to development problems (ibid: 18).

The key outcomes that the White Paper envisages developmental local government achieving are:

- provision of household infrastructure and services;

- creation of liveable, integrated cities, towns and rural areas;

- local economic development; and

- community empowerment and redistribution.

7.1.2 Local government institutions

South Africa's land mass spans around 1.2 million square kilometres, inhabited by close to 48 million people (Statistics South Africa 2007). Yet the country has only 278 municipalities, making South Africa home to some of the world's largest local governments in terms of both area and population.[3]

There are three types of municipalities: metropolitan, district and local. There are eight metropolitan municipalities, which are single-tier local government structures. Outside these areas the country is divided into 44 district municipalities. Each district comprises a number of local municipalities, usually between three and five. There are 226 local municipalities in total.

Municipalities are responsible for important services such as water and sanitation, local roads, refuse removal, town planning, electricity reticulation and environmental health services. They develop and maintain parks, recreational facilities, markets and local transport facilities. In addition to these constitutionally guaranteed functions, they often perform further functions including housing delivery, primary healthcare and community services such as developing and running libraries and museums. Taken together, these functions position local government at the epicentre of much-needed physical and social development in South Africa.

As directed in the *Local Government: Municipal Systems Act* (2000), municipalities must produce and annually review Integrated Development Plans (IDPs), which are intended to be the building blocks for the entire government's service delivery and infrastructure planning.

Property taxation

Property taxation is an important source of revenue for municipal services and, as indicated earlier, has been constitutionally guaranteed as a taxing power for municipalities. Historically, property rates have always been an important mechanism to fund municipal services, albeit as part of a diversified basket of revenue sources and not across the board. Kihato and Berrisford (2006: 33) note that under apartheid tax collection in white municipalities was 'generally high and well received', in part because residential owners enjoyed generous rebates and the substantial profits generated from the provision of electricity and water made up for the loss of income. Property taxation in rural areas was largely non-existent before the recent changes to the local government and property-rating regime. The White Paper remarks that 'while [it] is by no means the sole source of municipal revenue, it is an important source of discretionary own revenue' (Department of Constitutional Development 1998: 114). Municipalities rely on property rate income to fund other services, access to which is not limited to specific consumers.

Nevertheless, the White Paper expects municipalities to use their powers to levy property rates for more than simply raising revenue. It refers to the 'need to develop the criteria for evaluating alternative property valuation systems, within the framework of alleviating and addressing poverty' (ibid: 115). It also warns that this must be subject to clear policies and procedures, and that any tax relief 'should be clearly indicated in a transparent and consistent manner in the budget of a municipality' (ibid). Furthermore, the White Paper noted the importance of latitude for municipalities 'to make certain decisions concerning the nature of the property tax in their area of jurisdiction, which reflect their unique circumstances and local economic objectives' (ibid). By 1998 the policy intention was thus that municipalities would deploy the instrument strategically to achieve developmental outcomes. As discussed below, the legal framework still leaves considerable discretion to municipalities to make decisions in this regard.

7.1.3 The current context: local government 'in distress'

The constitutional, statutory and policy framework for local government in South Africa is sound and the progress made to date is impressive.[4] However, the challenges remain daunting. Many municipalities battle huge service delivery and backlog problems. Communication and accountability relationships with communities are often poor, and many municipalities experience internal governance issues and sometimes even corruption and fraud (Department of Cooperative Governance and Traditional Affairs 2009). Municipalities are often characterised by poor financial management, resulting in negative audit opinions (Department of Cooperative Governance and Traditional Affairs 2009). A lack of scarce skills such as engineering, financial management and planning seriously frustrates the ability of municipalities to implement their developmental mandate (ibid). Communities across South Africa are dissatisfied with the progress made. The image of communities protesting against service delivery backlogs, maladministration and corruption has become a common occurrence. Recent research indicates that, from 2007 to 2011, there was an average of 11.6 protests per month in South Africa, but the first eight months of 2012 averaged 28.3 protests. Not only is the number of protests on the increase, they are also becoming more violent, with 79.2 per cent of protests turning violent in the first eight months of 2012 (De Visser and Powell 2012). It is clear that local government is in distress.

Another manifestation of dissatisfaction with local government performance is the phenomenon of ratepayers withholding the payment of property rates and service fees. While community protests generally originate in the townships, the withholding of payments is led by well-organised ratepayers' associations, generally comprising middle- and upper-class residents. In response to administrative malaise and the lack of service delivery, ratepayers declare disputes with the municipality and cease paying their taxes. Instead, the moneys are paid into a common bank account and released to the municipality only when service delivery improves (Powell et al. 2009).[5]

Property rating by municipalities thus takes place within a context of a promising institutional framework, but with serious problems in terms of local government's capacity to implement the system effectively. Indeed, many rural municipalities do not levy any property rates at all, despite their constitutional authority to do so. High levels of poverty and the difficulties of valuing properties and administering the tax are cited as reasons for the absence of property rating in rural areas (National Treasury 2011).

7.2 Legal and policy framework for property rating

As noted earlier, section 229 of the constitution empowers a municipality to impose rates on property. This constitutional guarantee manifests itself in at least two ways:

- First, the power of a municipality to impose a rate on property stems from the constitution itself[6] and is described by the Constitutional Court as an 'original' power.[7] Before the interim constitution, all municipal powers, including the rating power, were 'delegated' powers conferred on a local authority by another organ of state.[8]

- Second, even though the constitution also enables the national government to regulate this power, such regulation must respect municipal discretion to establish policy and determine rates. For example, legislation in the Eastern Cape which required provincial permission for the imposition of a rate of over two cents in the rand was struck down in *CDA Boerdery (Edms) Bpk v Nelson Mandela Metropolitaanse Munisipaliteit*. The Supreme Court of Appeal held that this requirement was a product of the pre-1994 dispensation, 'tailored to its hierarchy and matched to the Administrator's supervisory control over municipalities and his executive role in relation to them.'[9] Under the 1996 constitution, the judge continued, the Premier enjoys no 'special supervisory powers over the exercise of local government functions, or special duties in relation to the determination of rates.'[10]

This does not mean that the municipality's power is unfettered. Section 229 of the constitution itself provides that the rating power 'may not be exercised in a way that materially and unreasonably prejudices national economic policies, economic activities across municipal boundaries, or the national mobility of goods, services, capital or labour'. Second, the *Local Government: Municipal Property Rates Act (MPRA)* of 2004 contains a framework within which municipalities must perform the property rating function.

Under the MPRA, only metropolitan and local municipalities may levy property rates. Rates are levied on land and improvements, and the owner of immovable property is liable to pay the property rates to the municipality. The market value of the property is the basis for valuation, which is carried out by professional valuers. Municipalities determine the tax rate and, importantly, the rate may differ from one category of properties to another. However, as indicated above, municipal discretion is subject to certain limitations imposed by the constitution and national government. For example, under the MPRA national government may set an upper limit on the percentage by which rates in the rand (R) for specific categories may increase. The national government may also set an upper limit on the percentage by which the total revenue derived from rates in all or specific categories may increase. Furthermore, the national government may determine maximum ratios with respect to differential rating and has indeed promulgated those.

7.2.1 Reliance on property rates

User charges (electricity, water, sanitation and refuse) are by far the largest contributors to municipal revenue (National Treasury 2011: 58; 2007: 13; Tshangana-Hickey 2009: 5). National transfers are the second largest source of revenue for local government, calculated at 32.6 per cent in the 2009/10 budget year (National Treasury 2011: 59). Property rates come in third, but the fact that a large proportion of user charges levied by municipalities has to be paid over to bulk providers (National Treasury 2011: 58) and that a significant proportion of national transfers are conditional[11] emphasises the important role that property rates income plays in the municipal budget. The municipality depends on this income to fund services for which no user charge can be levied. Examples are municipal roads, parks, street lighting and storm-water systems (National Treasury 2011: 40).

Broadly, property rates form about one fifth of the operating budget of a metropolitan municipality and about 15 per cent of the operating budget of a local municipality (National Treasury 2007: 14, 17; Tshangana-Hickey 2009: 5). Income from property rates grew at a modest pace between 2001 and 2009, and this income stream held up well during the Global Financial Crisis (National Treasury 2011: 58–59). Property rates as a percentage of the country's gross domestic product (GDP) have remained constant at about 1 per cent (National Treasury 2011: 50).

The introduction of the MPRA, with its full effects felt only from 2008, is predicted to accelerate the growth of property rates income. The National Treasury expected a 10 per cent increase in property rates income in the medium term (National Treasury 2007: 14, 17; 2011: 60).

The extent to which municipalities actually collect the property rates that are due to them is difficult to measure for a number of reasons. First, municipalities generally issue a composite account, which may comprise water, sewage and electricity charges along with property rates. Defaults on that account are not immediately attributed to any specific item, so that reporting on fiscal efficiency does not separate property taxation from service charges. Second, both the system and scope of property valuation have undergone drastic changes in recent years. Comparisons between the potential of these new valuation rolls and the actual collection of property rates have hardly been made yet, let alone aggregated to figures that represent general trends.

However, while the specific rates portion of consumer debt may not be easily identified, there is ample evidence for the assertion that the overall debt (including both property rates and service charges) is massive.[12] This consumer debt is a serious impediment to municipal operations. It can be attributed to a combination of failing revenue management (integrity and accuracy of billing systems) on the part of municipalities (National Treasury 2011: 68); unwillingness to pay on the part of consumers (National Treasury 2011: 209) and sometimes government departments; but also to the impact of poverty on the ability to pay. Any municipal efforts to use property rating for developmental purposes will need to be accompanied by improvements in fiscal efficiency.[13]

7.2.2 Municipal property rates policies

The MRPA requires every council to adopt a binding property rates policy, which must contain and give insight into policy choices the municipality is making when levying rates. The MPRA also instructs municipalities to pursue local, social and economic development in their property rates policies. The law thus envisages that municipalities use their property rates policies in a developmental manner. The MPRA more specifically places a number of demands on the content of the policy. For example, the policy must take into account the effect of rates on the poor[14] and include appropriate measures to alleviate their rates burden.[15] Relief cannot be granted other than in accordance with the policy. The impact on public benefit organisations must also be considered, and the policy must take into account the effect of rates on public infrastructure.[16] In addition, the Act requires special consideration of agricultural properties: the extent to which they receive services, contribute to the local economy and assist in meeting development obligations, and the contribution that is made by them to the welfare of farm workers, a particularly vulnerable group in South Africa.

The policy must furthermore set out the system of differential rates for different categories of properties,[17] and provide criteria for any differentiation between categories of properties or owners of properties for the purposes of rates exemptions, rebates or reductions, or increases in rates. Exemptions, rebates and reductions must be identified and motivated in the policy.[18] Finally, the policy must provide information about the impact that the MPRA and the municipality's own policy decisions will have on the level of rates revenue.

On the adoption of a rates policy, the municipality must pass a by-law to give effect to its implementation. This ensures that the choices made in the policy can be made legally binding on the municipal community. The policy and the by-law are long-term strategies. Actual rates are determined annually with the passing of a property rates resolution setting the rates for the different property categories.

This chapter focuses on the use of property rates as an instrument to facilitate development. It is therefore prudent to briefly introduce the menu of instruments from which a municipality may choose to differentiate or provide tax relief.

7.2.3 Differential rating

As indicated earlier, the law allows municipalities to apply differential rates, and municipalities have significant leeway in adopting differential rating regimes. They may choose a method of identifying categories, identify categories from a predetermined list and add their own categories (Steytler and De Visser 2007: 13–34). Forthcoming changes to the MPRA suggest this leeway will be reduced in that municipalities will be limited to choosing from a predetermined list of categories (Local Government: Municipal Property Rates Bill 2011). Also as noted previously, the extent to which the rating may differ across categories is curtailed by the promulgation of maximum ratios by the national government.

Bird and Slack identify three grounds to justify differentiated taxes. First, fairness may dictate that the tax should correlate to the benefits received from local public services (Bird and Slack 2004: 37). This is true for South Africa. Certain categories of properties, such as agricultural properties, tend to receive fewer benefits from local public services than residential properties or business properties. Second, the local government may want to impose a higher tax on the tax base that is 'least elastic' (Bird and Slack 2004: 37). In South Africa, the identification of business properties as a distinct category that is 'less elastic' has enabled municipalities to impose a higher rate on those properties. The third justification mentioned by Bird and Slack is particularly relevant in the context of this chapter, namely that variation can be used to achieve land use objectives (Bird and Slack 2004: 37). Property taxation then moves beyond the mere collection and redistribution of income to attempting to influence behaviour. The most common example in South Africa is the imposition of a higher rate on vacant land as a distinct category, in order to stimulate development and discourage speculation.

7.2.4 Exemptions

As with any property rating system, certain properties are exempt from rating. Municipalities may identify specific categories of properties or property owners for exemption, while some exemptions are already granted by the national government. The MPRA defines certain generic exemptions, such as nature reserves, mineral rights and places of worship.

Exemptions have been criticised in international literature because they narrow the tax base of municipalities. Therefore, the taxes on the remaining taxpayers must be increased or the level of local services must be decreased. Additionally, they are likely to result in disproportionate tax burdens. This is troublesome, especially when a higher-level government determines what is exempt (Bird and Slack 2004: 26).

In South Africa, it is becoming common for the national government to pursue its national policy objectives by imposing exemptions which municipalities are then obliged to follow. Its constitutional power to 'regulate' property taxation permits national government to do this. For example, nature conservation, a responsibility of national and provincial governments, may be pursued by prohibiting municipalities from levying property rates on property classified as such. This is discussed further below.

7.2.5 Reduction

As indicated earlier, rates are calculated annually on the full market value of a property. However, the municipality may, with respect to a category of properties or property owners, subtract an amount from the market value, thereby reducing the rates liability.[19] Some reductions are mandatory, but the municipality may also, in terms of its rates policy, add to the list.

In terms of developmental objectives, an important generic reduction is the so-called 'residential exclusion'. The MPRA excludes the first R15,000 of every residential property from the rateable value of that property, and thus introduces a very mild form of graduated property rates.

7.2.6 Rebates

Municipalities may grant rebates to specific categories of properties or property owners. These do not affect the rateable value of the property or the rate that applies to it. Rather, they are discounts granted by the municipality on the ultimate rates liability with respect to a specific property. Rebates are often granted on the basis of an application made to the municipality and may therefore involve considerable administrative effort. It is usually the profile of the owner, rather than the profile of the property, that attracts the rebate (Steytler and De Visser 2007: 13–39). The municipality must set out criteria for rebates in its rates policy. It is free to formulate its own categories, but the Act lists owners that are indigent, dependent on social welfare, temporarily without income or struck by disaster as examples of categories of owners that may be considered for rebates. Importantly, the Act also lists '*bona fide* farmers' as possible recipients of rebates.

7.2.7 Accounting for discounts

Transparency and accountability in the reduction of property rates liability for specific categories is critical (Bird and Slack 2004: 26). Bird and Slack advise that the properties in question should still be valued so that the municipality can be clear about the taxes that could have been collected.

This principle was already expressed in the 1998 White Paper (see above) and is followed in South African law. The MPRA requires all exemptions, reductions and rebates granted by the municipality to be listed and tabled by the municipal council. The municipality must indicate the implicit cost of all exemptions and rebates in an annual statement, and projections regarding revenue to be foregone must be included in the annual budget.

7.2.8 Expectations: South African national and provincial policy frameworks

Various national and provincial policy frameworks are expressing the expectation that municipalities use property rating as an instrument to stimulate local economic development. The White Paper on Local Government and its reference to the developmental use of property rating was discussed earlier in this chapter. The National Framework for Local Economic Development, a more recent policy statement, remarks that 'in promoting the local economy, the primary focus of municipalities should be upon [among other things] managing a progressive property tax system' (Department of Provincial and Local Government 2005). Furthermore, the framework lists property rating as an instrument that municipalities can use when they compete among themselves 'to get the best out of each area' (Department of Provincial and Local Government 2005: 15). The framework itself does not provide any advice to municipalities as to how best to use property rating to achieve these objectives.

Another example is the Western Cape Rural Land Use Planning and Management Guidelines, which envisage that municipalities will incentivise the consolidation of conservation estates through property rates discounts (Western Cape Department of Environmental Affairs and Development Planning 2009: 23). Therefore, there is an expectation that municipalities will choose to forfeit revenue to achieve nature conservation objectives, despite the fact that nature conservation is not part of a municipality's mandate.

7.3 Arguments against using property rates for developmental purposes

It is clear that South African municipalities must use their power to differentiate and offer property rates discounts in a balanced manner. However, the international literature appears to view differentiation and the granting of property rates relief with a dose of scepticism. Some of the most important arguments used to caution against liberal use of property rates differentiation and discounts are discussed below.

One of the most important determinants of a successful property rates regime is the administration of it. According to Bird and Slack, '[n]o area of taxation is more dependent on administration' (2004: 41). A property rating system should thus not be unduly complicated and it should be relatively easy for local officials to administer. The imposition of a myriad of different rates and instruments for granting tax relief could complicate the rating system. This dimension is particularly relevant in the South African context. The property rates regime is new, and skilful and experienced administrators, necessary to implement and administer complicated tax relief instruments, are in desperately short supply.

Transparency and certainty are also key values in property rating (Bird and Slack 2004: 40). If differentiation and tax discounts result in a lack of transparency and their administration is vulnerable to capture by local groups or individuals, they may become an instrument to benefit individuals or individual institutions rather than a strategy to achieve development. Similarly, property taxpayers should be able to ascertain, with a degree of certainty, how the property tax regime operates and how the criteria for differentiation or discounts will be applied to them. A lack of certainty will generally disadvantage taxpayers, and incentives do not work if it is unclear when they apply.

It is sometimes argued that property rates differentiation and rates relief are likely to create unwanted distortions. First, the differentiation is not always based on the level of municipal services received. Therefore, landowners may face different treatment while using the same level of municipal services. Second, the differentiation may have implications for economic competition: differential treatment means that owners or managers of taxed properties face higher costs than those of exempt properties (Bird and Slack 2004: 5).

Municipalities may want to use property rates relief to encourage activities that are particularly desirable from a developmental point of view. While acknowledging the need for favouring certain property holders to encourage their presence in the local community, Bird and Slack argue against the use of property tax exemptions to achieve this: they express a preference for direct grants in that context (2004).

Attempts to incentivise behaviour and mitigate rates liability often reduce the municipality's revenue from rates. It may be argued that local revenue generation is too precious a commodity to sacrifice at the altar of local policy-making and local redistribution. Local revenue generation is not only critical to enable the funding of local public services, but also indispensable to establish local accountability for those public services. Yet local governments are often the first to be requested or instructed to give up their own revenue, be it in response to national anxiety or as part of a tax relief effort.

One of the reasons for municipalities to use property rates differentiation or discounts is to redistribute resources from wealthier to poorer communities within their areas. However, in intergovernmental fiscal policy circles it is often argued that redistributive efforts are best administered at the central level. Decentralisation of revenue generation has the potential to aggravate regional inequity (Fjelstad 2001: 148), and sceptics of redistribution at the local level argue that localised decision-making surrounding revenue generation tends to ignore externalities (Ajam 2001: 126; Prud' Homme 1994: 15). Even property taxation, as an immovable tax, is not immune from that effect. For example, higher property taxation of businesses may make sense from a redistributive perspective, but the cost impact of that taxation may be exported to consumers of the relevant goods and services outside the municipality (Bird and Slack 2004: 39).

On the other hand, it may be argued that an outright rejection of any redistributive role for local government can no longer be supported, given the momentum towards a role for municipalities that moves beyond the quest for the most efficient retailer of services into a broader well-being or developmental objective that inevitably implies redistributive elements.[20]

In South Africa, both the policy context and the size of municipalities signal a clear departure from the position that local governments have no redistributive role. Policy and legislative instruments governing local government in South Africa are awash with references to redistribution. The White Paper on Local Government lists 'community empowerment and redistribution' as one of the developmental outcomes of local government.[21] Municipal boundaries must be demarcated with 'the need to share and redistribute financial and administrative resources' in mind.[22] Indeed, a radical transformation of local government boundaries has followed, as illustrated by Table 7.1.

As noted earlier, South Africa's municipalities rank among the world's largest and arguably are thus well positioned to perform a redistributive role. However, while the attempt to influence behaviour with taxation policy may be a dominant feature of national taxes, the same may not hold true for property taxation by local governments.

Table 7.1 Total number of municipalities in South Africa

Timeline	1994	1994/95	2000	2006	2011
Number of municipalities	> 2,000	842	284	283	278

Bird and Slack argue that the level of property rates is generally set to make up the shortfall between expenditure requirements and revenue from other sources: 'Local governments first determine their expenditure requirements. They then subtract non-property tax revenues available … from their expenditure requirements to determine how much they need to raise from property tax revenues. The resulting property tax requirements are divided by the taxable assessment to determine the property tax rate' (2004: 33; see also Steytler and De Visser 2007: 13). If property taxation is thus primarily aimed at ensuring that the municipality is able to fund service delivery and developmental activities from the expenditure side of its budget, the room to manoeuvre is necessarily limited when it comes to the setting of differential rates and the determination of tax relief measures.

This approach to setting a specific tax rate undoubtedly rings true for many local government practitioners in South Africa. Nevertheless, it is clear that the constitutional and legal framework expects more. Municipalities are tasked to carefully consider and consult communities on a property rates policy and pursue developmental objectives in that policy. This policy will have set the scene before the specific tax rate or differential tax rates can be set by the municipality.

Another concern is the danger of expecting too much impact from property rates variation and relief on, for example, business decisions (Bird and Slack 2004: 39). If property rates account for a small proportion of business costs, a tax variation or discount is unlikely to prompt businesses to change their behaviour or their location. In that context, it is important to note that in South Africa the overall municipal account (including rates and tariffs) falls below the international benchmark of 15 per cent of household income (Tshangana-Hickey 2009: 8). It is not unreasonable to deduce from that that property rates are also unlikely to take up large chunks of business expenditure.

In addition, the extent to which municipalities can link the property rates instrument to local economic development may be limited by the regulatory framework. For example, in South Africa municipalities are prohibited from rating any below-ground structures used for mining. This puts a large section of the economy beyond their reach. It prohibits municipalities from reaping the benefits of underground value and limits the municipality's ability to influence a mining company's decision-making through taxation policy.

7.4 A review of current South African practices

In order to examine how South African municipalities are making use of the opportunities for property rates differentiation and rates relief, and how they are mitigating the risks and concerns mentioned above, the policies of the 20 largest municipalities were examined. Policy strategies were organised into those that impact the demand side (efforts to mitigate rates liability for vulnerable groups) or the supply side (efforts to support or stimulate certain behaviour or enterprise) of the property market.

The analysis reveals from the outset that the new system of the MPRA, with its closely defined instruments for differentiation, has not yet fully translated into coherent property rates policies across the board. Some of the policies make use of the various instruments in a confusing manner. For example, when Ethekwini[23] promises to rate sporting bodies only on their buildings, this appears to be contrary to the MPRA's principle of rating land and improvements. A more innocuous example is Cape Town's 100 per cent rebate on religious properties, which is eclipsed by the MPRA's statutory exemption of religious properties. These are indications that municipalities are still coming to terms with the instruments contained in the MPRA property rates framework.

Many of the policies contain discretionary rebates, but often the actual discount offered by the municipality appears to be a matter decided on the basis of criteria that are not included in the property rates policy. This may give rise to disagreements, but more importantly it detracts from the transparency of the property rates scheme. For municipalities to maintain a credible property taxation system, more clarity needs to be provided in the policies themselves – lest the discount become simply a matter of negotiation between the property owner and the municipality.

What becomes clear upon comparing the policies is that, with regard to certain issues, there is considerable variation in approaches among municipalities. For example, some municipalities (such as Emfuleni and Mbombela)[24] impose a higher rate on vacant land in order to stimulate development and discourage speculation. However, municipalities such as Msunduzi[25] and Ethekwini appear to do the opposite by reducing the tax burden on vacant land. Another example is the treatment of state property: some municipalities offer rebates to state institutions (Johannesburg) while others levy additional rates (Emfuleni, Mbombela). Assuming that this variation is a result of well-considered policy choices, the importance and usefulness of local discretion is underscored.

Few municipalities appear to use property rates as an instrument to influence behaviour related to specific geographically determined areas within the municipality. In other words, few use property rating as a spatial planning instrument. Most geographically targeted discounts refer to areas that have been struck by disaster. The sample included only three rebates for property in designated areas such as industrial zones or urban development zones (Mbombela, Emahlahleni, Mangaung).[26] The City of Johannesburg's policy includes an incentive for people to move into the inner city: rezoning into residential use in the inner city is awarded with a rebate.

The property rates policies contain a variety of measures to mitigate the rates burden on institutions that perform activities that are socially desirable, such as:

- caring for the aged;
- offering education (public and private schools, universities);

- culture and history (museums, libraries, monuments, art galleries);

- performing charity and welfare activities;

- caring for animals; and

- providing sports activities.

Many municipalities in the sample include measures that target vulnerable groups. Most policies contain exemptions or rebates for indigent persons. Often, qualification for these rebates is linked to registration on the municipality's indigent register – a comprehensive list of residents maintained by the municipality to enable it to differentiate when it collects fees for services. Additional criteria (such as a maximum property value) may sometimes apply.

The extension of the statutory residential exclusion of R15,000 to a more generous level is a common occurrence in the sampled municipalities. This is a measure designed to mitigate rates liability for poor households. In an extreme case, Cape Town has increased the exclusion to R200,000. A number of other municipalities have set the level between R40,000 and R80,000.

Hickey-Tshangana discusses the residential exclusion and concludes that the effect is that many poor households escape the rates burden altogether. She concludes that the residential exclusion is by far the easiest form of rates relief to administer and that it is reasonably effective in targeting the poor. She also concludes that the effect on revenue generated is minimal, as the rates income from that property segment is modest. For example, while the residential exclusion in Johannesburg removed almost a third of the number of properties from the radar screen, their combined property value represented no more than 2 per cent of the entire valuation roll (Hickey-Tshangana 2009: 17). The conclusion may be that residential exclusions are a particularly attractive 'poverty alleviation' tool in a developing context. First, the demands on tax administration are modest. Second, large income and wealth disparities work in the municipality's favour by producing a large pool of beneficiaries while limiting impact on revenue.

Sometimes, specific vulnerable groups are identified in the policies that were reviewed. For example, 7 of the 20 policies contain specific rebates or exemptions for child-headed households, a particularly pernicious phenomenon often associated with under-development, migrant labour and the HIV/AIDS pandemic. Even more common is the rebate for pensioners and people with disabilities.

7.4.1 Encouraging developmental behaviour

Direct encouragement of 'developmental behaviour' can be found in the treatment of agricultural properties. Municipalities clearly attempt to incentivise decent treatment of farm workers, a particularly vulnerable group in South Africa. The sample includes rebates for:

- offering permanent employment (one case);

- providing housing to farm workers (four cases);

- providing water to farm workers (five cases);

- providing electricity to farm workers (five cases); and

- providing other educational/recreational services (four cases).

7.4.2 Stimulating local economic development

The sample includes a number of measures that are aimed at stimulating local economic development by reducing the rates liability of particular enterprises. Ethekwini and Mbombela encourage the tourism industry by including a rebate for bed and breakfasts and guesthouses. Mbombela also offers a rebate to micro businesses, plus one for farming activity that contributes to the local economy. Three local municipalities (Makhado, Matjabeng and King Sabata Dalindyebo)[27] have a rebate for enterprises that conform to their local social and economic development policies.

However, these examples of rates discounts that aim to directly stimulate economic development are not encouraging. Apart from the rebate for tourism accommodation, the discounts are loosely defined. It is not clear what a 'micro business' is. Similarly, a farmer's contribution to the local economy appears to be either a given or extremely hard to determine. Finally, it is unlikely that a local business will be able to make an informed assessment of whether it perhaps conforms to the social and economic development policy of the municipality and should therefore apply for a rebate, let alone include the rebate in its business calculations.

The sample also includes an interesting measure in Mbombela Municipality, which assists property owners to weather the storm of a recession by offering a rebate 'to assist owners with the current economic situation'.

7.5 Summary and assessment

The constitutional and statutory framework for property rates in South Africa permits and expects municipalities to use their authority to levy property rates in a developmental manner. In South Africa, property rates differentiation and rates relief are viewed as an expression of a developmental state, which is expected to intervene in a balanced manner to correct distortions in the economy and society. These include serious distortions in the South African economy, including gross racial imbalances, huge income disparities and a dominance of large economic institutions (African National Congress 2007). Municipalities thus operate from a firm ideological and policy basis when they engage in making policy on property rating.

International literature cautions against overzealous use of property rating to achieve developmental outcomes, and emphasises the need for municipalities to protect and carefully administer their revenue sources. However, the review of the property rates policies of the 20 largest municipalities shows that they are indeed making use of the opportunity offered by the legal framework to differentiate and offer rates relief to achieve policy objectives. The policies reveal a considerable array of differentiation between property categories, often with a view to redistribute resources. They also include a number of tax relief measures aimed at poverty alleviation and the promotion of economic, social and cultural development.

The policies can be critiqued for often employing differentiation and tax relief measures without a clearly stated policy rationale. The effectiveness of these instruments also varies. The exclusion of an initial amount of residential property value from rating is easy to administer and appears to assist in reducing poverty without resulting in huge amounts of revenue being lost to the municipality, particularly as part of the exclusion is for rates that the municipality would in all likelihood not be able to collect in any event. Some of the rebates to encourage local economic development are not particularly well designed and probably not realistic. Common criteria such as 'compliance with the local social and economic policy' and 'making a contribution to the local economy' are somewhat arbitrary and difficult to implement. From a tax administration point of view, they appear problematic and are not likely to go far in facilitating local economic development.

By providing relief to institutions that provide important social or cultural services, municipalities may encourage their presence and facilitate their work. These relief measures are not necessarily new and probably compare well with how local governments elsewhere levy property rates (albeit usually through centrally imposed limitations). The measures adopted to encourage the decent treatment of farm workers are examples of innovative use of the rebate instrument. It is important to note, however, that these mechanisms are suggested in the MPRA itself. This indicates that municipalities still rely heavily on the national framework for ideas.

Apart from the occasional reward for densification, few municipalities have included instruments directly aimed at encouraging sustainable use of resources. This appears to be an area where more policy innovation may be possible.

The apparent reluctance on the part of municipalities to innovate must be understood within its context. First, this assessment may have come too early. The property rates regime is new and required municipalities to implement significant technical reforms in, among other things, property valuation. To date, no comprehensive evaluation has been conducted of the impact of the new property rates regime and the policy objectives it is meant to serve. It is expected that over time attention will shift from managing the transition to exploiting the scope for policy innovation.

Second, a key question is to what extent the use of exemptions, rebates and exclusions is actually costing municipalities revenue. As indicated earlier, the municipality is instructed to make provision in its budget for revenue to be foregone as a result of rates alleviation, and to report on this item. Research on the computation of these municipal figures has not yet been conducted and falls outside the scope of this chapter. A system-wide assessment is thus difficult to make. However, it does appear that municipalities are reporting significant 'revenue costs' in the form of revenue foregone as a result of rates alleviation.[28]

Third, while municipalities in South Africa may enjoy constitutional protection, their own revenue sources are continuously under threat. For example, the national government seriously considered removing electricity distribution from local government. The perennial challenge of debt owed to municipalities may also make municipalities reluctant to be liberal with tax relief.[29]

Fourth, there are serious institutional constraints that prevent municipalities from using property taxation to its full potential. Property rating in rural areas is still in its infancy, given the levels of poverty, the difficulties in valuing properties and the challenge in administering the tax (National Treasury 2011: 208). The low level of trust in municipalities,[30] which has resulted in widespread unwillingness to pay, also seriously undermines property rating as a means to generate revenue and influence behaviour (National Treasury 2011: 209).

Fifth, many municipalities face capacity constraints in the area of financial management. The National Treasury bemoans 'a general lack of the technical skills and knowledge necessary for performing key duties in financial management from an operational perspective' prevalent in 'most' municipalities (National Treasury 2011: 87). Clearly, this lack of technical skills seriously hampers the policy-making potential of municipalities in the area of property taxation. However, it is suggested that the national and provincial governments are also partly to blame for the deficiencies in property rates policies. The constitution is clear that national and provincial governments must support local government in developing its capacity (sections 154 and 155), and the national government is usually quick to boast about the co-operative nature of its system of decentralisation. Yet the reality is that the national government is unable to reach all municipalities with effective tailor-made capacity building. Meanwhile provincial governments, which are better suited to provide direct hands-on assistance, have not provided any meaningful support with regard to property rating, because it is not an area where they have developed any real capacity themselves.[31] The result has been that most municipalities have had to rely on their own inadequate resources and capacity to craft property rates policies.

A more adequate system of supporting municipalities in drafting property rates policies would be likely to result in a more creative use of the scope offered by the MPRA. This support should take the form of not only training, guidelines and standardised templates, but also practical assistance to municipalities in making the necessary calculations and predictions in order to take informed policy decisions surrounding property rating.

The examination of municipality policies in this research project suggests that it may have been rather ambitious to expect them to make considered choices about the potential of property rating to influence specific behaviour relevant to the developmental trajectory of their areas. It may also have been a tall order to expect municipalities to implement and justify those choices in a refined policy, and even predict and weigh up the budgetary consequences of those choices without access to advanced policy-making and modelling capacity. Nevertheless, municipalities may over time further explore the possibilities offered by the constitutional and policy framework, moving towards a more progressive and developmental system of property rating.

Thus a key lesson for other jurisdictions would be that the successful deployment of property rating as a developmental instrument is contingent on the provision of strong support to municipalities. This should include a robust legal framework that provides the necessary tools to creatively use property rating, insists on transparent policy-making and demands good administration. However, because expertise in rating administration is hard to come by, particularly in a developmental context, support needs to go further. The South African experience shows that local discretion in designing rating policies may be desirable from a local democracy perspective, and offers opportunities for the adoption of policies that are tailored to local circumstances. But it also makes clear that the responsible design and implementation of instruments for rates alleviation that have a genuine developmental impact is a complicated task that may go beyond the capabilities of many a local authority. It is an activity that requires considerable capacity building through sector-wide initiatives and the close involvement of central (national or provincial) governments or international development bodies.

Notes

1   The author wishes to thank Jelani Karamoko, research intern from Harvard Law School, who provided invaluable research assistance, and Tinashe Chigwata for editorial assistance. The research for this contribution was made possible by South Africa's National Research Foundation, the Ford Foundation and the Charles Stewart Mott Foundation.
2   For a discussion of the history of local government and apartheid, see Steytler and De Visser (2007), De Visser (2005) and Ismail and Mpaisha (1997).
3   Compare, for example, Spain, with a population size of 44 million and a total number of 8,108 municipalities.
4   For example, access to electricity has increased by 10 per cent since 2001, flush toilets by 6 per cent and water by 4 per cent (Department of Cooperative Governance and Traditional Affairs 2009: 34).
5   The National Treasury cites a 'weak social contract at the local level, which finds expression in widespread unwillingness to pay for services' as a factor that compromises local government's ability to levy property rates (National Treasury 2011: 209). See also pages 23, 45 and 70 for references to the actions of ratepayer associations.
6   *City of Cape Town v Robertson* 2005 (3) BCLR 199 (CC) at para 62; *CDA Boerdery (Edms) Bpk en 'n Ander v Nelson Mandela Metropolitaanse Munisipaliteit en Andere* [2005] JOL 14785 (SE) at para 6.
7   *City of Cape Town v Robertson* 2005 (3) BCLR 199 (CC) at para 56.
8   *Fedsure Life Assurance Ltd and Others v Greater Johannesburg Transitional Metropolitan Council and Others* 1998 (12) BCLR 1458 (CC) at para 39.
9   *CDA Boerdery* (SCA) at para 35.
10 *CDA Boerdery* (SCA) at para 40.
11 The ratio between conditional and unconditional grants has moved from 35/65 in the 2006/2007 financial year to 45/55 in 2008/2009 financial year (National Treasury 2011: 56).
12 At the end of 2010, municipalities were owed a total of R62.3 billion, an increase of 10.8 per cent from the same month in 2009 (National Treasury 2011: 61). However, both the National Treasury (2011: 61) and the Financial and Fiscal Commission (2011: 45) note that municipalities are making inroads in managing consumer debt.
13 This is buttressed by a warning in the constitution that 'fiscal capacity and efficiency' of municipalities must be taken into account in the calculation of their share of nationally generated income (see Constitution of the Republic of South Africa 1996, section 214(2)(e)). The fact that fiscal capacity and efficiency has not yet found a place in the equitable share formula points towards a failure to implement this constitutional instruction.
14 It has been suggested that municipalities should exempt owners who are recipients of old age or disability grants (Department of Provincial and Local Government [DPLG] 2005: 8).
15 For example, it has been suggested that indigents' properties should not be attached and sold because of their inability to settle rates liabilities (DPLG 2005: 7).

16 The Department of Provincial and Local Government (DPLG) suggests that excessive rating of public service infrastructure may compromise the 'competitiveness of the local (municipal) economies and the entire South African economy vis-à-vis the international economy' (2005: 9).

17 Section 8(2) of the MPRA includes a list of categories, including categories such as residential, industrial, business and commercial, farm properties, smallholdings, state-owned properties, public service infrastructure, state trust land, communal land, properties owned by public benefit organisations etc. However, municipalities are free to determine their own categories, based on use, permitted use or geographical location.

18 S 3(3)(e) MPRA as amended by s 21(a) Local Government Law Amendment Act 19 of 2008.

19 See s 1(1) 'reduction' MPRA.

20 See, for example, McKinlay Douglas (2006: 39–46) for an overview of the criticism of the public choice theory as the single platform for explaining local government's use. Section 2(1) of England's Local Government Act 2000 (c.22) postulates the economic, social and environmental well-being of the area of jurisdiction as the object for which local governments ought to use their powers. Section 174 of the recently adopted Constitution of Kenya posits 'equitable sharing of national and local resources throughout Kenya' as one of the objects of devolution of government. See also De Visser (2005: 19–32).

21 See, for example, Department of Constitutional Development (1998, paragraph 2).

22 S 25(d) Local Government: Municipal Demarcation Act 27 of 1998.

23 A large metropolitan municipality incorporating Durban.

24 Emfuleni is one of three local municipalities comprising the Sedibeng District Municipality situated in Gauteng Province. Mbomela (Nelspruit) is a middle-sized municipality and capital of Mpumalanga Province.

25 Msunduzi (Richard's Bay) is a large coastal municipality in KwaZulu-Natal.

26 Emalahleni is a local municipality situated in Mpumalanga Province, and is one of six in the Nkangala District Municipality. Mangaung (Bloemfontein) is a metropolitan municipality and capital of the Free State Province.

27 Makhado (Louis Trichardt) is in Limpopo province. King Sabata Dalindyebo (Umthata) is a middle-sized municipality in the Eastern Cape. Matjhabeng (Welkom) is in the Free State.

28 For example, during the 2010–11 financial year the City of Cape Town forfeited R840 million in property rates revenue, which amounts to 16 per cent of its total property rates income. Its neighbour, Drakenstein Municipality, reported having foregone close to R41 million, which amounts to 21 per cent of its total property rates income. See City of Cape Town (2011: 167) and Drakenstein Municipality (2011: 165).

29 As at 31 December 2010, municipalities were owed a total of R62.3 billion. See National Treasury (2011: 60).

30 Confidence levels in local government are lower than in national and provincial governments, and have not been higher than 50 per cent since 2006. See Lefko-Everett et al. (2011: 14).

31 The proposed Local Government: Municipal Property Rates Amendment Bill (9 June 2011, Government Gazette 34357) includes provisions to compel provincial governments to take a greater interest in supporting municipal property rating. The Explanatory Memorandum is telling in that it predicts that, in order to implement these provisions, provincial departments responsible for local government 'will have to augment their establishments … to perform hands-on monitoring of municipal implementation of the Act'. At the same time, the memorandum emphasises that they 'should ideally [already] have commensurate establishments if they are to fulfil their constitutional monitoring and support role'. See page 48 of the Bill. At the time of writing, the Bill had not been passed.

References

African National Congress (2007), *ANC Economic Transformation Policy Discussion Document*, African National Congress, Johannesburg, available at: www.anc.org.za/show.php?id=5246, (accessed 6 February 2013).

Ajam, T (2001), 'Intergovernmental fiscal relations in South Africa', in Levy, N and C Tapscott (Eds), *Intergovernmental Relations in South Africa: The Challenges of Co-operative Government*, IDASA/School of Government, Cape Town, 125–142.

Bird, RM and E Slack (2004), 'Land and property taxation in 25 countries: a comparative overview', in Bird and Slack (Eds.), *International Handbook of Land and Property Taxation*, Edward Elgar, Cheltenham/Northampton, UK, 19–56.

City of Cape Town (2011), *Annual Report 2010–11*, City of Cape Town, Cape Town.

De Visser, J (2005), *Developmental Local Government: A Case Study of South Africa*, Intersentia, Antwerp.

De Visser, J and D Powell (2012), *Service Delivery Protest Barometer 2007–12*, Multi-level Government Initiative, Community Law Centre, Cape Town, available at: www.mlgi.org.za/barometers/service-delivery-protest-barometer (accessed 6 February 2013).

Department of Constitutional Development (1998), *White Paper on Local Government*, Government Printers, Pretoria.

Department of Cooperative Governance and Traditional Affairs (2009), *State of Local Government in South Africa National State of Local Government Assessments*, Department of Cooperative Governance and Traditional Affairs, Pretoria.

Department of Provincial and Local Government (2005), *Robust & Inclusive Municipal Economies, Policy Guidelines for Implementing Local Economic Development in South Africa Pretoria*, Department of Provincial and Local Government, Pretoria.

Drakenstein Municipality (2011), *Annual Report 2010–2011*, Drakenstein Municipality, Paarl.

Financial and Fiscal Commission (2011), *2012/2013 Submission for the Division of Revenue*, Financial and Fiscal Commission, Pretoria.

Fjeldstad, OH (2001), 'Intergovernmental fiscal relations in the developing world: a review of issues', in Levy, N and C Tapscott (Eds), *Intergovernmental Relations in South Africa: The Challenges of Co-operative Government*, IDASA/School of Government, Cape Town, 143–162.

Hickey-Tshangana, A (2009), *Municipal Rates Policies and the Urban Poor – How can Municipal Rates Policies Promote Access by the Poor to Urban Land Markets?*, SA Cities Network, Johannesburg.

Ismail, N and CJJ Mphaisha (1997), *The Final Constitution of South Africa: Local Government Provisions and Their Implications*, Occasional Papers Series, January, Konrad Adenauer Stiftung, Johannesburg.

Kihato, M and S Berrisford (2006), 'Regulatory systems and making urban land markets work for the poor in South Africa', paper prepared for the Urban Land Seminar, available at: http://www.urbanlandmark.org/downloads/04_Kihato_Berrisford.pdf (accessed 12 June 2012).

Lefko-Everett K, A Nyoka and L Tiscornia (2011), 'SA reconciliation barometer', available at: reconciliationbarometer.org/ (accessed 6 February 2013).

McKinlay Douglas (2006), *Local Government Structure and Efficiency*, McKinlay Douglas, Tauranga.

National Treasury (2007), *Local Government Budgets and Expenditure Review 2001/2–2007/8*, National Treasury, Pretoria.

National Treasury (2011), *Local Government Budgets and Expenditure Review: 2006/07 –*
    2012/13, National Treasury, Pretoria.
Powell, D, A May and P Ntliziywana (2010), *The Withholding of Rates in Five Local*
    Municipalities, Community Law Centre, Cape Town.
Prud'Homme, R (1994), *On the Dangers of Decentralisation*, World Bank, Washington,
    DC.
Statistics South Africa (2007), *South African Statistics*, Statistics South Africa,
    Pretoria.
Steytler, N and J De Visser (2007), *Local Government Law of South Africa*, LexisNexis,
    Durban.
Western Cape Department of Environmental Affairs and Development Planning
    (2009), *Western Cape Provincial Spatial Development Framework – Rural Land Use*
    Planning & Management Guidelines, Department of Development Planning and
    Environmental Affairs, Cape Town.

Legislation

Local Government: Municipal Property Rates Act, Act 6 of 2004.
Local Government: Municipal Property Rates Bill, 2011.
Local Government: Municipal Systems Act, Act 32 of 2000.
Constitution of the Republic of South Africa, 1996.

Case law

CDA Boerdery (Edms) Bpk en 'n Ander v Nelson Mandela Metropolitaanse Munisipaliteit
    en Andere [2005] JOL 14785 (SE).
City of Cape Town v Robertson 2005 (3) BCLR 199 (CC).
Fedsure Life Assurance Ltd and Others v Greater Johannesburg Transitional Metropolitan
    Council and Others 1998 (12) BCLR 1458 (CC).

Chapter 8

Municipal Partnerships for Prosperity: Empowering the Working Poor in Local Economic Development

Alison Brown

This chapter addresses the crucial relationship between local government and the urban informal economy, both to support local economic development and in the fight against poverty. The chapter focuses on street vending as one of the most visible and contested domains of the informal economy, which the author has studied over many years (see, for example, Brown 2006; 2010; Brown et al. 2010).

Widespread informality has now become a structural characteristic of low-income urban economies and contributes significantly to gross domestic product (GDP; see International Labour Organization [ILO] 2007: 8). In many cities of the developing world, the informal economy provides 60–70 per cent of urban jobs and up to 90 per cent of new jobs (ILO 2011). Informal work provides a crucial source of urban livelihoods, particularly for young people entering the job market and new migrants to cities. Although individual incomes are often low, cumulatively these activities make important contributions to urban economies.

The term 'informal economy' embraces a wide range of occupations: the street traders and porters of Asia, Africa and Latin America; service workers such as transport operators, domestics or waste pickers; construction workers employed on day rates; or home-based workers undertaking manufacturing piecework. An *enterprise-based* description includes legal activities taking place either fully or partly outside formal regulatory frameworks (Chen et al. 2002), such as enterprises that are not registered or do not maintain formal accounts (ILO 2011). This includes, for example, selling vegetables or T-shirts without a trading permit or site license. The term excludes criminal activities, such as drug peddling or prostitution. Many informal enterprises are small, with fewer than 10 workers, although not all micro-enterprises are informal. The *worker-based* definition of the International Labour Organization (ILO) includes non-wage, own-account workers, the self-employed in micro-enterprises and disguised wage workers such as home-based and sweatshop workers, working in either the formal or the informal sector, who generally lack social or legal protection (ILO 2002: 3; 2011; Carr and Chen 2001).

Local governments are at the forefront of managing informal economies, and in most jurisdictions have significant legal and management responsibilities that impinge on the urban working poor. Typically these include market management, highway maintenance and safety, public health, public order and policing, town planning regulations and local economic development. However, local governments are often heavily constrained in the creative management of local economies because of fragmented departmental responsibilities, weak management capacity, outdated or conflicting legislation or erratic financing. Policy is often poorly co-ordinated, with several local authority departments having competing responsibilities, and as a result many of the working poor face erratic enforcement, fines, bribes or evictions which increase their vulnerability.

Within globalised economies, city governments have only limited scope to influence local economic development, because external factors influence where investments are made. However, what matters for urban poverty reduction is the extent to which economic growth is labour-intensive and benefits local micro- and medium-sized enterprises (Devas 2004). City governments have a critical role in ensuring access to basic infrastructure and a secure place of operation if the economic potential of micro-enterprises is to be realised (ibid), but there are major challenges for those faced with large informal economies and competing claims over city space. The vested interests of powerful property owners and developers, and aspirations to create a modern city image, give little priority to the enterprise of the poor, whose potential to contribute to a vibrant local economy is sometimes forgotten. It is easy to destroy jobs, but much more difficult to create them.

The lack of reliable data on the scale of the informal economy – its employment potential and economic contribution – means that policy and practice is often ad hoc, with a limited information base on which to address needs and priorities. The complexity of the informal economy is rarely understood – both the value chains within which workers operate and their extended network of dependents. The claim that those involved in the informal economy are not taxed is often untrue – many pay daily fees and tolls to municipal collectors for the space they use. Unfortunately there are few examples of good management practices on which to draw as precedent, and where these exist they are easily reversed with a change in political power.

This chapter first establishes a theoretical basis for examining relationships between local government and informal economy workers, discussing urban regime theory and debates on modernity and post-modernity as a conceptual framework. It then explores approaches to managing the informal economy and street vending in the Commonwealth countries of Tanzania, South Africa and India, asking why gains which initially seemed favourable to informal economy workers were so difficult to sustain.

In making recommendations for strengthening local government's role in improved management of the urban informal economy, the chapter draws on the work of the global advocacy network – Women in Informal Employment: Globalizing and Organizing (WIEGO), a network of member-based organisations of poor workers (MBOs) supported by researchers, statisticians, practitioners and development agencies – which campaigns for improved visibility and recognition for the working poor, especially women (WIEGO 2012). WIEGO's MBO groups are active in Asia, Africa and Latin America, and together represent around 3 million workers.

8.1 Conceptualising governance contexts

Why is it that from Dar es Salaam to Durban to Delhi street vendors are under threat? Or, as Cross and Karides ask, what makes it acceptable to sell oranges from a shop but not from a stall in the street (2007)? The concept of 'governance', referring to the 'mechanisms, processes, relationships and institutions through which citizens and groups articulate their interests' (United Nations Development Programme [UNDP] 1997, ch. 1), is used here to mean the collective institutions and mechanisms, both formal and informal, through which decisions over urban management and development take place. This section explores how urban regime theory[1] and debates on economic modernisation explain the persistent exclusion of the informal economy from urban policy agendas.

Urban regime theory, first introduced by Stone (1989) in his study of Atlanta, Georgia, has become the dominant paradigm for describing the relationship between governance and urban economies. Stone (2001) defined an urban regime as the 'set of arrangements through which a community is governed', including the key elements of a 'purpose' or slogan, and a governing 'coalition of interests', often between the local state and private actors, that goes beyond a single organisation with no overall chain of command and where power is seen as fragmented (Stone 2001; Elkin 1987: 18).

Stone (1989; 2005) suggests that governing arrangements stem from an alignment of strategic connections in which elections, although important, are not the defining factor. Such alignments have four key elements:

- an agenda or purpose addressing a distinct set of problems;

- a governing coalition formed around the agenda, often with both government and non-government members;

- resources for addressing the agenda; and

- a scheme of co-operation through which the governing coalition's members align their contributions.

Thus power is exercised by elites who have the resources to pursue agendas, and, while the composition of power may vary over different issues, elite power has an ongoing existence and commonality.

In addressing the persistence of social inequalities, Stone argues that lower-status groups are weakly positioned to contribute to governance (2005). Thus, developing agendas that effectively tackle social problems requires an understanding of two key questions: first, how can lower-status populations mobilise as active partners for change; and, second, under what conditions can local government and non-government actors partner to expand opportunities? Many measures by governments intended to reduce inequality are merely token efforts rather than a genuine long-term expansion of opportunity (Stone 2005).

Critics have highlighted the limitations of urban regime theory, first in analysing local governance where politicians, rather than the local administration, are dominant

(Dowding 2001; Dowding et al. 1999); and second because of its focus on the developed world. Some argue that the theory's original application in examining public–private sector relationships was useful, but its use to study societal settings and the make-up of governing coalitions is less appropriate (Mossberger and Stoker 2001; Stoker 1998). Of note in urban regime theory is the assumption that the market economy is the best economic system available, but that social equity is not a dominant objective (Davies 2002). Nevertheless, the notions of 'elite power' and 'coalitions of interests' in analysing local economies are useful in exploring why gains initially supportive for the urban poor are so hard to sustain.

Debates on modernity and post-modernity also suggest an agenda of exclusion of informal economy workers from development agendas. Modernisation theory is based on seventeenth-century ideals of the Enlightenment. From a Marxist perspective, the industrial revolution and modernised economic growth mobilised the masses. A competing version of modernisation was based on capitalism, although both ideologies were based on the idea of economic growth. More recently the term has become associated with the modernisation of industrial processes and the specialisation of production.

Within the modernisation project, the role of the state was to foster economic growth through large-scale industrial investment, with a view that small-scale enterprises are inherently inefficient and thus not part of the modern dream (Cross and Karides 2007). The powerful alliance of interests between the state, land-owning classes and capitalism drove the modernisation project forward. The petty economy was seen either as 'parallel' or as a 'transient' phenomenon that would disappear once industrial-led growth prevailed. Although there is now more emphasis on the potential of small businesses to contribute to local economic development, this does not usually stretch to encompass the 'street entrepreneurs' identified by Cross and Morales (2007).

Urban planning was among a number of instruments developed to enable modernisation, with a belief that towns could be designed and planned by an interventionist state. In the late nineteenth century, 'modern' urban planning emerged to support the privatisation of urban land, and as a response to the unsanitary conditions of early industrial cities (UN Human Settlement Programme [UN-HABITAT] 2009: 10). Planning was seen as a technical and design-led process often implemented through the legal instrument of the zoning plan, particularly in the United States and many other planning regimes, which served the coalition of power between city governments and elite economic and land-owning interests to the exclusion of the mixed-use activities of poor neighbourhoods.

Post-modernity, argue Cross and Morales, represents an economic change resulting in increasingly flexible systems of exchange and fragmented power relations, a movement in which individuals attempt to regain control over their lives, reflected in the renewed growth of small businesses since the 1980s (Cross and Morales 2007; Inglehart and Welzel 2005). Far from being 'backward, inefficient and detrimental to national development' as often perceived, Cross and Morales see informal economy workers as 'adopting reasoned reactions to local manifestations of today's economic, cultural and social world', partly a response to over-regulation which forces entrepreneurs to circumvent the rules (Cross and Morales 2007: 7–10).

The key issue here is how local governments manage large numbers of independent operators, and how informal economy actors create coalitions of interest as a basis for negotiation. It is difficult for poorly resourced local governments to process large numbers of small transactions – for example, collecting fees from street vendors – and for the disparate enterprises in the informal economy to combine interests: their bargaining power is often weak, and in general they lose out from major urban development and the privatisation of public services. For example, street vendors are often dispossessed in historic area improvements (Crossa 2009; Middleton 2003; Walton 1998; Bromley and Mackie 2009), or by the introduction of new urban freeways and rapid transit routes.

Furthermore, as is apparent from the case studies, participatory planning does not always achieve lasting change, as powerful coalitions act to block the voices of the poor. In Dar es Salaam, Durban and Delhi, participatory processes that gained fleeting influence for grassroots organisations have established only fragile leverage in the alliance of interests between state, land-owning classes and capitalist entrepreneurs. Local governments continue to miss out on the potential for economic growth, while the modernisation agenda does not allow space for micro-enterprises or recognise their actions as a post-modern and 'reasoned' reaction to economic trends.

8.2 Approaches to the informal economy and street vending

The examples in this chapter examine initiatives in three different Commonwealth countries to legitimise and manage the informal economy and street vending. Each case demonstrates willingness by local government to innovate through enabling national or city-level policies, but all have suffered setbacks in implementation when broader interests came into play. The case studies also illustrate the crucial problems of a vision that excludes the informal economy, and the lack of evidence to demonstrate its innovation and reach. In Dar es Salaam an innovative pilot and national formalisation project faltered; in Durban environmental improvement projects have taken precedence over street vending; and in India a top-down national policy is proving controversial in its implementation.

8.2.1 Petty trade in Dar es Salaam

In Tanzania, national and local policy towards street vending has fluctuated with economic and political change. The 1967 Arusha Declaration heralded a process of 'socialism and self-reliance' that led to the nationalisation of major industries and the introduction of a one-party state. Local government was abolished in 1972. However, following a decline in local services, elected local government was re-established in 1984, as was a national multiparty system in 1992. In most urban areas, local government is a single-tier system (municipal, city or town level) supported by administrative committees at ward and street (*mtaa*) level (Prime Minister's Office [PMO] 2008).

By-laws dating from the 1960s and 1970s made petty trading illegal, but the 1980s economic crisis forced some accommodation, facilitated by three key factors (Brown et al. 2010). First, the 1983 *Human Resources Deployment Act* required every able-bodied person to work, and established the *nguvu kazi* hawker license (Tripp 1997). Second, the Sustainable Dar es Salaam Project (SDP), a strategic planning project initiated by UNDP and UN-HABITAT with Dar es Salaam City Council, heralded a participatory approach to city planning. The SDP's 1992 city consultation defined 'petty trading' as one of nine critical urban issues, leading to physical and management innovations for street vending and a strengthening of traders' associations (Nnkya 2004; Msoka 2007). Third, the near bankruptcy and suspension of Dar es Salaam City Council in 1996 was followed in 2000 by the division of the city into three new district municipalities, Ilala, Temeke and Kinondoni, which took over land-use planning and market management, leaving the city council with reduced influence (Brown 2006: 71).

In recent years Tanzania has seen strong economic performance, recording 52 per cent cumulative growth of GDP between 2001 and 2007. Although the proportion of people living in 'basic needs' poverty declined from 38 per cent in 1991/92 to 33 per cent in 2006/07, persistent poverty among specific groups drives further urbanisation and informalisation (United Republic of Tanzania [URT] 2002; Tideman 2009). The 2001 Labour Force Survey estimated that 34 per cent of male and 30 per cent of female household heads worked in the informal economy (Lerise and Kyessi 2002).

From the late 1990s, several important reports on the informal economy pursued an agenda of formalisation. The ILO's Roadmap Study (ILO et al. 1999) highlighted the costs and complexity of business registration, and sought to simplify registration and absorb informal enterprises into the mainstream. In 2005 the well-known Peruvian economist and strong proponent of land titling Hernando de Soto visited Tanzania. His consultancy ILD undertook a major study of small-scale enterprise, finding that that 98 per cent of all businesses in Tanzania operated 'extra-legally' and providing recommendations that encouraged legalisation (ILD 2005a, 2005b). Meanwhile, attitudes towards street vending hardened; it was seen by municipal officials both as a public health risk and as undermining trade in designated markets (Mfaume and Leonard 2004). In 2003 the *nguvu kazi* was cancelled, effectively making street vending illegal, and from 2006 widespread evictions were ordered. In Temeke Municipality alone there were 40,000 prosecutions of street vendors (out of an estimated population of 250,000 vendors) in the six months from February 2007 (Lyons with Msoka 2007).

Several major new projects are now shaping the face of Dar es Salaam. Construction contracts are being established for the Dar Rapid Transit system (DART), a 21-kilometre bus-based system running along major arterial roads, with costs for Phase 1 estimated at US$92 million (ITDP 2008). The routing through busy markets has displaced street vendors. In a commercial initiative designed to solve the problem of street vending, Dar es Salaam City Council constructed a new 12-storey market building for street vendors, but this is not located near a main pedestrian route and vendors are reluctant to move in; it remained largely empty several months after completion (*Tanzania Daily News* 2011).

The new district municipalities in Dar es Salaam lack capacity, and, despite the gains of the 1990s and the revenue raised in market fees, street vending is seen by municipal government as a management problem rather than a potential growth sector. A recent study suggests that poverty eradication policies in Tanzania have not paid enough attention to the growth of poor and very poor people's incomes, and that the poor operate in labour, service and commodity markets which are over-subscribed and lack institutional support (Shepherd 2010).

8.2.2 South Africa and Durban's informal economy policy

In South Africa a similar story of ambivalent policy on informal business is evident, as illustrated through the struggles of Durban. From the late 1980s growing political awareness in South Africa culminated in the *1991 Business Act*, which removed the barriers to informal activities and prohibited use of the 'move-on' regulations. This resulted in a dramatic increase of street vending in all major cities (Lund and Skinner 2004; Skinner 2008). Local authorities reacted by calling for more powers of control, and in 1993 an amendment to the Act permitted by-laws that designated 'restricted' and 'prohibited' trading zones, which enhanced local authorities' ability to regulate street vending and restrict the areas in which traders operate (Yale Law School 2011).

After the African National Congress (ANC) government was elected in 1994 there was considerable emphasis on rethinking the role and constitution of local government, and in Durban from 1996 various transitional arrangements were put in place. At first this was a series of local councils and a metropolitan council, leading to the interim UniCity in 1999 and finally to the establishment of the unitary eThekwini Municipality in 2000. The emerging municipality put considerable emphasis on economic development, preparing a set of policy papers including the 1996 *Green Paper on Economic Development* (Robbins 2005). The Economic Development Department was created in 1998, and between 1999 and 2004 an 'economic development flagship fund' and 'regeneration fund', with a peak operating budget of more than 350 million rand (R) in 2002/03, supported capital investment in more than 30 projects, about half of which were pro-poor in intent (Robbins 2005).

The emphasis of this programme was influenced by early work at Warwick Junction, a major city centre market near the bus and railway terminals, which attracts perhaps 300,000 commuters a day. In the late 1980s trading at Warwick Junction had grown rapidly, and by the mid-1990s a special team was set up to address the chaos in the area. Officials rapidly concluded that the use of public space for trading was essential to the future of the precinct, and embarked on an urban renewal programme based on extensive consultation between city officials and traders (Robbins 2005).

The innovative programme at Warwick Junction included the provision of shelters, a series of pedestrian walkways over dual carriageways, closure of a street to increase trading space, a market for traditional medicine sellers and improvements to the fresh produce market. By the mid-2000s Warwick Junction accommodated around 4,000 traders, generating an estimated annual turnover of R1 billion (Devey et al. 2006; Lund and Skinner 2004; Skinner 2008).

The success of initiatives at Warwick Junction encouraged the newly formed Economic Development Unit to allocate significant research funds to a pioneering study into informal traders in the city, which in 1997 identified 19,301 street vendors, of whom about 10,000 were in the city centre and the majority (59 per cent) were women (Skinner 2008).

The city council also developed the 2001 Durban Informal Economy Policy through a participatory process, which recognised that the informal economy was critical to economic development and should be recognised in the city's economic strategy. The policy committed the city to providing support for very small enterprises, recognising the importance of worker organisations and exploring improved management practices (Lund and Skinner 2004). For street traders the policy sought easier registration, site allocation and area-based management based on experience at Warwick Junction.

Unfortunately the policy was not translated into effective implementation, while at Warwick Junction lack of ongoing management and internal restructuring within the municipality resulted in erratic enforcement and poor communication between the municipality and traders (Robbins 2005). In November 2004 a Public Realm Management Project was allocated major funding, and 50 additional police officers were appointed to improve the image of the city. By 2005 armed constables were deployed to stop 'illegal, unlicensed street trading', evicting all traders without permits – although only 872 permits had been issued for the estimated 19,000 traders (Horn 2005).

Activists see the 2004 announcement that South Africa was to host the 2010 soccer World Cup as a turning point, although the press cited conflict with city centre businesses as the reason for the crackdown. In response, street vendor organisations launched a 'World Class Cities for All' campaign, and mounted a successful legal challenge to redevelopment plans that would have replaced part of the Warwick Junction trading space with a mall (StreetNet 2006).

8.2.3 India's national street vendor policy

In India, management of street vending is a state function. The federal government has been proactive in establishing a new policy context in response to lobbying by street vendors, but its implementation is erratic. In October 2010 the Indian Supreme Court affirmed that hawking is a fundamental right under the Indian Constitution, requiring the enactment of new legislation on street vending to respect that right (Yale Law School 2011). The judgement came after more than a decade of action by street vendors, providing new legitimacy in the relationship between street vendors and the state.

The National Association of Street Vendors of India (NASVI) was formed in 1998 with the objective of achieving national recognition for India's estimated 10 million street vendors. NASVI is a coalition of more than 540 trade unions and community-based organisations of street vendors, representing more than 3.5 million vendors. Over the last decade NASVI has successfully lobbied for the introduction of a *National Policy for Urban Street Vendors* (NPUSV), published in 2004 and revised in

2009 (Ministry of Housing and Urban Poverty Alleviation [MHUPA] 2009), and it is now campaigning for the introduction of legislation protecting street vendors. The NPUSV draws on Articles 39a and 39b in the Indian Constitution, stating that:

- citizens, men and women equally, have the right to an adequate means of livelihood; and

- ownership and control of the material resources of the community are so distributed as to best serve the common good.

The aim of the policy is to recognise the contribution of street vendors to society, and to respect street vending as a major initiative for urban poverty alleviation (MHUPA 2009). Its objectives include:

- giving vendors legal status through amending relevant laws and regulations;

- providing legitimate hawking zones with nominal fee-based regulation;

- including spaces for street vending in urban development and zoning plans; and

- encouraging participatory conduct of urban vending activities.

The policy introduces an interesting concept of 'natural markets', where a significant flow of pedestrians or general traffic creates a commercial demand (e.g. at bus stations). The policy recognises that demand for street vendors' wares is often at highly specific locations, and argues that city authorities should provide for natural markets in layout plans and that hawking should be permitted elsewhere except in areas designated as 'no-vending zones'. Designation is established by a town vending committee, made up of representatives from municipal government, traffic and local police, and market and vendors' organisations (MHUPA 2009). Unfortunately the 'no-vending zones' can be quite extensive and have been used as a prohibitive tool, rather than as part of a wider enabling approach.

The 2009 draft of the National Policy was accompanied by model legislation, which has to be enacted by states. NASVI has been critical of the lack of progress, as the policy was implemented in only eight states by 2010. Meanwhile in New Delhi the 2010 Commonwealth Games was used to justify evictions, which are explicitly prohibited by the policy (Yale Law School 2011). About 50 street-vending sites were closed and around half of these have not been re-established.

The crucial importance of the National Policy is its recognition that vending is a legitimate urban activity to be supported in the process of urban development. However, the policy leaves much unresolved. The relationship between state, urban local bodies and town vending committees is unclear, and the balance of trader interests on the vending committees is not specified. The policy suggests a simple process of registration for a nominal fee without quota restrictions or prior residential requirements, which may be difficult to enforce. However, local designation may lead to large swathes of land where street trading, once tolerated, is now prohibited. The choice of department with enforcement powers is also crucial, as eviction is the threat that most traders fear. As Skinner has said, 'moving street trading responsibilities from the traffic department is essential if local authorities are to manage and develop the informal sector, rather than simply enforce by-laws' (1999: 27), yet effective enforcement is often carried out by traffic police under s.283 of the *Indian Penal Code 1860*.

8.3 Developing capabilities

It is evident from the case studies that local governments have a number of problems in managing informal economies. First is the difficulty of finding ways to generate revenue from the informal economy, as street vending and other informal work is usually managed by the lowest tier of local government, which may be the least well equipped to collect fees or set up accessible licensing processes. Many street vendors, for example, can only afford to pay daily fees, but collecting the fees and payment details is difficult when authorities themselves lack capacity (such as access to computers).

Second is the problem of conflicting responsibilities of different local government agencies. For example, municipal police may wish to keep streets open for traffic circulation but, as in Durban, economic development policy may favour use of the public realm by micro-enterprises.

Third is the lack of data on the informal economy, which is usually difficult to capture because of the large number of small operations involved. WIEGO has developed programmes on urban policies and statistics to improve understanding of the potential role that the informal economy can play in local economic development, and to strengthen the capacity of local government in effective and pro-poor urban management (WIEGO 2012). But measurement of the informal economy is inherently difficult, partly because of definitional problems and partly because of paucity of data. Residual methods are being developed to combine statistical data from economic surveys measuring formal employment, and household surveys or census data (labour force surveys or population censuses). Informal employment is calculated as the difference between total employment and formal employment (in non-agricultural sectors). Sometimes data can be disaggregated to show employees and the self-employed (Heniz and Vanek 2010; Wills 2009).

WIEGO's urban policies programme is undertaking informal economy budget analyses which, drawing on traditions of participatory budgeting, explore how different government budgets address the needs and interests of informal workers, and identify opportunities for informal workers to participate during budget preparation (Budlender 2009). Pilot studies have been undertaken in Belo Horizonte, Brazil; Ravi Town, Lahore, Pakistan; Quezon City, the Philippines; and Lima, Peru. Different methodologies are adopted for different contexts, and the analysis covers central, state and local programmes (Budlender 2009; Budlender et al. 2004).

The programme is also exploring how training curricula can equip the next generation of urban professionals to support the informal economy, and WIEGO has signed a Memorandum of Understanding with the Association of African Planning Schools to provide training support. However, the most crucial problem is the political will to explore the needs of informal economy workers, and recognise their economic potential.

8.4 Conclusion

The challenges for 'new century' local government are legion, and the case studies demonstrate the extraordinary difficulties of embedding pro-poor approaches to the informal economy in municipal policy development. Mayors and city directors often strive to improve the quality of life for their citizens, but the discourse of modernisation based on notions of order imported from the developed world ignores reality on the ground, and tentative gains are often reversed where more powerful coalitions of interest come into play.

Lack of effective fee collection means that the revenue potential of the informal economy is not fully exploited. Although local officials may see the informal economy as avoiding taxation, in practice street vendors and others pay significant amounts in local authority fees or bribes. Vendors often indicate a willingness to pay more for the security to trade and access to basic services. The challenge is to capture payments within the local government revenue stream – for example, through co-operative or private management of major trading sites or through the creation of an arms-length body with a specific mandate to promote the informal economy and generate revenue to cover its costs.

In Durban success was based on the existence of a fairly well-resourced unitary authority, a strong political emphasis on economic development and excellent pilot work undertaken in partnership with street vendors at the busiest vending location in the city. By contrast, in Dar es Salaam the creation of a two-tier system of local government meant that powers to manage the informal economy were mostly moved to the less well-resourced lower tiers, and the emphasis on business formalisation created a new coalition of interest between elite businesses and government that gave less priority to urban street vendors. In India street vending comes under a state/local government jurisdiction, so the well-researched federal policy is only advisory.

All three case studies illustrate fluctuating commitment towards the informal economy, which may be tolerated or even accommodated until it comes into collision with more powerful interests. As was especially the case in Durban and Dar es Salaam, tentative measures to accommodate street vending eventually reverted to a more conventional elite-focused role. This illustrates both the potential and the difficulties of embedding pro-poor approaches to development in municipal policy development, and the importance of understanding how elite power may undermine innovative local government initiatives.

Urban regime theory suggests that strong coalitions of socially excluded groups combined with a fundamental rethinking of the role of local government are essential to consolidate effective pro-poor change. A shift by local authorities from 'government' to 'governance' would require a corresponding attitudinal change in the exercise of their powers and responsibilities, so that local government's role goes beyond mere service delivery to holding powers in trust for communities and supporting them in pursuing their goals. This also means a shift from positioning local government as an outpost of central administrations, to one of community leadership in enhancing local well-being.

The crucial issue remains that the informal economy is too often perceived as backward, marginal and disconnected from economic innovation and global value chains. Yet in many instances the reverse is true. Many street vendors adopt flexible strategies to survive and adapt to changing trading patterns and demands, provide outlets for locally produced goods or are linked into global value chains (Lyons et al. 2008). Local government is potentially the single most important catalyst to support this community-level change, but unleashing its potential requires a rethinking of its role through practical demonstrations of the new agenda if the potential of the informal economy to contribute to local economic development is to be realised.

Notes

1   As a framework for analysing power relations between the state and other actors.

References

Bromley, R and P Mackie, (2009), 'Displacement and the new spaces for informal trade in the Latin American city centre', *Urban Studies*, Vol. 46 No. 7, 1485–1506.

Brown, A (2006), *Contested Space: Street Trading, Public Space and Livelihoods in Developing Cities*, ITDG Publishing, Rugby.

Brown, A (2010), 'Requiem for stability: impact of the global recession on the world's working poor', *International Planning Studies*, Vol. 15 No. 3, 175–190.

Brown, A, M Lyons and I Dankoco (2010), 'Street-traders and the emerging spaces for urban citizenship and voice in African cities', *Urban Studies*, Vol. 47 No. 3, 666–687.

Budlender, D (2009), 'Informal economy budget analysis in Brazil, Peru, Pakistan and the Philippines', Urban Policies Research Report No. 1, WIEGO, Women in Informal Employment – Globalizing and Organizing, available at: www.wiego.org/program_areas/urban_policies/ic_researchReports.php (accessed January 2011).

Budlender, D, C Skinner and I Valodia (2004), *Budgets and the Informal Economy: An Analysis of the Impact of the Budget on Informal Workers in South Africa*, School of Development Studies, University of Kwazulu-Natal, available at: www.thaigoodgovernance.org/upload/content/286/budgets%20and%20the%20informal%20economy.pdf (accessed January 2001).

Carr, M and M Chen (2001), *Globalization and the Informal Economy: How Global Trade and Investment Impact on the Working Poor*, available at: http://sed-trade-forum.itcilo.org/eng/Papers/Other/carrchenglobalization.pdf (accessed June 2009).

Chen, M, R Jhabvala and F Lund (2002), 'Supporting workers in the informal economy: a policy framework', Working Paper on the Informal Economy, Employment Sector, International Labour Office, Geneva.

Cross, J and A Morales (2007), 'Introduction: locating street markets in the modern/postmodern world', in J Cross and A Morales (Eds.), *Street Entrepreneurs: People, Place and Politics in Local and Global Perspectives*, Routledge, London and New York, 1–14.

Cross, J and M Karides (2007), 'Capitalism, modernity, and the "appropriate" use of space', in J Cross and A Morales (Eds.), *Street Entrepreneurs: People, Place and Politics in Local and Global Perspectives*, Routledge, London and New York, 15–35.

Crossa, V (2009), 'Resisting the entrepreneurial city: street vendors' struggle in Mexico City's Historic Center', *International Journal of Urban and Regional Research*, Vol. 33 No. 1, 43–63.

Davies, J (2002), 'Urban regime theory: a normative-empirical critique', *Journal of Urban Affairs*, Vol. 24 No. 1, 1–17.

Devas, N (Ed.) (2004), *Urban Governance, Voice and Poverty in the Developing World*, Earthscan, London.

Devey, R, C Skinner and I Valodia (2006), 'Definitions, data and the informal economy in South Africa: a critical analysis', in V Padayachee (Ed.), *The Development Decade? Economic and Social Change in South Africa, 1994–2004*, HSRC (Human Sciences Research Council), Cape Town.

Dowding, K (2001), 'Explaining urban regimes', *International Journal of Urban and Regional Research*, Vol. 25 No. 1, 7–19.

Dowding, K, P Dunleavy, D King, H Margetts and Y Rydin, (1999), 'Regime politics in London local government', *Urban Affairs Review*, Vol. 34 No. 4, 515–545.

Elkin, S (1987), *City and Regime in the American Republic*, University of Chicago Press, Chicago.

Heniz, J and J Vanek (2010), 'Women and men in the informal economy 2010 – a statistical picture: plans for an updated report', paper to the conference on The Informal Sector and Informal Employment: Statistical Measurement, Economic Implications and Public Policies, Hanoi, Vietnam, 6–7 May, available at: www.wiego.org/pdf/Hanoi-meeting-paper.pdf (accessed January 2011).

Horn, P (2005), 'From best practice to pariah state', *StreetNet News*, No. 6, September, available at: www.streetnet.org.za/wp-content/uploads/2010/06/Streetnetnews61.pdf (accessed January 2011).

ILD (2005a), *Volume I: Executive Summary, The Diagnosis*, available at: http://MKURABITA-DiagnosisReportExecutiveSummary-ILD.pdf (accessed January 2011).

ILD (2005b), *Volume II: The Extra-legal Economy: Its Archetypes and Sizes*, available at: http://MKURABITA-DiagnosisReportVolumeII-ILD.pdf (accessed January 2011).

International Labour Organization (ILO) (2002), 'Decent work and the informal economy: Agenda Item 6', International Labour Conference 90th Session, International Labour Organization (ILO), Geneva.

ILO (2007), 'The informal economy, Agenda Item 4', International Labour Office, Governing Body, March, International Labour Organisation (ILO), Geneva.

ILO (2011), *Statistical Update on Employment in the Informal Economy*, International Labour Organisation (ILO), Geneva, available at: www.ilo.org/public/libdoc/ilo/2011/111B09_241_engl.pdf (accessed October 2012).

ILO, UN Industrial Development Organization (UNIDO) and UNDP (1999), 'Roadmap study of the informal sector in mainland Tanzania', available at: www.ilo.org/wcmsp5/groups/public/—ed_emp/—emp_policy/—invest/documents/publication/wcms_asist_8365.pdf (accessed January 2011).

Inglehart, R and C Welzel (2005), *Modernization, Cultural Change, and Democracy: The Human Development Sequence*, Princeton University Press, Princeton, NJ.

Institute for Transportation and Development Policy (ITDP) (2008), 'Recent developments on bus rapid transit in Africa', *Cities for Mobility*, Stuttgart, eMagazine of the global network for sustainable urban mobility', available at: www.itdp-europe.org/assets/documents/Cities_for_Mobility_2.pdf (accessed January 2011).

Lerise, F and A Kyessi (2002), 'Trends of urban poverty in Tanzania', unpublished report, University College of Lands and Architectural Studies, Dar es Salaam.

Lyons, M with C Msoka (2007), 'Microtrading in urban mainland Tanzania: the way forward', report for HTSPE Development Consulting Services for the Development Partner Group, Tanzania.

Lyons, M, A Brown and Z-G Li (2008), 'The "third tier" of globalization', *City*, Vol. 12 No. 2, 196–206.

Lund, F and C Skinner (2004), 'Integrating the informal economy in urban planning and governance: a case study of the process of policy development in Durban, South Africa', *International Development Planning Reviews*, Vol. 26 No. 4, 431–455.

Mfaume, R and W Leonard (2004), 'Small business entrepreneurship in Dar es Salaam – Tanzania: prospects for future development', paper to the workshop on African Development and Poverty Reduction: the Macro-Micro Linkage, 13–15 October 2004, Somerset West, South Africa, available at: www.tips.org.za/files/Small_Business_Entrepreneurship_in_Dar-es-salaam_rashid_mfau.pdf (accessed January 2013).

Middleton, A (2003), 'Informal traders and planners in the regeneration of historic city centres: the case of Quito, Ecuador', *Progress in Planning*, Vol. 59 No. 2, 71–123.

Ministry of Housing and Urban Poverty Alleviation (MHUPA) (2009), 'National policy for urban street vendors', MHUPA, available at: http://mhupa.gov.in/policies/natpol.htm (accessed August 2011).

Mossberger, K and G Stoker (2001), 'Regime theory: the challenge of conceptualization', *Urban Affairs Review*, Vol. 36 No. 6, 810–835.

Msoka, C (2007), 'An assessment of the informal economy associations in Tanzania: the case study of VIBINDO Society in Dar es Salaam', paper to the conference on Informalising Economies and New Organising Strategies in Africa, Nordic Africa Institute, 20–22 April.

Nnkya, T (2004), 'The Sustainable Dar es Salaam Project, 1992–2003', UN-HABITAT and UNEP, Nairobi, available at: www.un-habitat.org/pmss/getElectronicVersion.aspx?nr=1809&alt=1 (accessed January 2011).

Prime Minister's Office (PMO) (2008), 'History of local government system in Tanzania', Prime Minister's Office, Government of Tanzania, available at: www.pmo.go.tz/mawaziri.php?cat=12&subcat=81 (accessed September 2011).

Robbins, G (2005), 'Pro-poor urban led case study: eThekwini Municipality (Durban)', available at: http://siteresources.worldbank.org/INTLED/Resources/339650-1144099718914/ProPoor_eThekwini.pdf (accessed May 2012).

Shepherd, A (2010), 'Growth and poverty reduction: policy implications from qualitative research in Tanzania', briefing paper – Chronic Poverty Research

Centre (CPRC) Policy Briefs 21, Overseas Development Institute (ODI), London.

Skinner, C (1999), 'Local government in transition: a gendered analysis of trends in urban policy and practice regarding street trading in five South African cities', CSDS Research Report No. 16, University of Natal, Durban, available at: http://sds.ukzn.ac.za/files/rr18.pdf (accessed September 2011).

Skinner, C (2008), 'The struggle for the streets: processes of exclusion and inclusion of street traders in Durban, South Africa', *Development Southern Africa*, Vol. 25 No. 2, 227–242.

Stoker, G (1998), 'Public partnerships and urban governance', in J Pierre (Ed.), *Partnerships in Urban Governance: European and American Experience*, Macmillan, Basingstoke, 34–51.

Stone, C (1989), *Regime Politics: Governing Atlanta, 1946–1988*, University Press of Kansas, Lawrence.

Stone, C (2001), 'The Atlanta experience re-examined: the link between agenda and regime change', *International Journal of Urban and Regional Research*, Vol. 25 No. 1, 20–34.

Stone, C (2005), 'Looking back to look forward: reflections on urban regime analysis', *Urban Affairs Review*, Vol. 40 No. 3, 309–341.

StreetNet (2006), 'International campaign: World Class Cities for All', StreetNet International, available at: www.streetnet.org.za/wp-content/uploads/2010/06/WCCA-Campaign-launch-press-release-December-2006.pdf (accessed January 2011).

Tanzania Daily News (2011), 'Machinga complex: trades complain over high fees', 21 September, available at: http://allafrica.com/stories/201009220025.html (accessed September 2011).

Tideman, P (2009), *Sector Budget Support in Practice. Desk Study: Local Government Sector in Tanzania*, Overseas Development Institute, London, available at: www.odi.org.uk/resources/download/4581-english.pdf (accessed September 2011).

Tripp, AM (1997), *Changing the Rules: The Political Economy of Liberalization and the Urban Informal Economy of Tanzania*, University of California Press, London and Los Angeles.

UN Development Programme (UNDP) (1997), *Governance for Sustainable Human Development: A UNDP Policy Document*, United Nations Development Programme (UNDP), available at: http://mirror.undp.org/magnet/policy/ (accessed October 2012).

UN Human Settlement Programme (UN-HABITAT) (2009), *Planning Sustainable Cities: Global Report on Human Settlements*, United Nations Human Settlement Programme, Earthscan, London and Sterling, VA.

United Republic of Tanzania (2002), *National Labour Survey*, United Republic of Tanzania, Dar es Salaam.

Walton, J (1998), 'Urban conflict and social movements in poor countries: theory and evidence of collective action', *International Journal of Urban and Regional Research*, Vol. 22 No. 3, 460–481.

WIEGO (2012), 'Women in Informal Employment – Globalizing and Organizing', available at: http://wiego.org/publications-resources (accessed October 2012).

Wills, G (2009), 'South Africa's Informal Economy, a statistical profile', Urban Policies Research Report, No. 7, Women in Informal Employment – Globalizing and Organizing, available at: www.wiego.org (accessed January 2011).

Yale Law School (2011), 'Working paper: developing national street vendor legislation in India: a comparative study of street vending regulation', prepared for the Self-Employed Women's Association, unpublished report.

PART III. NEW APPROACHES TO GOVERNANCE

Chapter 9

New Pathways to Effective Regional Governance: Canadian Reflections

Brian Walisser, Gary Paget and Michelle Dann[1]

Across the globe, there is considerable interest in federated local government systems (Slack 2007; Fahim 2009). In the Canadian province of British Columbia (BC), institutions for federated regional governance – known as regional districts (RDs) – date back more than four decades. When established, RDs were not viewed as 'governments', but were heralded merely as forums to reduce the transaction costs of inter-local co-operation for mutual benefit in service delivery. This chapter initially examines these institutions, explaining why regional districts on the whole have been successful with their service delivery mission.

Some regional districts in BC have sought to build on their success with service delivery to take on more of a governance orientation (while still maintaining their service mission). For instance, using 1995 legislation, ten urbanised regions have developed 'regional growth strategies', policy documents that are negotiated in the context not of mutual benefit but of unequal implications for the localities affected. The experience of such regions – those attempting to migrate from the administration of services to the governance of issues with differential impacts – must be interpreted through a different lens.

Therefore, this chapter will secondly widen its focus and rise to a higher plane: it goes on to discuss what happens when matters requiring a regional response cannot be addressed purely on the basis of inter-local co-operation for mutual benefit. Such matters may cut across numerous localities, diverging interests, multiple institutions and a complex regional geography. New pathways are presented that, if implemented, might enable jurisdictions to more successfully tackle regional issues that are contested and political – issues often verging on irresolvable when approached using customary governance techniques. On this higher plane, regional governance is invariably polycentric, such that the quest for good governance must move beyond co-operation for mutual benefit to the quest for acceptable decision outcomes, even when local interests are unaligned and no single institution is, or can ever be, 'in charge' (Torfing et al. 2012).

9.1 British Columbia's layered system for local governance

Canada is a federal state with ten provinces and three province-like territories. Provinces have exclusive jurisdiction for the varying architecture of the local government systems within their boundaries, and there is no national statute for local government per se. However, the federal government has an interest in urban (as opposed to strictly municipal) issues and has used its considerable spending power over the past two decades to address local government infrastructure challenges in fields such as environmental and energy sustainability, water and air quality, and transportation (Berdahl 2006).

In most parts of Canada local governments have similar roles in providing core community services, including transportation and communications, water/wastewater, refuse collection/disposal, recreation and culture, land use planning and building regulation. Fire and police protection are local responsibilities, although in most provinces a national police force is available to provide local policing by contract. Local government spending on health, education and social services is minimal, as these services have, with the exception of Ontario, been taken over by provinces (Commonwealth Local Government Forum [CLGF] 2009; Kitchen and Slack 2006; Kitchen 2002).[2]

9.1.1 Creating British Columbia's regional districts

British Columbia, on Canada's west coast, is large and mountainous. Only a small fraction of the land mass is suitable for settlement. About three-quarters of BC's 4.5 million residents are concentrated into three urbanised territories: the Vancouver area, known as the Lower Mainland; the area around the provincial capital, Victoria, on Vancouver Island; and the Okanagan Valley in the south-central interior. Elsewhere, municipalities and rural communities are scattered mostly along the river valleys that carve through the province. The typical municipality is small, the median population among the roughly 160 municipalities being a mere 5,000 persons.

After a comprehensive, decade-long search for a politically palatable regional governance system, legislation to establish a federated framework for regional service delivery was adopted in 1965 (Brown 1968; Collier 1972; Tennant and Zirnhelt 1972, 1973; Ministry of Community, Sport and Cultural Development [MCD] 2010). Through a series of intergovernmental negotiations in the late 1960s, each region was established with local consent (Local Government Knowledge Partnership [LGKP] 2009). Expressly designed for BC, the legislation relied on local choice not only for establishing individual RDs, but also for determining their functions thereafter. The philosophy of the system required that there be little in the way of mandated service responsibilities. Rather the legislative framework would embody a 'strategy of gentle imposition': it would enable regions to tailor functions to their own evolving needs (Tennant and Zirnhelt 1973; MCD 2010). Today, through incremental decisions based on a region's unique characteristics and service needs, each RD has been able to develop a distinct service personality.

9.1.2 Attributes of British Columbia's regional districts

More than 40 years on, much of the philosophy that guided the creation of RDs remains relevant, and they have become integral to BC's local government landscape. Nevertheless, the RD system is misunderstood by many and is underappreciated for the role it plays in arranging solutions to what had been troubling gaps in service provision. Bish (2002, 2006) points out that, while the system is difficult to fit into the standard lexicon of regional governance, its capacity to provide any service, at any scale, using any mode of provision, offers a practical set of institutional arrangements for dealing with a variety of boundary issues. He judges the system to have fostered fiscal equivalence, lowered inter-local co-operation costs and improved the overall performance of BC's local government system.

Except for the remote north, 27 regional districts blanket the province, layered over the pre-existing system of municipalities. All municipalities are now federated within one of these regions. RDs serve three hybrid purposes. First, they provide a region-wide forum for members to discuss issues while capturing scale economies by delivering large-scale services. Second, they provide the principal framework for inter-local service delivery in both metropolitan and non-metropolitan areas. Third, they provide democratic representation and local community services for populations residing outside municipalities (MCD 2006).

Like municipal governments, RDs provide a range of services including utilities and other infrastructure, recreation and culture, and regulatory services (Bish and Clemens 2008). An essential element of the RD model is that different services may have different boundaries, which also act as financial and decision-making boundaries, helping minimise 'free-rider' problems. Each service is independent and there is no cross-subsidisation; service areas are tantamount to 'special districts' (Phares 2009). However, all such 'special districts' inside any particular RD are managed by a common board of directors, thus also minimising problems of political fragmentation.

As federations, regional district boards (known collectively as 'directors') are composed of councillors appointed from member municipalities plus directly elected representatives from unincorporated members outside municipalities. To ensure municipal and non-municipal members are fairly represented in regional decision-making, the number of directors is made roughly proportional to each member's population, and then multiple votes are assigned to directors from the more populous members to better reflect population differences. System-wide legislation prescribes how unweighted votes and weighted votes (used primarily for money matters) are employed.

Despite sharing a common legislative foundation, the 27 RDs are far from homogeneous. In land area, they vary in size from around 2,000 to about 120,000 km². They range in population up to 2.4 million for the Greater Vancouver Regional District;[3] five other RDs have populations exceeding 100,000. Together, the six most populous RDs contained 77 per cent of the total BC population in 2012. By contrast, the ten least populous RDs are each 40,000 or fewer in population and together account for just 6 per cent of the BC total population.

9.2 Inside three regional districts

Looking in depth at regional districts is the best way to understand the differences in their character and the manner in which they have implemented their power of self-organisation. Three RDs of varying size and with distinctive service personalities are discussed in detail this section: Columbia Shuswap Regional District (CSRD), Thompson Nicola Regional District (TNRD), and Capital Regional District (CapRD) (Tables 9.1 and 9.2).

Table 9.1 Comparison of selected RDs: Columbia Shuswap (CSRD), Thompson Nicola (TNRD), Capital (CapRD)

	CSRD	TNRD	CapRD
Location	Southeastern interior	Central interior	Southern tip of Vancouver Island
Geography	• Crosses three spectacular mountain ranges • Shuswap Lake dominates the region's western half • Hot summers, cold winters	• Vast, sparsely populated rural area anchored by a large city • Rugged mountains, rolling grasslands and forests • Hot summers, cold winters	• Coastal geography/climate • Contains the southern Gulf Islands – but the population is mostly settled on mainland Vancouver Island
Land area (comparator)	29,004 km² (similar to Lesotho)	45,279 km² (smaller than Sri Lanka)	2,367 km² (larger than Mauritius)
Pop. 2012	53,600 (rank 16 of 27)	132,450 (rank 6 of 27)	376,400 (rank 2 of 27)
Rural/urban mix	Large rural population; only 60 % resident in municipalities	About one-third resident in small towns or rural areas; two-thirds in Kamloops	Small rural population – only 7 %; four core cities contain 62 % of total population
Municipal members	• 4 municipalities • 5 directors and up to 14 votes	• 11 municipalities • 15 directors and up to 37 votes (incl. Kamloops: 5 directors/25 votes)	• 13 municipalities • 20 directors and up to 70 votes (incl. core: 11 directors/46 votes)
Rural members	• 6 rural members • 6 directors and up to 12 votes	• 10 rural members • 10 directors and up to 11 votes	• 3 rural (or island) members • 3 directors and up to 6 votes
Expenditure (C$/2009)	• $23 million ($451/person) • About 44 % of total local government spending in RD	• $37 million ($304/person) • About 22 % of total local government spending in RD	• $128 million ($370/person) • About 27% of total local government spending in RD
Staff size	45	120	750

Table 9.2 Comparison of selected RDs: examples of self-organised services, 2010

Services (#)	CSRD 95	TNRD 115	CapRD 200
Drivers of service personality	• Geography: large area, divided by mountain ranges • Small population in subregional clusters • **Result**: focus on subregions	• One dominant municipal member (two-thirds of population) • Large number of smaller urban and rural members • **Result**: 'service bureau' approach primarily aimed at smaller members	• Small territory, concentrated and relatively large metro population • Surrounded by several, small rural or island communities • **Result**: service focus for rural/island communities • **Result**: strategic focus for metro subregion, focus on regional planning and scale economies
Water	• Community systems (rural) • Strategy for takeover of additional systems	• Community systems (11, rural)	• Bulk supply (region-wide) • Distribution (non-core cities) • Community systems (11, rural)
Sewerage	• Planning, liquid waste (rural, inter-local) • Community systems, liquid (2)	• Community systems (2, rural)	• Trunk, treatment, planning (regional) • Community systems (subregional)
Parks	• Parks, trails (30, regional) • Community parks (subregional)	• n/a	• Parks (30), trails (3) (regional) • Recreation complex (subregional) • Parks, recreation (islands)
Solid waste and recycling	• Solid waste planning (regional) • Landfills (subregional) • Recycling depot (regional)	• Solid waste planning (regional) • Garbage collection (inter-local) • Recycling (regional) • Landfills/transfer depots (regional)	• Solid waste services (regional) • Landfill (regional) • Residential recycling (regional)
Emergency services	• Emergency phone (regional) • Emergency services (local)	• Emergency phone (regional) • Volunteer fire support (rural)	• Emergency dispatch (subregional) • Emergency planning (regional)

(continued)

Table 9.2 Comparison of selected RDs: examples of self-organised services, 2010 (continued)

Services (#)	CSRD	TNRD	CapRD
	95	115	200
Library and culture	• Film commission (regional)	• Film commission (regional) • Library (regional)	• Arts grants, theatre (inter-local) • Museum (funding, inter-local) • Community library (rural, local)
Planning and Development	• Community planning (rural) • Building inspection (rural)	• Growth strategy (regional) • Building inspection (contract) • Planning (contract, rural)	• Growth strategy (regional) • Transportation planning (regional) • Building inspection (rural)
Other services	• Economic development (subregional) • Mosquito control (rural) • Airport (subregional)	• Economic development (subregional) • Pest/weed management (inter-local)	• Climate action (regional) • Housing trust + corporation (regional)

9.2.1 Geography, demographics and corporate composition

CSRD crosses three mountain ranges, making it a region of subregions. Its large rural population is clustered mainly around four non-contiguous municipalities. Each subregion is centred on a municipality, but no municipality is a dominant political actor in the region as a whole: the board is well balanced between municipal and rural members in terms of the number of directors and their respective voting power. CSRD accounts for about 44 per cent of all local government spending in this region (in Canadian currency, about C$451/person).

By land size, TNRD is the largest of the three regional districts discussed here. Its population is split among 10 rural members and 11 non-contiguous municipalities – with Kamloops accounting for about two thirds of the TNRD total. In contrast, all but one of the remaining municipalities has a population of less than 5,000. Reflecting the uneven population distribution, Kamloops alone appoints 20 per cent of the 25-member TNRD board and its representatives together control more than 50 per cent of weighted votes. TNRD accounts for about 22 per cent of all local government spending in this region (C$304/person).

CapRD is a mid-sized metropolis with an overwhelmingly urban population of 354,000 on a land area just 5 per cent that of TNRD. The populations of its 13 contiguous municipalities range from fewer than 2,500 to more than 110,000. Its central city, Victoria, is the capital of British Columbia. CapRD can be imagined as three concentric rings, resulting in a divided service personality. Four larger municipalities form an urban core wielding a majority of weighted votes. A surrounding suburban ring consists of nine smaller municipalities, casting about a third of weighted votes. Finally, there is an outer ring of rural and island communities. CapRD accounts for about 27 per cent of all local government spending within this region (about C$370/person). Its staff total of 750 far exceeds that of the other two regions profiled here. One idiosyncrasy is that the urban core municipalities have a long history of co-operation on certain joint services that were not folded into CapRD upon its creation, and these continue to operate without RD participation.

9.2.2 Self-organised service profiles

Table 9.2 shows that the service profiles of the three regions reflect incremental choices made in response to differing circumstances. CSRD's service personality is explained largely by its geography and subregional population clusters. It has a strong rural services role in both land-use planning and regulation, while also being instrumental in the provision of basic local services such as water supply. At a subregional level, CSRD delivers services such as recreation and fire protection.

Being composed of one large regional centre and many small towns and rural communities, TNRD tends to be focused on the issues faced by its smaller jurisdictions, which have challenges achieving scale economies and attracting technical staff in areas such as planning and engineering. The region aspires to be a 'regional service bureau' for its smaller members. At the same time, TNRD performs important region-wide roles such as operating the regional library system and having responsibility for the regional growth strategy.

As might be expected the CapRD narrative is rather complex, given that it faces the need to intervene in service provision and issue management in both rural and metropolitan domains (Capital Regional District 2012). Region-wide, members expect strategic leadership from CapRD and have given it responsibility for a robust set of key region-shaping services, including regional land-use and transportation planning, regional water supply and sewage treatment. While benefiting from these region-wide activities, the suburban ring has additionally defined a clear inter-local role for the RD, for example, providing recreation facilities and household water and sewerage services. Finally, within the outer ring of small or island communities, CapRD has assumed an important role in arranging local or rural services, such as water, sewerage and fire protection.

9.3 Responding to place, need and scale

There are 27 different stories about BC regional districts – and, since those districts continue to evolve, the stories are not final. Across BC, more than 3,000 local and partnership services have been formed, operating at different scales and employing different modes of provision.

The RD system's characteristic flexibility has been achieved through enabling rather than prescriptive legislation. As shown in Table 9.3, RDs employ a structured decision methodology when establishing a new local or partnership service. The first step is to define the service and service component of interest: they have discretion not only to choose the service spheres in which they will be active, but also to select the precise components of a service that will be produced or provided. For example, in the case of fire services the distinct components of the service include administration, procurement, regulation, inspection, prevention, investigation, training and suppression – any combination of which could be regionalised.

The second and third steps in the methodology involve defining service scale and service mode respectively. Services may be established at a local or rural scale, serving single communities, or at an inter-local or regional scale, serving multiple communities. More rarely, services can be created at a multi-RD scale if warranted by circumstances. In terms of service mode, alternative service delivery methods include direct production, public–public or public–private contracting, and production through an autonomous entity with an arm's-length relationship to the RD.

Table 9.3 also presents a selection of individual service arrangements from across BC revealing scale differences, differences in mode or services not typically associated with local governments. The examples were chosen from regions with vastly different characteristics. The self-organising behaviour of individual regional districts is apparent. One example is the case of fire services provided by the Columbia Shuswap Regional District; this shows how individual RDs have handled different components of the same service using different scales and modes. A second example contrasts transit services in the RDs serving the Central Okanagan and Nanaimo regions respectively; this shows that the same service may be delivered in different ways depending on regional circumstances.

Table 9.3 Self-organised service examples from across BC

Step 1: Choose service component (all or part of a service)		Step 3: Choose service mode…			
Step 2: Choose service area…		**Direct production**	**Public/public contracting**	**Public/private contracting**	**Autonomous corporation or entity**
Local or rural		• CSRD rural fire • TNRD water (Sorrento)	• CSRD suburban fire • TNRD small town building regulation	• KBRD (Big White) recycling and garbage	• CRD (Saturna Is.) fire protection–funding
Inter-local		• CSRD fire co-ordination • TNRD rural building regulation • CapRD water delivery	• CapRD town and fringe recreation (*two cases*) • CORD suburban transit	• CapRD town and fringe recreation (*one case*) • NRD waste collection • South CapRD airport	• CapRD theatres • BV-EDA (economic development)
Regional		• CapRD bulk water • NRD transit • NRD landfill • TNRD regional library	• CORD landfill • PRRD solid waste disposal	• GVRD waste-to-energy • NRD composting	• NRD recycling (public education) • CapRD housing
Multi-regional		• Lower Mainland (GVRD) regional parks	• NI-911 service contracts	• Lower Mainland (GVRD) regional parks	• NI-911 management of service contracts

Legend:		**Population ('000)**	**Central city**
CORD	Regional district: Central Okanagan	185	Kelowna
CapRD	Regional district: Capital	372	Victoria
CarRD	Regional district: Cariboo	65	n/a (3 centres)
CSRD	Regional district: Columbia Shuswap	54	Salmon Arm
GVRD	Regional district: Greater Vancouver	2,375	Vancouver
KBRD	Regional district: Kootenay Boundary	32	n/a (2 centres)
NRD	Regional district: Nanaimo	150	Nanaimo
PRRD	Regional district: Powell River	20	Powell River
TNRD	Regional district: Thompson Nicola	132	Kamloops
BV-EDA	Autonomous entity: Bulkley Valley Economic Development Association	n/a	n/a
NI-911	Subsidiary corporation to six RDs: North Island 911	n/a	n/a

9.4 Coping with complex, divisive issues at a regional scale

The institutional architecture of the BC regional district system has had its greatest success in the service delivery sphere (MCD 2010). However it was inevitable that some RDs, especially the more urbanised, would eventually encounter the need or opportunity to face issues more conflicted or inherently political in nature. These are issues where benefits and costs are not equally distributed among localities. Examples from BC include the development and implementation of regional growth strategies, regional transportation planning, affordable housing and economic development. Entry into these conflicted, more political spheres of activity has proved challenging. Such challenges are commonplace across the globe – examples abound of inter-institutional rivalries and contested decision-making in the regional domain. Thus the remainder of this chapter widens its focus beyond regional service delivery to regional governance. Governance requirements are reconsidered in the case where regional issues cannot be handled on the basis of inter-local co-operation to achieve mutual benefit, and nor can they be addressed by any single institution.

9.4.1 How polycentricity and rivalry affects decision-making

Decision-makers struggle when the incentive of mutual benefit cannot overcome the barrier of legitimate differences in interests – as so often happens regionally. In such cases, questions of 'who gets, who pays and who decides' might well provoke intense inter-local rivalries and disagreements, potentially leading to decision-making stalemate and perceived failures in regional governance.[4] Further, there is an especially complex mix of interests and institutions, both public and private, with a stake in decision outcomes. 'The basic point is that no single actor can alone account for contemporary governance' (Torfing et al. 2012: 5).

A region is an elastic concept that is always in flux. Any given region takes meaning from context and circumstance, and therefore has different meanings at particular times and for certain purposes. Political boundaries seldom coincide with those of social, economic and environmental territories. Governance systems must therefore cope with many 'regions', which co-exist, overlap and at times even collide (Seltzer and Carbonell 2011).

Regional governance is always a problem regardless of how responsibilities are divided among public institutions, either *de jure* or *de facto*. Many of the most challenging issues on the domestic agenda play out in the regional space – not locally within individual municipalities or at the territorial span of central governments. Such issues typically include heavy infrastructure for water and sewage treatment; transit and arterial transportation; aspects of protective services; environment, conservation and farmland preservation; competitiveness and economic development planning; affordable housing; and hospitals, health and social service systems. Major regional issues of this kind tend to present themselves in different ways to the multiple local communities of interest that together form a region. Such issues have differential implications across space. Since costs and benefits are seldom distributed in a perfectly even fashion, regional decisions tend to create area-based winners and losers. Thus the issues are inherently tough or 'wicked' and, when problems arise, are difficult to resolve.

9.4.2 How polycentricity and rivalry affects system architecture

The example of Canada illustrates a common occurrence – that the regional level is typically the most weakly developed and variable component of the governance apparatus (Sancton 2009). Canadians seem not to have settled how they want their regions to be governed: each province differs in the allocation of provincial and local responsibilities. Where they exist, the form of regional institutions varies; a considerable amount of experimentation in regional governance continues (while experimentation in relation to municipal governance is comparatively rare); and, finally, individual provincial governments play a highly variable role in regional decision-making.

Although this seldom seems to be fully appreciated, architects of regional governance systems almost always face three quite distinct problems:

* establishing institutions capable of delivering physical services at an economic scale larger than municipalities;

* designing regional institutions capable of resolving major boundary-crossing problems in a legitimate and democratic manner; and

* where the nature of their issues causes them to intersect, linking various institutions operating in the same regional space to achieve joined-up governance horizontally and vertically.

In our experience as public officials, it is clear that the first and easiest of these challenges tends to receive the most emphasis. The two latter challenges, however, need more focused attention.

Writing on how metropolitan areas blend into mega-regions, Innes et al. observed that, despite their many linkages and interdependencies, mega-regions are poorly linked in terms of governance:

> Hundreds of jurisdictions, federal and state sectoral agencies, and regulatory bodies make independent and conflicting decisions. The result is a complex system without a government or public agency that focuses on the metropolitan region's overall welfare much less on that of a mega-region. Instead the policy decisions of one agency or jurisdiction often push their problems onto others. In addition a myriad of public and private players whose actions have large and small impacts on the region have no incentive to work together to address shared problems. The result is a region that is unable to adapt to changing conditions in a productive way and unable to be resilient in the face of stressors (2009: 2).

Virtually all regional territories to some degree share the governance attributes Innes and colleagues described.

The extent of the natural, inevitable fracturing of regional space is easy to illustrate with Canadian examples. At some point over the past half-century, initiatives have been taken in most Canadian provinces to rationalise or consolidate regional governance (Sancton 1993, 2011; Lightbody 2006). As heroic as such efforts may be, they inevitably address only a fraction of the institutions engaged in making the most significant regional decisions.

One example is from Ontario, where Toronto is the major city. The modern City of Toronto was consolidated in 1998 by the legislated merger of all municipalities in the former federated regional organisation. However, recent data shows that the consolidated city now represents less than half the population of the Toronto census metropolitan area, and less than a third of the population covered by the Ontario government's growth plan for the wider Toronto region. A multitude of institutions still vie for influence within southern Ontario.

In a second example, a tally of local governance institutions was undertaken in two economic regions in BC. Both the Lower Mainland (anchored by Vancouver) and the Thompson-Okanagan (anchored by Kelowna and Kamloops) have a complex organisation of regional space. A range of entities has been identified covering the spectrum from municipal governments with a full suite of responsibilities to numerous functional or subregional institutions having a single role. There are at least 75 relatively autonomous bodies contributing to governance in each of the two regions.[5]

Such examples suggest that the notion of all key regional-scale decisions flowing through a single, overarching political forum is simply unreal. Regional space is inevitably carved up by a plethora of institutions, large or small, multi-functional or uni-functional, democratic or otherwise. Horizontal and vertical bonds between institutions are often weak and usually fragile – and, if reliance is placed solely on traditional governance techniques, these bonds are subject to degradation or failure at any time and for any number of reasons.

9.4.3 Regions as 'arenas of contention'

It will by now be clear that polycentric regional governance unfolds in 'arenas of contention'. Decision-making in the context of complex, divisive regional issues is one of the hardest things asked of our domestic political system. The governance requirements for an arena of contention can be described generically. A governance architecture is needed that copes with at least these requirements:

- the motivation (either 'natural' or 'manufactured') to coalesce;

- an inter-institutional forum: a place for regional dialogue and decision-making based on balancing contending institutional and area-based interests in the context of regional strategies;

- a 'brain' to undertake situational assessments and planning, and to communicate visions, issues, threats, opportunities and accomplishments;

- provision (possibly vicarious) for implementation capacity;

- the 'glue' to hold the regional coalition together in the face of contention and stress of implementation; and

- the capacity over time to adapt to new circumstances and regenerate.

These criteria presuppose neither a particular governance strategy nor any fixed structural solution.

In British Columbia, several RDs have been building their regional governance capacity, even while perpetuating their responsibilities for regional service delivery. As one example, 10 of the 13 RDs in the most heavily urbanised parts of BC, representing 83 per cent of the total provincial population, have adopted regional growth strategies. Those strategies link the planning interests of municipalities with larger regional and provincial interests. The legislation establishes RD boards as forums for cross-region dialogue and decision-making, while avoiding traditional hierarchical relationships between regional and municipal governments. It has not always been 'plain sailing' for regional districts: some growth-related issues have naturally triggered inter-local disputes. These have been addressed with 'soft-power' tools such as facilitation and mediation, plus 'harder' tools such as arbitration. Participants have been able to enact growth strategies and complementary local plans, even in a divisive setting.

Another example is an issue that cuts across social, economic and environmental sectors and political boundaries: affordable housing. Inherently regional in scope, the issue intersects with regional planning, job location, public transit, transportation and greenhouse gas emissions. In BC, however, the issue comes into focus primarily at a local rather than regional level. The issue can be divisive: suburban municipalities tend to favour sprawling, low-density residential and commercial development patterns yielding good property tax returns, while central cities face high land costs, densification pressures and, increasingly, the effects of poverty and homelessness. Meanwhile, dispersal of jobs and houses puts tremendous pressure on transportation and transit. Although local interests are not harmonious, the Capital Regional District has achieved a measure of success in addressing housing regionally. It has tackled this issue by establishing a 'housing trust', which redistributes capital resources contributed by members to the most needy municipalities, and by ensuring that regional land-use, transportation and social policy are integrated with housing solutions.

9.5 New pathways for regional governance

The literature on governance of complex systems (Innes et al. 2009: 13–18) and interactive governance (Torfing et al. 2012) is growing. Around the globe, much attention is being given to designing effective regional governance arrangements. However, genuine success stories are comparatively rare (Sancton 2008).[6]

A feature of complex regions is the inability of any single institution to successfully act unilaterally – none has the requisite span of control and all are subject to vital interdependencies. As the complexity of regional decision-making environments increases and the relative influence of individual institutions declines, the more likely it is that decisions will actually emerge from self-organising networks of institutions. According to Innes and colleagues, such networks are fluid in terms of space, time and membership. When simple, traditional governance processes fail, networks are needed to strengthen linkages between people, ideas and knowledge. 'These linkages facilitate the self-organisation of nodes of interaction, dialogue and collaboration to address emerging problems or crises' (2009: 14).

Network linkages must be established and sustained in both horizontal and vertical planes. Respecting vertical linkages, Innes, Torfing and their respective colleagues both cite the need for central government to play new roles (Innes et al. 2009: 16–17; Torfing et al. 2012: 122–44). Central governments must adopt a meta-governance paradigm in their interactions with regions, seeking influence without reverting to traditional statist forms of top-down control and command (Sørensen and Torfing 2012: 9). In this context, 'meta-governance' refers to the orchestration of complexity and plurality, that is, co-ordinated actions to encourage self-organisation and build capacity. Primary capacity-building mechanisms include such things as offering incentives for co-operation, creating forums for dialogue on multi-party issues, and establishing visions and expectations for regional development. Torfing et al. refer to this as the 'art of governing interactive governance' (2012: 122).

Confronting wicked issues in the regional space is unlikely to be successful if action is predicated on the governance environment being simple and static. Rudimentary remedies are often attempted involving such things as changing governance structures, adjusting the allocation of functions and powers among the various orders of government, and redefining the service mandates of different institutions. These are conventional or 'hard-power' solutions. Such measures have met with a degree of success since, it is true, dysfunctional structures and illogical allocations of functions must indeed be addressed. However, merely rearranging institutions or resorting mandates will not ordinarily change the character of underlying issues. As shown in Figure 9.1, it is more realistic to view the regional space as a complex and dynamic governance arena compartmentalised by legitimate differences in interests. In a complex arena, the need for high levels of vertical and horizontal co-ordination must be anticipated. In arenas of contention, governance approaches must move beyond conventional 'hard-power' remedies and toward issue-focused 'soft-power' solutions. New pathways to effective regional governance must enhance leadership and co-ordination, expand the regional decision toolkit and enable meta-governance.

Aware of the challenges of importing solutions from abroad – generally only the kernel of an idea is transportable, a kernel that will require moulding for the culture and circumstances of any adopting jurisdiction – a set of case studies is presented below, designed to suggest ways forward. The case studies are brief. They sketch the

Figure 9.1 Making the shift: governance in arenas of contention

SHIFT FROM...	SHIFT TO...
Assumes:	**Anticipates:**
Simple, static governance environment Low levels of inter-local conflict Institutions are independent	Complex, dynamic governance environment Inter-local conflict normal and legitimate Vital need for inter-institutional co-ordination
Focus on:	**Focus on:**
Structure / functions / mandates Conventional tools optimised for localities (not regions) Traditional governance mechanisms	Enhancing regional leadership and co-ordination Enhancing regional decision-making using tools optimised for regions (not localities) Meta-governance: vertical facilitation

relevant issue or problem, identify the need for a new approach, and paint a picture of new pathways in action, together with pointers to further information. The case studies explore a number of ideas, principally that regions need:

- more astute regional leadership and improved mechanisms for co-ordinating decisions, both horizontally and vertically;

- 'smart' incentives and 'smart' procedures designed to make decisions for regional betterment more feasible and realistic for those asked to make tough choices or resolve issues at the regional level; and

- deft, enabling and supportive interventions by central governments.

9.5.1 Enhancing regional leadership and co-ordination

Leadership

The complex, conflict-ridden problems facing regions demand an understanding of polycentricity. Leadership training must emphasise horizontal relationships, influence management, and processes of negotiation and mediation (Innes and Booher 2010). Canadian elected officials get scant training of this sort; for non-elected officials, leadership training generally focuses merely on the needs of unitary organisations and emphasises hierarchy, central planning, control and direction.

Thomas, Foster and Siegel[7] have complementary ideas about the skills for working or forging agreements in polycentric regional governance settings. Thomas argues for a curriculum emphasising the smart use of power, relations between elected and non-elected officials, and horizontal governance. Foster seeks proficiency in crossing jurisdictional, functional and sectoral borders. Siegel emphasises the importance of moving past the traditional notion of 'leading downward': leaders must now add 'leading upward' and 'outward' to their repertoire.

Both Georgia and British Columbia provide complementary illustrations.[8] The Regional Leadership Institute is mandated to reach beyond elected officials to include Atlanta's business, education and social sectors. The curriculum combines training in leadership skills, application to concrete regional problems, and developing regional awareness. BC's Local Government Leadership Academy has a specific mandate to cultivate the leadership competencies of elected and senior non-elected officials. Developing skills in intergovernmental relations and in negotiation and conflict management are emphasised.

Co-operation

Regions usually must fend for themselves in their efforts to forge viable internal and external relationships. Lack of co-ordination vertically with central governments, and horizontally among local governments and between sectors, prevents regions from reaching their full potential.

Effective management of issues in the regional space requires 'joined-up governance'. Without intergovernmental and cross-sector involvement, regions are severely limited in their ability to develop and implement viable plans. Horizontal and vertical co-ordination is needed. Central governments in particular must focus on improving both intergovernmental and inter-ministry co-ordination practices to help make 'joined-up governance' a reality.

Illustrating this approach, Québec brings provincial, regional and local elected officials together to achieve 'joined-up' decision-making in its regions and at the centre. Regional co-ordination occurs through 21 regional conferences of elected officers – which may also include delegates from the economic, culture, education and science sectors. In addition, an oversight body has been created, the Table Québec-régions (TQR), formed by the presidents of the regional conferences and Québec's local government minister.[9]

Articulation of regional interests

With their passion and commitment, local officials are often 'local patriots', assiduously defending the interests of their community. Local patriotism is a healthy, natural phenomenon unless it manifests as parochialism or complete insensitivity toward broader regional interests. However, there is often another factor at play: what if nobody has the opportunity or responsibility to articulate regional interests?

Regions are complex spaces where communities, institutions, interests and governments interact. Amid such complexity, it is often difficult (even where formal regional governance mechanisms do exist) to clearly articulate regional interests. McDavid and Vakil[10] ask probing questions about one region endowed with formal institutions: Greater Vancouver. In regions without the benefit of formal institutions, the challenge of articulating regional interests escalates. The architecture of regional governance systems must somehow enable regional interests to be heard amid the cacophony of locally oriented demands and ambitions.

Illustrating the capacity to span multiple local and regional institutions, the Columbia Basin Trust has oversight in a territory heavily impacted by hydroelectric infrastructure. In practice, the governance model effectively balances local interests in the context of regional strategies.[11] According to Travers,[12] the Greater London Authority (GLA) shows the pivotal role of regional strategies. Boroughs retain local service responsibility, yet the GLA has vital responsibilities to articulate region-wide strategies for the environment, planning, transport, economic development and culture. This model appears to enable articulation of regional interests better than most.

9.5.2 Enhancing regional decision-making

Challenge grants and rewards for results

In contentious policy arenas, decisions protecting local interests more often than not win out over regional betterment. A second problem is that regional decisions are often unrewarding or politically punishing to the officials who make them: the benefits from a 'tough' regional choice may be enjoyed in windfall fashion in other jurisdictions or by other orders of government.

Regions need mechanisms to reliably capture benefits derived from their decisions. They also need incentives designed to support regional betterment and thus make it feasible for decision-makers to set aside their natural inclination toward local protectionism. Challenge grants have this purpose and thus have preconditions attached to them: grants are issued on a competitive basis only to those localities able to 'join-up' and demonstrate they possess a common vision and have agreed on objectives, co-ordinating mechanisms and implementation plans.

The UK and US governments show how regional decision-making can be enhanced in this way. The UK government is concluding City Deals[13] with the largest and fastest-growing regional centres in England. The objectives are to accelerate the pace of decentralisation and unlock new and innovative ways to drive growth. Avoiding top-down imposition, each deal is customised and could represent a genuine transaction – with 'asks' and 'offers' from both sides. Significantly, the City Deal for Greater Manchester includes an earn-back or 'rewards-for-results' model – the region will capture tax receipts from the added economic activity resulting from its actions. Meanwhile, the US government's Jobs and Innovation Accelerator Challenge[14] seeks to stimulate collaborative, cluster-based regional growth. To win a subsidy, applicants must be self-organised and present a 'united front'. They must also articulate a clear plan and measurable outcomes.

Dispute resolution and streamlining co-operation

With ever-changing demographics, service economics, institutions and politics, self-organisation of working relationships in regional environments sometimes needs a boost. Once relationships are established, relentless change is likely. Lacking the requisite resilience, bitter conflicts can ensue within and between institutions. The absence of formal procedures can make it difficult to resolve such differences.

Formal dispute resolution systems can aid in 'manufacturing' agreement, despite differences in narrow, local interests. In order to sweep away barriers to co-operation, the root of the obstacle must first be identified. Only after understanding a barrier can it be matched with a specific remedy. For example, legal obstacles may come to light only as a result of failed attempts at solving a problem. In such cases, legislative amendments may be required. However, addressing capacity issues may also include incentives for neighbouring communities or municipalities to team up.

Supported by provincial advice and subsidies, British Columbia uses alternative dispute resolution (ADR) to resolve differences in developing, implementing and updating regional growth strategies and in operating regional services.[15] As another example, arcane federal regulations or an inability to contact the right people were found to create barriers for US city halls when accessing federal support. The Strong Cities, Strong Communities (SC2) initiative is designed to streamline co-operation in six economically struggling cities. SC2 also seeks to help the cities create and maintain critical regional partnerships.[16]

Mandates, structures, functions

Central governments often resort to such 'hard-power' solutions, such as imposing spending mandates or forcing reform of structures and allocation of functions – often with disappointing results. Regional issues tend to be too complex to be addressed with simplistic, directive interventions.

Nevertheless, regional officials may sometimes recognise circumstances where central government leadership via imposed mandates can be beneficial. The recognition is, however, circumscribed. Typically, mandates are viewed positively only where the matter is of genuine strategic importance, is accompanied by provisions addressing resource impacts, and leaves regions with some flexibility to manage implementation. Similarly, central leadership in structural or functional realignment, while not seen as a panacea, can facilitate (rather than force) agreement on difficult structural issues.

Revealing an instinct toward 'soft-power' intervention, the BC government resorted to strategic use of provincial mandates in the case of solid-waste planning. Initially controversial, opposition to compulsory planning was tempered by provincial incentives and technical assistance. Strategic restructuring has been used when existing structures are a clear barrier to performance. The Fraser Valley Regional District is the result of one such intervention. Service realignment is another, albeit rare, intervention strategy. Provincial leadership was instrumental when consolidating an old, independent water delivery agency with the Capital Regional District.[17]

9.5.3 Meta-governance role of central governments

Often regions are left on their own to deal with their polycentric, conflict-ridden decision-making setting. They lack the active support and engagement of a central order of government.

Resolution of the complex challenges facing regions requires deft, but not domineering, support and engagement from central government. Engagement must be enabling in nature and supportive of self-organisation at the regional level – what is termed 'meta-governance' or the governance of plurality and complexity (Innes et al. 2009: 16–18). Central governments can build regional capacity in a variety of ways including establishing a vision, setting targets and direction, providing incentives and creating forums for direct action.

As an example, Québec's flexible, leading-edge *Politique nationale de la ruralité* (rural strategy) began developing in 2002. Partnership-focused, it is designed to foster bottom-up innovation. The strategy models meta-governance: a provincial policy framework guides progress while maintaining a voluntary, democratic, facilitative approach. More than inspirational, the policy is backed up by customised institutional processes that seek to harness or 'join-up' energies across a broad spectrum of parties with a stake or interest in rural development.[18]

9.6 Effective regional governance for the twenty-first century

9.6.1 Reflections on effective regional service delivery

To deliver inter-local and regional services for mutual benefit among localities, the BC government created an innovative system of regional districts that has been relatively successful in its service-oriented mission. RDs have resolved hundreds of inter-local servicing problems. This is a singular achievement in that, while often encouraged in local government systems worldwide, successful implementation of joint servicing schemes is comparatively rare. Based on the BC experience, we contend that an effective system for regionalised (inter-local) service delivery must be:

- **Self-organised** and **capable.** Top-down imposition of standardised service solutions will often fail to produce service schemes adapted to the widely varying circumstances encountered in different regions. A better approach revolves around self-organised solutions, where partnerships and financial/operational parameters are set by local participants. At the same time, self-organisation is a near insurmountable hurdle if it means every detail of each individual inter-local service must be negotiated from a zero-base; thus built-in measures are necessary to sharply reduce the cost of negotiation (e.g. templates for agreements).

- **Evolving** and **resilient.** The environment for regional service delivery is dynamic. Systems must be designed to enable regional servicing issues to be addressed as they arise, case-by-case, in a process of continuous, system-wide evolution. However, a solution once adopted also exists in a dynamic environment, and so over time, if conditions change sufficiently, service solutions may need adaptive rearrangement. Service systems therefore need to have learning capacity.

- **Sustainable.** Durable service partnerships will exist only if collective action is seen to be fair (successful service solutions are usually fiscally equivalent), rewarding (scale economies are captured) and accountable (to the partners).

- **Connected** and **intelligent.** An enormous challenge is to arrange for satisfactory co-ordination among individual joint servicing schemes – since one may affect others and excessive service fragmentation can itself become a problem. While many approaches are theoretically viable, BC's strategy of managing distinct individual services under a common board has proved to have merit: (a) as a means for accumulating collective regional intelligence; (b) by providing a political forum for issue identification and problem resolution among partners; (c) by acting as a channel for vertical co-ordination; and (d) by facilitating the provision of expert, professional administration of even the smallest individual services.

While the design objectives cited can be met by systems of near unlimited diversity, it nevertheless will be vital for adopting jurisdictions to carefully consider the extent of institutionalisation required for effective joint service provision. There are critical choices about the necessary degree (amount of structure) and nature (amount of hard power or authority) of institutionalisation. There are three generic approaches:

- **'Light' institutions – weak authority.** In the first case, central governments may use persuasion to bring about joint service delivery, but the local participants have only soft-power tools at their disposal. Some will overcome institutional limitations and, with sufficient entrepreneurial leadership, devise creative and practical ways to provide inter-local services. However, since this is an almost purely *laissez-faire* strategy, regional partnerships will generally emerge only after protracted, sometimes fraught, negotiations – or will fail to emerge at all.

- **'Heavy' institutions – strong authority.** In the second case, joint service delivery may be strongly encouraged or even mandated by central government. The frameworks will generally be legislated, with regional service delivery institutions imbued with considerable statutory authority vis-à-vis localities. This is a challenging approach in jurisdictions with strong local self-rule traditions and, if attempted, a degree of instability must be anticipated due to incessant regional/ local conflict of a type 'power' cannot resolve.

- **'Heavy' institutions – weak authority.** The third case is a consensus-based rather than power-based approach – effectively a middle path between the first and second cases. This is the path followed by British Columbia. It institutionalises inter-local service delivery at a regional scale, but through a loosely coupled, consensus-based federation of localities that is designed to deal with issues best managed co-operatively.

Success at regionalism does not necessarily depend on having a formal regional government structure. Many of the factors that make BC's regional districts successful could be replicated in the absence of formal regional institutions. A problem-by-problem, service-by-service, incremental approach can lead in effect to a 'virtual region' or 'regionalism without regions'. Derived from BC's experience and other Canadian-based research (Martin et al. 2012), practical suggestions for any lightly institutionalised strategy include the following:

- BC's approach substantially reduces the costs of negotiation by employing default 'templates' for joint service agreements, defined statutorily. If statutory mechanisms are impractical, 'implementation kits' and 'self-help guides' can be substituted, together with the provision of best practice advice through central governments and/or local government associations.

- Central government and local government associations can agree on a strategy of collaborative steering of joint service systems. Collaborative steering can speed innovation and enable efficient issue resolution. Ideally, a 'regionalism without regions' strategy will use incremental adaptation as a strategy for avoiding cataclysmic disruptions.

- Central government impetus and support in terms of direction can speed implementation. Well-thought-out and sensitively delivered mandates can accelerate inter-local collaboration. Well-designed incentives can make it feasible for local elected officials to represent regional betterment positively to sceptical local voters.

9.6.2 Reflections on effective governance in arenas of contention

As noted earlier, some of the more urbanised regional districts in British Columbia have begun to migrate from their original mission, the administration of services, to a more challenging endeavour, regional governance. Not every regional matter lends itself to resolution through co-operation for mutual benefit. When matters are controversial or costly, or when the impacts of decisions have important differential effects on localities, interests or people – thus creating 'winners' and 'losers' – problems can turn 'wicked' and become resistant to resolution. Such problems we find will stubbornly remain if any central, regional or local government relies exclusively on hard-power mechanisms to force desired outcomes.

Looking broadly at the experience of RDs throughout British Columbia, it is by no means clear that success in arranging for co-operative services will necessarily position regional institutions for success in regional governance. Regional governance is often fraught and, with the elastic boundaries of regions and the potential for clashing interests, is inherently difficult. The BC experience strongly suggests the journey toward regional governance is arduous – and will not be accomplished successfully without a fundamental rethinking of how regional governance might be approached.

In our estimation, success in regional governance demands a paradigm shift – reorienting the entire regional governance system to enable deft, astute and prolonged action toward region building.[19] This involves strengthening an element of the governance apparatus that, in Canada and perhaps elsewhere, has received far less attention than it deserves. Merely to construct institutions is insufficient. More importantly, institutions with a slice of regional decision-making authority must be able to continuously assemble, confront wicked issues and negotiate durable solutions. Region building means anticipating and taking action on the simultaneous need for vertical and horizontal co-ordination. It also means moving beyond conventional 'hard-power' remedies. Issue-focused 'soft-power' solutions must be advanced – i.e., solutions must be designed to coax better outcomes from regional decision-makers, without depriving them of the opportunity to be creative and without exhausting their local political capital. Solutions arrived at in this manner will have more chance of success than those imposed from above.

Thus while we have no clear blueprint for the future, our analysis suggests that future pathways to effective regional governance must focus on enhancing leadership and co-ordination, expanding the regional decision toolkit, and meta-governance or the orchestration of complexity and plurality. Unless governance systems improve along those three dimensions, struggles with regional decision-making will persist.

Notes

1 The views expressed are those of the authors and do not reflect the views of the Government of British Columbia or Ministry of Community, Sport & Cultural Development. The authors benefited and appropriated certain insights from two anonymous reviewers.

2 In Canada, school districts are treated as part of the system of local government for statistical and other purposes. In this chapter, 'local government' is used with only its municipal connotation.

3 The Greater Vancouver Regional District (GVRD) has in recent years operated under the brand name Metro Vancouver. The official corporate name for Metro Vancouver (metrovancouver.org) remains the GVRD.

4 An anonymous reviewer has pointed out that stalemate is not an unusual or remarkable outcome in a voluntary system in the absence of mutual benefits that create incentives to conclude agreements; nor is there empirical evidence that a stalemate may not be the best outcome. True as this is, a state

of government in apparent paralysis is in the authors' experience rarely an acceptable outcome in the partisan political environments that generally prevail. For this reason, government officials rarely have the luxury of defending stalemated decisions as being optimal purely in economic terms.

5   In the Lower Mainland: 30 municipal governments, 12 first-nation (aboriginal) governments, all or part of 3 regional districts, and 36 functional regional or subregional entities (such as regional hospital districts and other like service entities, council-controlled bodies, economic development entities, school districts and so forth). In the Thompson Okanagan: 23 municipal governments, 18 first-nation governments, all or part of 5 regional districts, and 29 functional regional or subregional entities.

6   However, both Sancton (2011) and Bish (2002, 2006) credit the BC system of regional districts as being comparatively successful in a Canadian or North American context.

7   Several sources for further information have been identified. See Paul Thomas, available at: www. ipac.ca/2008/docs/presentation/2608PM-Paul-Thomas-LeadingPublicSector.pdf (accessed February 2013). Kathryn Foster published 'A Region of One's Own' in *Regional Planning in America* by Seltzer and Carbonell (Eds. 2011). David Siegel's 'Leadership Role of the Municipal CAO' is in *Canadian Public Administration* Vol. 53 No. 2, 139–161, June 2010.

8   The training institutions discussed here have websites available at: rli.atlantaregional.com/rli and lgla.ca respectively (both accessed February 2013).

9   La Conférence de l'Outaouais, one specific example of a regional conference, is available at: www. cre-o.qc.ca/index.php. La Table Québec-régions (TQR) is at www.mamrot.gouv.qc.ca/ministere/ table-quebec-regions (both accessed February 2013).

10 Regarding Greater Vancouver, Jim McDavid and Thea Vakil have an analysis of decision-making available at: www.uvic.ca/hsd/publicadmin/professionalDevelopment/home/localgovernment/Gov_ conf2011.php (accessed February 2013).

11 For information about the Columbia Basin Trust, see: cbt.org (accessed February 2013).

12 An analysis of Greater London by Tony Travers is available at: http://78.41.128.130/ dataoecd/52/63/35565616.pdf (accessed February 2013).

13 For information on City Deals, see: www.dpm.cabinetoffice.gov.uk/resource-library/wave-1-city-deals. From there, follow links to information on Wave 2 deals and other ancillary sources. On the Manchester 'earn-back' scheme, see: www.lgcplus.com/budget-2012-manchester-earn-back-details-emerge/5043169.article (all accessed February 2013).

14 The Centre for Cities, available at: www.centreforcities.org also has a wealth of relevant information. Information about the Accelerator Challenge is available at: www.eda.gov/challenges/jobsaccelerator (both accessed February 2013).

15 Dispute resolution is the subject of two publications from British Columbia: the first is available at: http://cscd.gov.bc.ca/lgd/intergov_relations/library/Reaching_Agreement_Growth_Strategies.pdf; the second is available at: http://cscd.gov.bc.ca/lgd/intergov_relations/library/Reaching_Agreement_ Services_2005.pdf (both accessed February 2013).

16 For further information use the search term 'epa strong cities communities' in a search engine.

17 See: http://env.gov.bc.ca/epd/mun-waste/index.htm for an illustration of the strategic use of provincial mandates. For strategic use of restructuring, see: www.fvrd.bc.ca. Information about the strategic use of service realignment is available at: www.crd.bc.ca/water/index.htm (all accessed February 2013).

18 Use the search term 'quebec national policy rurality' in a search engine to access information on Québec's 2006 rural policy framework. A 2008 discussion of the policy framework will be found by navigating from: www.muniscope.ca/home/Symposium/index.php (accessed February 2013).

19 Katz (2009) suggests a similar strategy with reference to American metropolitan areas, inviting policy designers to imagine a reversal of federal interventions. Instead of operating traditional locality-focused and application-based programmes which overlook the regional nature of most challenges facing urban America, he proposes shifting federal interventions to a regionally focused and results-based strategy.

References

Berdahl, L (2006), 'The Federal Urban Role and Federal-Municipal Relations' in Young, R and C Leuprecht (Eds.), *Canada: The State of the Federation 2004:*

Municipal-Federal-Provincial Relations in Canada, available at: www.ppm-ppm.ca/ publicationssotf04.asp (accessed March 2013).

Bish, RL (2002), 'Accommodating multiple boundaries for local services: British Columbia's local government system'. Retrieved from *Workshop in Political Theory and Policy Analysis*, Indiana University, available at: www.indiana.edu/~workshop/ papers/bish_102102.pdf (accessed March 2013).

Bish, RL (2006), 'Inter-municipal cooperation in British Columbia', *Public Manager*, Vol. 35 No. 4, 34–9.

Bish, RL and EG Clemens (2008), *Local Government in British Columbia*, 4th ed., Union of British Columbia Municipalities, Richmond, BC.

Brown, JE (1968), 'Regional Districts in British Columbia', *Municipal Finance*, Vol. 41 No. 2, 82–6.

Capital Regional District (2012), *Capital Regional District Strategic Plan 2012–2014*. Retrieved from Capital Regional District, available at: www.crd.bc.ca/about/docu ments/1710StratPlanBookletALTonline.pdf (accessed March 2013).

Commonwealth Local Government Forum (2009), *Local Government System in Canada*. Retrieved from CLGF (Country Profiles), available at: www.clgf.org.uk/ index.cfm/PageID/13/ViewPage/Country-profiles (accessed March 2013).

Collier, R (1972), *The Evolution of Regional Districts in British Columbia*. Retrieved from BC Studies Archives, available at: ojs.library.ubc.ca/index.php/bcstudies/ article/view/754/796 (accessed March 2013).

Fahim, M (2009), *Multi-Tier Local Government Systems Adopted in Many Parts of the World*. Retrieved from City Mayors, available at: www.citymayors.com/ government/multitier_system.html (accessed March 2013).

Innes, J, S Di Vittorio and D Booher (2009), *Governance for the Megaregion of Northern California: A Framework for Action*. Retrieved from Institute of Urban and Regional Development, University of California, Berkeley, available at: metrostudies. berkeley.edu/pubs/reports/GMS-WP09-01.pdf (accessed March 2013).

Innes, J and D Booher (2010), *Planning with Complexity: An Introduction to Collaborative Rationality for Public Policy*, Routledge, New York.

Katz, B (2009), *The White House Office of Urban Policy: Form and Function*. Retrieved from The Brookings Institution, available at: www.brookings.edu/research/ speeches/2009/02/12-housing-katz (accessed March 2013).

Kitchen, H (2002), 'Canadian municipalities: fiscal trends and sustainability'. Retrieved from *Canadian Tax Journal*, available at: www.ctf.ca/ctfweb/Documents/ PDF/2002ctj/2002ctj1_kitchen.pdf (accessed March 2013).

Kitchen, H and E Slack, (2006), *Trends in Public Finance in Canada*. Retrieved from The Institute on Municipal Finance and Governance, available at: http://munkschool. utoronto.ca/imfg/uploads/102/trends_in_public_finance_in_canada___june_1. pdf (accessed March 2013).

Local Government Knowledge Partnership (2009), *40 Years: A Regional District Retrospective – Summary of Proceedings*. Retrieved from LGKP, available at: www. uvic.ca/hsd/publicadmin/assets/docs/professionalDevelopment/pdfs/Mar%2009/ Summary.pdf (accessed March 2013).

Lightbody, J (2006), *City Politics, Canada*, Broadview Press, Peterborough, ON.

Martin, J, G Paget and B Walisser (2012), 'Rural municipal development and reform in Canada: policy learning through local-provincial collaboration'. Retrieved from *Commonwealth Journal of Local Governance*, available at: http://epress.lib.uts. edu.au/journals/index.php/cjlg/article/view/2687 (accessed March 2013).

Ministry of Community, Sport and Cultural Development (MCD) (2006), *Primer on Regional Districts in British Columbia*. Retrieved from MCD, Government of British Columbia, available at: www.cscd.gov.bc.ca/lgd/gov_structure/library/ Primer_on_Regional_Districts_in_BC.pdf (accessed March 2013).

MCD (2010), *Regional Districts, Parts 1 to 3*. Retrieved from Ministry of Community and Rural Development, Government of British Columbia, available at: www. cscd.gov.bc.ca/lgd/history/mini_histories (accessed March 2013).

Phares, D (2009), 'Prologue: on metropolitan government and governance', in Phares, D (Ed.), *Governing Metropolitan Regions in the 21st Century*, ME Sharpe, Armonk, NY.

Sørensen, E and J Torfing (2012), 'Introduction: collaborative innovation in the public sector'. Retrieved from *Innovation Journal*, available at: www.innovation. cc/volumes-issues/vol17-no1.htm (accessed March 2013).

Sancton, A (1993), *Local Government Reorganisation in Canada since 1975*. Retrieved from Muniscope (ICURR Press Publications Archive), available at: www. muniscope.ca/library/publications/index.php#Municipal (accessed March 2013).

Sancton, A (2008), *The Limits of Boundaries: Why City-Regions Cannot Be Self-Governing*, McGill-Queen's University Press, Montreal and Kingston.

Sancton, A (2009), *A Review of Canadian Metropolitan Regions: Governance and Government*. Retrieved from Local Government Knowledge Partnership (University of Victoria), available at: www.uvic.ca/hsd/publicadmin/assets/docs/ professionalDevelopment/pdfs/Dec%2009/Sancton.pdf (accessed March 2013).

Sancton, A (2011), *Canadian Local Government: An Urban Perspective*, Oxford University Press Canada, Don Mills, ON.

Seltzer, E and A Carbonell (2011), 'Planning regions'. Retrieved from *Regional Planning in America: Practice and Prospect*, available at: www.lincolninst.edu/pubs/ dl/1893_1239_RPA_WebCh.pdf (accessed March 2013).

Slack, E (2007), 'Managing the coordination of service delivery in metropolitan cities: the role of metropolitan governance (WPS4317)'. Retrieved from *Policy Research Working Paper Series*, World Bank, available at: http://ideas.repec.org/p/ wbk/wbrwps/4317.html (accessed March 2013).

Tennant, P and D Zirnhelt (1972), *The Emergence of Metropolitan Government in Vancouver*. Retrieved from BC Studies Archives, available at: http://ojs.library.ubc. ca/index.php/bcstudies/article/view/753/795 (accessed March 2013).

Tennant, P and D Zirnhelt (1973), 'Metropolitan government in Vancouver: the strategy of gentle imposition', *Canadian Public Administration*, Vol. 16 No. 1, 124–38.

Torfing, J, BG Peters, J Pierre and E Sørensen (2012), *Interactive Governance: Advancing the Paradigm*, Oxford University Press, Oxford.

Chapter 10

Long-term Strategic Planning in New Zealand: Will Compliance Crowd Out Performance?

Michael Reid

Strategic planning is a management tool introduced during the recent period of public sector reform intended to improve the efficacy and efficiency of public organisations. Councils in New Zealand, like elsewhere, were quick and enthusiastic adopters and a range of innovative approaches was developed. However, 20 years on, that innovation is at risk of being lost because of an increasing emphasis on accountability and compliance.[1] Long-term council planning is required to address multiple objectives, with the risk that 'strategy' will be crowded out. It is not clear whether the emphasis on accountability and financial planning allows sufficient space for innovative engagement with citizens about possible futures.

While we treat strategic planning as a relatively new technique, one of a bundle of tools loosely termed 'New Public Management' (Rhodes 1997), it would be a mistake to assume that local government has never engaged in long-term planning. Since their creation councils have planned for, and invested in, the future development of infrastructure and amenities that growing settlements will require. Yet formal strategic planning is a recent phenomenon, appearing in New Zealand local government only after the comprehensive reform of the sector in 1988/89, which both modernised its processes and created larger and more competent units.[2] One legacy of reform was a much smaller number of local councils, and these larger authorities were willing and able to experiment with new and innovative approaches to organisational matters. Strategic planning (entirely discretionary) was one of those innovations, with almost all councils having produced some form of strategic plan by the mid-1990s.

Strategic planning can be understood as the 'disciplined effort to produce fundamental decisions and actions that shape and guide what an organisation (or other entity) is, what it does, and why it does it' (Bryson 2004: 6). In the public sector, strategic planning is commonplace, and sits among the tools that local governments employ to ensure they provide the appropriate services at the right quality level in order to meet the expectations of their publics. It is one of a suite of related techniques that include strategic management and strategic thinking. The terms are closely interrelated: while strategic management is concerned with developing a continuing commitment to the mission and vision of the organisation and ensuring a clear focus on the organisation's strategic agenda, strategic thinking is more concerned with synthesis, questioning conventional assumptions and seeking integration around broadly crafted visions (Local Futures 2006).

Some form of requirement to undertake strategic planning in local government can be found in most national jurisdictions; however, the way this is done varies considerably, with obvious implications for council practice. One area of diversity is the degree of prescription; does empowering legislation spell out in detail how strategic planning should occur or are provisions broadly written, leaving room for innovation? Nowhere is this question better realised than the way in which New Zealand councils have approached strategic planning. In the space of 20 years, strategic planning has gone from a matter of local authority discretion, under which councils developed approaches framed to address the circumstances of their communities, to a prescribed tool which requires all councils to follow the same template. The change from a discretionary to mandatory approach, and what this means in practice, has broad lessons for local authorities and their governments internationally.

10.1 The New Zealand local government system

New Zealand local government exists within a parliamentary democracy with a single house of parliament. As it is one of three countries in the developed world that does not have a written constitution, powers and roles are defined by statute and consequently lack the protection often found in countries with constitutional recognition. For most of its existence local government's power was defined by the *ultra vires* principle (councils were allowed to undertake only roles defined in statute), but with the *Local Government Act 2002* tightly prescribed powers were replaced by a form of general competence, an approach commonly found in other OECD countries.

The local government sector consists of 78 local authorities. These include 11 regional councils and 67 'territorial' authorities (cities and districts). Regional councils are responsible for environmental policy, pest control and in some cases public transport, regional parks and bulk water supply. Territorial authorities provide local services including roads, water reticulation, sewerage and refuse collection, libraries, parks, recreation services, local regulations and community leadership. Six of the territorial councils also have regional council functions and are known as 'unitary' councils. Total expenditure in local government is approximately 4 per cent of gross domestic product and just under 10 per cent of all public spending. Local government has a low 'task' profile (activities such as the police, education and social services are provided by the national government), but a high level of autonomy – councils raise approximately 90 per cent of their own income. Reflecting this narrow range of mandatory local functions, *The Economist* has described New Zealand as the most centralised state in the OECD (*The Economist* 2009: 59).

While the sector's mandatory tasks are minimal, councils have considerable autonomy from central government due to their ability to levy property taxes. To enhance accountability, parliament has prescribed detailed processes to ensure that citizens' views are taken into account in council decision-making, such as when adopting annual budgets and work programmes. The predominant role of councils is one of place-shaping[3] (Lyons 2007) and, except for a small number of regulatory functions undertaken on behalf of the central government, legally made council decisions cannot be overturned by the central government without legislation. Councils are also responsible for undertaking a number of plans and policies that provide coherent and joined-up governance at the local level. These include, for example, annual plans, district plans (for land use), regional policy statements, land transport plans, emergency management plans, gaming strategies and long-term plans. More recently some areas have developed regional spatial strategies, and in New Zealand's largest city – Auckland – the adoption of a spatial plan[4] is mandatory.

10.2 The rise of strategic planning

Over the last few decades successive governments in New Zealand have endorsed a programme of public sector reform, which has sought to shift public agencies from a narrow focus on services to a more strategic view of the outcomes services are intended to achieve. In addition, a new focus on effectiveness has required public organisations to better align their activities to the goals and outcomes articulated by government ministers and, in local government's case, communities. The 2002 Act required councils, in a manner similar to the framework applied to government agencies, to take a more strategic view towards their roles and functions, and ultimately their focus. A new range of competencies was required, including an ability to apply new techniques for fostering community participation and leveraging other actors in order to ensure a more joined-up approach to the achievement of community well-being.

Strategic planning was one of those techniques. Often discussed in terms of New Public Management or modernisation (Boston et al. 1996; Naschold 1997), it is one of a menu of tools that governments have adopted to improve responsiveness and ensure scarce resources are employed efficiently and effectively.[5] In New Zealand the modernisation process began with the election of the fourth Labour Government in 1984, and reflected a view that 'at least from the standpoint of management, the differences between the public and private sectors are not generally significant; hence public and private organisations can, and should, be managed on more or less the same basis' (Boston et al. 1996: 26). The modernisation applied to both central and local government.

The modernisation project set out to organise the bureaucracy so that departments: had clear and consistent objectives; had a high standard of accountability; made trade-offs transparently; were less likely to be 'captured' (unduly influenced) by the service providers they were supposed to regulate, monitor or commission; and operated trading activities in a manner which was free from direct political control. As Boston says, changes to the machinery of government sought to achieve 'consistency, accountability, transparency, contestability, complementarity, co-ordination, economy, efficiency, the minimisation of capture and improved bureaucratic representation for dis-advantaged groups' (Boston 1991: 239). In short, the objective was a public sector that was more likely to be responsive, arranged in a way that reflected a greater plurality of voices and more focused on outcomes.

In this context the introduction of strategic planning enabled local public decision-makers to focus on outcomes and take a more discerning approach when considering the outputs and inputs required to achieve them. It represented an attempt to reconcile the 'rational' approach to decision-making with the predominantly 'political' approach to decision-making found in public organisations (see Figure 10.1).

Figure 10.1 Rational planning and political decision-making models

Rational planning model	Political decision-making model
Goals Policies Programmes Actions	Most general policies More general policies Policies and programmes Issue area
• Based on organisation • Key decision-makers are internal, facilitating co-ordination and reconciling differences	• Starts with issues across boundaries • Involving conflict, not consensus • Politically rational policies and programmes emerge • More generalised policies emerge over time to capture, frame, shape or guide programmes • 'Policy as Treaty' – policies represent reasonable level of agreement between parties

Source: Bryson (2004: 18–20)

Rational decision-making is a deductive process that begins with a clear statement of goals from which policies, programmes and actions to achieve those goals are then 'deduced' (Bryson 2004). A precondition for the model to work is agreement on the overall goals; this is an assumption not always found in public organisations, which reflect diverse views about the 'good life'. Political decision-making on the other hand is inductive; it begins with issues that inevitably involve disagreement. In contrast to the rational approach, decisions made in the political model emerge through the political process itself. This process requires agreement among key stakeholders and a degree of consensus building. Bryson describes the resulting policies and programmes as essentially 'treaties' negotiated between various stakeholder groups.

Promoters of strategic planning argue that it marries both the rational and political decision-making models by focusing on identifying and resolving what they describe as 'strategic issues'. Political decision-making is essential in order to achieve agreement on the programmes and policies to address key issues, while the rational planning approach provides a framework to recast that agreement in terms of goals, policies and actions. Strategic planning provides tools for addressing and resolving the issues that political decision-making identifies. In doing so it highlights inconsistencies where different approaches might have been adopted to address issues and achieve goals. In contrast to the purely rational approach, strategic planning does not assume a consensus. Rather, it provides a process that involves stakeholders and interested parties in a negotiation or conversation that takes into account interests and issues, and so ensures that actions agreed upon are more likely to be 'politically wise' (Bryson 2004: 20).

While modernisation has been a major driver behind reform in many developed countries, the way in which strategic planning frameworks have been designed for local governments varies considerably. Some countries have broadly worded requirements that allow for local experimentation and innovation, while others – for example, England and New Zealand – have adopted more prescriptive approaches that have resulted in a greater consistency of approach. In the New Zealand case, strategic planning developed voluntarily after the reorganisation of local government in 1989 and was regarded as an example of good practice (see Local Futures 2006). Strategic planning complemented a statutory corporate planning framework, which was based on a regime of annual planning. The reforms of 1989 required councils to publish a draft annual plan and budget, outlining major activities planned for the coming 12 months, and to seek community views on the draft before adoption. A further obligation was the publication of an annual report describing whether budgetary and work-plan forecasts were met or not, including performance measures. Annual reports were also made subject to an official audit by the Office of the Auditor General, with results reported to parliament.

The requirement to publish an annual plan and budget was the first step towards making the business of local government transparent, so as to enable citizens to have a greater say on council priorities. Unfortunately it also encouraged councils to think and plan on an annual basis, which was a problem given that many activities, such as providing infrastructure, require long-term decision-making. Consequently, councils began to turn to strategic planning as a mechanism to help elected members and officials think about the 'big picture' and to provide a long-term context for annual plans. Some councils sought to be innovative – for example, Porirua City Council and Manukau City Council, which used their new strategic plans not only to help their own decision-makers think about the longterm, but also to help focus non-council agencies, such as government departments, align their priorities with those of the city as a whole. Waitakere City, for instance, was well known for its 'eco city' theme, which sought to examine not only the council's activities but those of other agencies as well through a sustainability lens.

10.3 Long-term council community plans

While councils experimented with strategic plans as a way of providing decision-makers with a context for their annual planning, the government had concerns about a lack of long-term infrastructure planning at the local level. In particular there was a concern about a growing infrastructural deficit, and in 1996 the government passed the *Local Government Amendment Act (No. 3)* to address the issue. This Act was remarkable in a number of respects, in particular for its requirement that councils develop and publish long-term financial strategies based on financial forecasts for the forthcoming ten years and revised every three years. While long-term financial strategies were to be based on assumptions about future growth or decline, underpinned by detailed asset management plans and environmental scans, they were not in themselves strategic plans as understood in this chapter. Their primary goal was to make councils' performance in asset maintenance more transparent and to provide citizens and elected members with information about the fiscal implications of current decisions – ultimately strengthening the ability of citizens to hold their elected members to account. In practice, these financial strategies sat alongside council strategic plans with little if any acknowledgement.

A change of government at the end of 1999 signalled a new approach to local government policy, and almost immediately work began on a full rewrite of the *Local Government Act*. The cabinet was sympathetic to requests from some in local government that the new legislation should make strategic planning mandatory, but was reluctant to create yet more planning obligations. Its solution was to enhance the long-term financial strategies (LTFS) by creating a strategic 'front end', a requirement that councils identify 'community outcomes' (longer-term goals for the city or district articulated through extensive community consultation) and show how the activities in the LTFS contribute to those outcomes. As the Cabinet Policy Committee commented, the LTFS failed to:

> ...recognise and integrate the Council's social, cultural and environmental reasons for undertaking activities. As a result, the way that these social, cultural and environmental plans and activities fit into the whole Council programme is not clear (Cabinet Policy Committee 2001).

The Cabinet Policy Committee was concerned that the LTFS placed too much reliance on fiscal matters and failed to integrate social, cultural and environmental considerations. In the cabinet's mind the shortcoming of the LTFS was its failure to provide a sufficiently broad strategic framework to steer council activity, particularly in relation to citizen expectations and the promotion of community well-being. It believed that councils should be engaging in dialogue with their communities, and that local government was a crucial leader in determining how community assets should be used. This issue was addressed with the passage of the new *Local Government Act 2002 (LGA02)*, which was a full rewrite of the sector's empowering legislation. The new statute reframed the purpose of local government to emphasise democratic local decision-making by, and on behalf of, communities, and stressed councils' roles in promoting the social, economic, environmental and cultural well-being of communities – in the present and for the future. The critical mechanism for delivering on this new purpose was the Long-Term Council Community Plan (LTCCP), the successor to the LTFS.[6] Unlike the LTFS, which emphasised financial accountability, the purpose of the LTCCP was to:

- set out the community outcomes and the local authority's intended contribution to those outcomes;

- set out the things the local authority will be doing over the life of the plan;

- co-ordinate the activities of the local authority;

- provide a long-term focus for the local authority;

- provide a means for communities to hold the local authority accountable; and

- provide an opportunity (potentially the primary opportunity) for the public to participate in local decision-making (LGNZ 2003: 32).

The LTCCP contains most of the elements of the LTFS, but with a number of enhancements. Like the LTFS the LTCCP has a planning horizon of at least ten years, with a review period of at least once every three years. A key difference was the introduction of community outcomes in order to provide a strategic context for council financial strategies, a gap identified by cabinet. The new statute was quite specific that councils should undertake a process at least once every six years to enable the community to identify their outcomes; in contrast, the LTCCP must be reviewed every three years. As envisaged in the LGA02, the council's role when identifying outcomes should be one of facilitator, enabling communities to determine their own outcomes. The nature of the process led some commentators to suggest that the community outcomes process was a forum for community governance (Leonard and Memon 2008).

Underpinning the design of the LTCCP was a concern held by ministers that elected members and/or their officials might seek to control or at least influence the outcome-setting process, and substitute a community's aspirations with their own. Consequently the legislation required councils to invite other organisations to assist with both the design of the process for identifying outcomes and its implementation. This provision resulted in a view that the new framework heralded a shift to a more participative form of democracy, in which elected representatives were likely to be sidelined (Thomas and Memon 2007). A more considered view described the new framework as a form of community strategic planning and drew parallels with the approach to community strategic planning prevalent in English and Welsh councils:

> The community governance mandate in the LGA has opened a window of opportunity for community engagement and intergovernmental collaboration to an extent that has not been witnessed before in New Zealand (Leonard and Memon 2008: 44).

10.4 Identifying community outcomes

Following the passage of the LGA02 and the introduction of the new LTCCP with the requirement to identify community outcomes, the LTCCP essentially became a council's strategic plan. Within a few years only a handful of councils were doing any other form of strategic planning. A critical aspect of the new model concerned the way in which councils went about identifying community outcomes. A number of observations can be made, including that practice has varied – some councils have clustered together and taken a regional approach to the community outcomes process, while others have been happy to manage the whole process within their own jurisdictions. Other councils have placed greater emphasis on the inter-agency nature of the process, and have invested in strong collaborative relationships with the not-for-profit sector and government agencies. By focusing on outcomes rather than council or organisational services, the new strategic planning model was inherently collaborative, encouraging councils to work with other agencies that contributed to the achievement of outcomes.

The way in which the provisions were drafted encouraged councils to experiment and use a range of initiatives to identify the issues their citizens considered important. Suggestions included using focus groups to develop draft outcomes, which could then be used as a basis for more traditional public consultation processes. Kapiti District

Council, a medium-sized semi-rural local authority north of Wellington, was one council that designed an innovative community-based process to assist residents think about the district's future. Called 'Choosing Futures', the project departed from traditional approaches to consultation by involving citizens as both leaders and participants in the strategic planning process, with independent facilitators engaged to run more than 40 community meetings, many held in local neighbourhoods. One of the techniques employed was to encourage residents to talk about their own neighbourhoods and the issues that were important to them before thinking about the issues facing the district as a whole. Results were collated into an overall vision for the district, which set out the council's leadership role, how it would work with the community and suggested investment priorities for the next 20 years (Burke 2004). Copies were sent to all residents, along with information on what the council intended to do to achieve the vision.

Following the passage of the LGA02, Manukau City, a large urban city in the Auckland metropolitan area (now part of the new single Auckland Council), was able to utilise its existing strategic plan, 'Tomorrow's Manukau', as the basis for consultation on community outcomes. To identify the issues facing the city, the council developed a consultation strategy that operated at a number of levels and involved numerous public meetings and a survey of approximately 1,000 residents. The survey was undertaken to provide not only a broad public perspective, but to understand the preferences of the city's various population groups. Leadership roles were given to government agencies and not-for-profit organisations, the latter to improve engagement with more marginalised groups in the city. The council's process goals were to stimulate a sense of direction for the city; to identify what was important to citizens; to ensure a participative process; and to take a multi-stakeholder approach (Burke 2004). Seven high-level outcomes were identified, ranging from an 'educated and knowledgeable population' to a 'thriving economy'. To advance each of the outcome areas, teams of council officials and external stakeholders were formed to lead specific action plans. Manukau City Council sought to use the new LTCCP as a vehicle not only to integrate the council's different services towards a common objective, but also to encourage the broad range of public and non-public agencies active in the city to work towards the same aspirational goals.

By 2006 all councils had completed their first LTCCP, including having identified community outcomes. The similarity of outcomes is worth noting. Many were of the general 'healthy, wealthy and wise' style of outcome and it was often difficult to distinguish between cities and districts, although the frequency with which some outcomes arose probably reflects citizens' common aspirations to live in safe, healthy and comfortable communities. Some councils approached the exercise by starting with a blank slate and simply asking citizens what they wanted to see. Others prepared a list of draft outcomes and asked local citizens to rank them and give preference. While the blank page approach was seen to reduce the risk of council 'capture', in practice council officials played a critical role in shaping outcomes, regardless of the approach taken. What was often lacking, however, was any sense of the strategies required to achieve aspirational outcomes, particularly since councils themselves were often minor players in relation to the achievement of goals that involved other agencies.[7]

In setting outcomes not just for councils but for communities, the LTCCP could only be an effective form of strategic planning to the degree that the organisations and agencies that actually took part were able to influence the achievement of those outcomes. Previous discussion in this chapter noted that, under the LGA02, councils had an obligation to invite other agencies – those able to influence the achievement of outcomes – to assist with the design and implementation of the outcomes process. Ensuring that such agencies contributed to outcome achievement was another challenge, as councils have few statutory levers to require them to do so. Despite the difficulty, a range of models has been developed through which councils and agencies seek to align local, regional and national priorities in order to bring about community outcomes, many of which are still in operation.[8]

Following the enactment of the LGA02, the central government, despite failing to *require* its departments to contribute to the achievement of outcomes, actively sought to *encourage* them. This took the form of appointing lead agencies for each of the four well-being areas – social, cultural, economic and environmental; forming a deputy secretaries group to oversee local–central government collaboration; and establishing a small group of advisers whose task was to facilitate the involvement of government departments in the community outcome process, essentially helping councils make contact with departments.

Not surprisingly collaboration was easier in some areas, particularly large urban jurisdictions, than others. One rural council, Rangitikei District Council, found it had little government presence in its district, so organised a seminar for relevant government departments in the capital, Wellington, at which a presentation on the council's community outcomes was given. The exercise engaged government officials in a conversation about the future of the district, including concerns highlighted by local citizens about the lack tertiary education opportunities, in a way that had never before occurred.

10.5 The problem of complexity

With the enactment of the LGA02, the LTCCP became councils' primary strategic planning document, with previous strategic plans essentially folded into the new framework. The LTCCP, however, is a consolidated framework with multiple objectives, only one of which could be said to be strategic planning; it also contains elements of a corporate plan, financial plan and accountability document. Consequently it faces the classic dilemma faced by any enterprise seeking to achieve multiple objectives; that is, it risks achieving none. The difference between the discretionary strategic plans prepared before 2002 and the multi-objective long-term council community plan is well illustrated by Ashburton District Council, a medium-sized council of approximately 30,000 residents situated in the centre of the South Island. The council's first strategic plan was published in 1995 and revised in 2000. Comparing the 2000 strategic plan with its 2009–2019 LTCCP illustrates the problem.

The 2000 strategic plan is a focused document containing the type of material you would expect in a strategic plan, namely:

- mission, vision, strategic goals, strategies and actions;

- an assessment of the targets achieved from the 1995 strategic plan;

- an environmental scan; and

- a description of the council's main activities, grouped under five strategic goals with key performance indicators.

The process used to adopt the strategic plan involved a series of elected member and staff workshops; consultation was not a statutory requirement. The plan was 31 pages long. In contrast, the 2009 LTCCP consists of 372 pages divided into two volumes. The content of the LTCCP includes:

- information about the council and its community;

- the results of the recent round of public submissions on the draft LTCCP (the LTCCP also acts as an annual plan in the year that it is adopted);

- a statement of community outcomes, strategic objectives and the council activities that contribute to each;

- the council's strategic vision (adapted from the 2000 strategic plan);

- a community outcomes monitoring report;

- a key issues and major projects section;

- a description of planned council activities grouped under five headings (similar to the strategic plan);

- a schedule of fees and charges;

- a financial strategy;

- financial policies (40 pages);

- a development contribution policy (23 pages);

- forecasting assumptions; and

- the Auditor General's report.

There are certainly significant strategic elements contained within Ashburton's LTCCP; however, they are spread throughout the 372 pages. Although councils have discretion as to how they structure their plans, and most attempt to separate out the 'strategic' content from the purely administrative and financial material, there is a constant risk that the strategic elements will be lost in the detail. While the Ashburton District Council attempts to address this risk by publishing a 'strategic' volume, this still stretches to more than 200 pages. Many councils have made the decision to divide their LTCCPs into discrete volumes to make them more accessible to readers, but the law requires that councils also publish a summary LTCCP. The summaries are the documents that most citizens read and respond to. They contain information on the major issues facing each community, a description of the community outcomes, major projects proposed by the council and a summary of the council's finances. While more accessible, and more obviously future-focused, the LTCCP summary is still some distance away from being a strategic plan.

Not surprisingly given the diversity of the local government sector, the New Zealand approach to community planning has resulted in variable practice. Some councils have sought to be innovative, collaborative and inclusive, while others have treated the exercise as a matter of compliance which simply gets in way of the important business of providing services. Part of the challenge facing councils is the complexity of the LTCCP itself, and the decision by parliament to aggregate diverse planning and accountability documents into the one process. While aggregation is attractive because it brings information and material together into one place, it risks overwhelming readers with the amount of information provided and encouraging a focus on compliance as opposed to innovation. Other countries have made different choices, and the next section discusses some of this international experience.

10.6 International experience

Jurisdictions with similar local government systems to New Zealand, and which require their councils to undertake strategic planning, include New South Wales (NSW) in Australia, England and South Africa.

10.6.1 New South Wales

In New South Wales, the *Local Government Act 1993* specifies the way in which councils should undertake their planning and reporting functions. The framework, which previously involved separate social and management plans, was recently amended to include a community strategic plan with a focus of ten or more years; a resourcing strategy that focuses on financial and asset management, as well as workforce planning; a four-year delivery programme covering the term of each elected council; and an operational plan which is essentially based on the budget, sets out in detail the individual programmes and activities that will be undertaken, and is reviewed annually. Councils must also adopt an engagement strategy, which determines their approach to engaging citizens and communities. One purpose of the framework is to draw existing plans together in an integrated framework, such as social, environmental and infrastructure plans.

Official guidelines describe the community strategic plan as the highest-level plan that a council will prepare, intended to identify the community's main priorities and aspirations for the future and plan strategies for achieving these goals (Department of Local Government 2010). As with New Zealand, there is no assumption that the council should be wholly responsible for the implementation of the strategic plan, as other partners – for example, state agencies and community organisations – are likely to have similar objectives and will need to take the lead on particular issues. Key features of the NSW community strategic plans include:

- the main priorities and aspirations for the future of the local government area;

- strategic objectives together with strategies to achieve those objectives;

- social, environmental, economic and civic leadership issues and how they will be addressed in an integrated manner;

- the social justice principles of equity, access, participation and rights; and

- due regard to the State Plan and other relevant state and regional plans.

Councils' community strategic plans must be reviewed every four years (local government has a four-year term in NSW), with reviews completed by 30 June in the year following local government elections. As noted above, plans are accompanied by a resourcing strategy comprising three other documents: a long-term financial plan; an asset management plan; and a workforce plan. The resourcing strategy is primarily, but not entirely, inward-focused on matters that are council responsibilities. While the long-term financial plans and the asset management plans are similar to the requirements found in New Zealand, there is no New Zealand equivalent to the workforce plan.

10.6.2 England

Under the *Local Government Act 2000*, councils in England were required to develop community strategies, later modified to become 'sustainable' community strategies.[9] The purpose of these strategies was to enhance the quality of life of local communities, as well as contribute to the achievement of sustainable development by improving the economic, social and environmental well-being of the area and its inhabitants (ODPM 2004). In order to meet this purpose, a sustainable community strategy was to:

- allow local communities to articulate their aspirations, needs and priorities;

- co-ordinate the actions of the council and of the public, private and community organisations that operate in the council's area;

- focus and shape existing and future activity of those organisations, so that they effectively meet community needs and aspirations; and

- contribute to the achievement of sustainable development with local goals and priorities relating, where appropriate, to regional, national and even global aims.

The legislation required a community strategy to include four components: a long-term vision for the area focusing on outcomes; an action plan identifying shorter-term priorities and activities that will contribute to the achievement of long-term outcomes; a shared commitment for implementing the action plan; and arrangements for monitoring and review (ODPM 2004). Compared with the approaches taken in New Zealand and New South Wales, the English approach was less concerned with the financial implications of its strategy and more focused on aligning agencies towards the achievement of identified outcomes – what might be described as a 'community governance approach'. An additional difference was the requirement to form local strategic partnerships (LSP), a joined-up approach with local agencies to develop and implement each community strategy. LSPs can be viewed as over-arching local institutions within a multilevel governance framework, and were mandatory if localities wished to access various national funding streams and to secure a whole-of-government response to addressing local priorities and targets. An example of good practice identified by the Egan Committee (ODPM 2004) was Manchester City. Its approach consisted of three tiers, ranging from regional to neighbourhood – see Table 10.1.

Sustainable community strategies can be described as a form of meta-governance; that is, umbrella processes designed to deal with the 'highly fragmented jungle of organisations and institutions which have grown up over the past two decades' (Geddes 2005: 6). By setting out the strategic vision for localities, community strategies provided a mechanism for addressing difficult cross-cutting issues. As indicated, when preparing strategies, councils were expected to consult with local citizens, communities and the voluntary, community and private sectors; to reflect the views of other partner agencies; to take into account key local and regional plans; and to have regard to the government's national sustainable development strategy. While the framework was very much the creation of the former New Labour government, the underlying concepts continue to apply insofar as they fit with the new government's approach to localism.

10.6.3 South Africa

Strategic planning in South Africa is guided by the *Municipal Systems Act 2000* (MSA 2000). It requires each municipal council to have a single, inclusive strategic plan for the development of the municipality (Section 25, MSA 2000). The emphasis on inclusiveness highlights the importance the government places on what it refers to as integrated development planning (IDP), essentially the preparation of a 'super plan' able to provide an overall framework for development.[10] The plans are required to consider the economic and social development of specific areas, with particular emphasis on how land should be used, necessary infrastructure and services, and environmental protection.[11]

IDPs must be prepared by all municipalities, but are not limited to municipal concerns. Other stakeholders – those who can impact on and/or benefit from

Table 10.1 The Manchester City approach

Tier One	Describes regeneration strategies, set at the level of each participating local authority, which connect opportunities for economic and infrastructure development to regional and subregional strategies
Tier Two	For each local authority, themed strategies and quality of life partnerships are developed, focusing on, for example, public safety, transport and housing
Tier Three	Operates at the ward or neighbourhood level, where the partnerships are brought together in various forms of joined-up service delivery initiatives

Source: ODPM (2004: 37)

development – must be invited to contribute. In this way the plan is intended to align and enhance co-operation between the three spheres of government – national, provincial and local. It seeks to promote policy coherence among agencies and across common issues. IDPs are therefore essentially an attempt to create a joined-up approach to tackling local, provincial and national issues (Padarath 2006). As well as alignment and integration within councils, and with external stakeholders, the plan is also a key mechanism for citizen participation.

The IDP is designed to be a comprehensive tool, with councils required to follow a standard process which begins, as with many strategic planning exercises, with the definition of a vision and mission; the identification of key objectives and priorities; and the development of strategies to address the issues and priorities identified (Padarath 2006). Like New Zealand's LTCCP, the IDP is expected to provide a context for all other municipal plans and projects, as well as influencing the plans of government departments in each area. It must be reviewed annually and has a lifespan of five years, consistent with the political term of councils. Thus, as in NSW, one of the first tasks facing each incoming council is the future of the IDP, which can be adopted, reviewed or amended.

The task of addressing cross-cutting and co-ordinating multiple stakeholders has, however, made the planning framework increasingly complex to manage. Padarath (2006) argues that harmonisation is made more difficult by the fact that federal and provincial governments operate on different timeframes to local governments; do not have a shared approach to analysis and information; and struggle to participate in a joined-up way. In other words sector priorities can often conflict with the goal of integrated planning, an issue which has also been identified with the LTCCP in New Zealand and its attempt to create a more joined-up approach to local governance (Leonard and Memon 2008; Local Futures 2006).

10.7 Balancing compliance and performance

Strategic planning frameworks have a number of common themes, including identifying community aspirations, articulating goals and priorities, and integrating existing plans and policies towards the achievement of those goals. Current thinking about strategic planning frequently eschews mechanical or rational approaches, which treat the exercise as a technical one of mapping out linear steps to goal achievement (Bryson 2004). Rather, strategic planning tends to be regarded as a more organic and pluralistic exercise, in which diverse values and goals are subject to compromise and adjustment. To be effective it requires effective engagement with citizens and stakeholder organisations, and a willingness to focus on a limited number of significant matters. This is an issue for the New Zealand strategic planning framework, given its multiple objectives and agglomeration.

The complexity and size of LTCCPs creates a challenge for councils that seek to engage citizens in strategic conversations about possible futures, a challenge recognised by the Office of the Auditor General (OAG). In its 2010 report on the 2009–2019 Long-Term Council Community Plans, the office highlights the importance of engaging communities in the 'right debate'. This, according to the office, involves consulting citizens on the major issues affecting their communities:

> An important role of the LTCCP is to provide information about significant issues facing a community so that the community can provide feedback on the choices facing it … local authorities still need to improve how they present and explain their financial strategies (OAG 2010: 9).

In the view of the Auditor General, information should be presented so that strategic and other major issues are presented first; choices and options for addressing the issues should be presented next; and these should be followed by the implications of those choices, namely implications for financial strategy, levels of service and impact on well-being. Only by engaging communities in a discussion on these strategic issues and their implications will the right debate be seen to have taken place. Yet the existence of the audit regime itself is not without effect. LTCCPs are subject to an audit opinion commenting on the underlying assumptions of the plan, financial efficacy and the accuracy and quality of its performance management system. The approach taken to the audit, and in particular the requirements of the International Financial Reporting Standards (IFRS), has diminished the ability of councils to promote strategic conversations with citizens, often because legislative compliance takes precedence over deliberative strategy.[12] Again, the size and sheer detail contained within the draft LTCCPs limits the ability of councils to engage in open-ended discussions of a strategic nature; the exception are those councils that go beyond the defined requirements of the LGA02 and develop 'bottom-up' strategies to engage citizens in discussions about their future.

Despite the OAG's desire to have councils focus on the 'right debate', it has also acknowledged the tendency of some councils to take a risk-averse approach. '… an LTCCP is a large document containing a great deal of detail. Therefore, local authorities need to effectively communicate the strategic and other important issues, choices, and implications so that these are readily apparent to the community' (OAG 2010: 10). Reflecting a similar theme, Leonard and Memon (2008), who based their analysis on the 2006–2016 LTCCPs, identified a number of shortcomings that diminished performance, namely:

- A failure by both local and central government to understand the full significance of the paradigm shift that was the LGA02. As a result the promise of the community outcomes process has not been realised.

- A failure to appreciate the importance of taking a participatory approach to the community outcomes process and to develop 'intermediate' outcomes which would better replicate the 'managing for outcomes' approach of central government departments.

- A failure to ensure those participating in the community outcomes process, such as elected members and staff, were adequately informed 'of the substantive issues in the community' (OAG 2010: xii).

- A lack of understanding, by the community and business sectors, about the collective ownership of community outcomes and a lack of resourcing for these sectors, including Maori organisations, to adequately participate in the process of identifying outcomes (ibid.: p xii).

Underpinning many of these concerns is a belief that councils were not given sufficient guidance to implement the new focus on outcomes adequately, and that there was a lack of national leadership to champion the new community outcomes paradigm, within both central and local government and in the community (Leonard and Memon 2008). It was suggested that the approach to framing outcomes taken by most councils resulted in 'high level outcomes [which] cannot provide effective tools for guiding local decision-making' (Local Futures 2006: 208). Local Futures also expressed concern that the majority of councils tended to use passive methods for identifying outcomes, such as surveys, rather than deliberative processes involving extensive citizen engagement, the result being akin to a list of issues, rather than a considered vision of the future.

The complexity and size of LTCCPs also has implications for the cost of preparing plans, with officials beginning work at least 18 months before adoption. A survey undertaken by Local Government New Zealand (the national association of councils) found that councils in total spent 897,629 hours on the preparation of their 2009–2019 long-term plans (LGNZ 2009).[13] It is an exercise that involves almost every aspect of a local authority's organisation, administratively and politically, a problem that began with the decision in 2002 to go with an aggregated model of planning. It is interesting to compare the New Zealand approach with that taken by the state of Victoria in Australia, in which councils' long-term financial strategies and strategic plans are stand-alone separate documents. The City of Bayside in Melbourne, for example, has a strategic planning framework that includes a number of stand-alone documents:

- the municipal strategic statement;
- the council plan/strategic resource plan (18 pages);
- budget (56 pages);
- an annual action plan (11 pages); and
- the Long-Term Financial Plan (86 pages).

In comparison to an average LTCCP, Bayside's strategies are clear and focused, with each placing emphasis on a single objective, resulting in documents that are easy to read and engage with.

New Zealand councils have sought to address the problems caused by the scale and complexity of the aggregated long-term plan by placing more emphasis on the community outcomes process, such as the process used by the Kapiti Coast District Council, or by enhancing the quality of the summaries. Yet aggregation has not only caused administrative challenges for councils and 'readability' challenges for citizens: it has also been less successful than some of its supporters had hoped in terms of integrating the plans and policies of other agencies.

In their work on community strategic planning, Leonard and Memon (2008) argue that both local and central government have failed to understand the full significance of the paradigm shift that was the LGA02. In their view the new emphasis on community well-being, sustainable development and participatory democracy has been overlooked, with the effect that the promise of the community outcomes process has not in fact been realised. In addition, councils faced challenges when seeking commitments from government departments and other agencies towards making outcomes real.

10.8 Strategic planning: where is it heading?

In a global world, cities and towns are forced to compete to attract new investment and skilled populations. Local authorities in particular must ensure that their localities have the physical infrastructure, amenities and social capital that make them attractive to skilled migrants. Strategic planning is critical if councils are to prepare their communities for the challenge of the future – it is one of the ways by which councils and communities differentiate themselves and make choices about the sort of place they wish to be. It is an essential tool for place-shaping (Lyons 2007).

Councils in New Zealand were quick to utilise strategic planning and related techniques as a way of better understanding the environment in which they work and the unique roles that local authorities play, and of identifying the objectives to which citizens and communities might aspire. Policy-makers saw the revision of the Local Government Act in 2002 as an opportunity to cement strategic planning into the fabric of the new statute. The decision was made to combine it with the previous requirement to develop long-term financial strategies, disclosure policies and a performance framework to create the LTCCP. The result was a plan that, while having strategic elements, was dominated by objectives primarily concerned with accountability, transparency and prudent stewardship of assets – a document that practice has shown as being relatively unwieldy and far from sympathetic to average citizens. The weight of the accountability requirements, in terms of the information collected and presented in the LTCCP, effectively hinders efforts by local authorities seeking to undertake innovative strategic planning.

To some degree the complexity of the LTCCP and its inhibiting effect on citizen engagement was identified by the National Party-led government elected in 2008. The then Minister of Local Government, the Hon. Rodney Hide, stated:

> The LTCCP purpose was to address strategic planning issues. However, most LTCCPs include large amounts of detail, have multiple volumes and contain hundreds of pages. Even with summaries documents of this size and complexity make it harder for ratepayers and citizens to engage on strategic issues (Hide 2009).

Unfortunately for the minister, his solution to improve transparency, accountability and fiscal management involved an inherent tension:[14] how do you deliver better engagement on strategic issues while also enhancing transparency, accountability and fiscal management? New Zealand has not yet found a solution to the multiple objectives issue. Councils already have the authority to go beyond statutory requirements and undertake good participatory strategic planning, and a number have shown themselves ready to use it. However, only a minority appear willing to go this extra mile, while the majority appear to be constrained by the scope of the statutory long-term plan and the degree to which it is subject to an inspection regime. The policy question that arises concerns the impact of specific frameworks on institutional behaviours, and the degree to which higher authorities are prepared to relax prescription to encourage both innovation and more 'bottom-up' approaches.

Strategic planning is essentially a technique to assist councils to think about and plan for the future of their communities. That local governments should be leading the strategic discussion in localities is not a new idea; they are ideally placed to foster and facilitate a place-based vision for their communities, as well as to promote alignment between public, private and third sector organisations. However, countries such as New Zealand, which have minimalist task profiles for local government, face unique challenges, as many of the significant players in their communities are national government departments, and their willingness to participate in local strategic conversations and be bound by desired local outcomes is far from certain. In addition, local strategic planning frameworks do not always align with strategic planning approaches taken nationally, and this is also the case in New Zealand. It is not easy to deliver future-focused strategic plans with minimal information on the future plans of higher-level governments and what they might mean for localities.

Finally, the success or failure of strategic planning will be heavily influenced by the manner in which higher governments 'craft' particular obligations. This chapter has highlighted the issue of aggregation and inspection as factors in the performance of the New Zealand framework, especially its ability to move beyond formal planning to the more deliberative practice of strategic thinking. The greater the degree to which strategic plans are seen as mechanisms for accountability and financial management and seek to achieve multiple objectives, the greater the risk that real 'strategy' will be pushed to the background.

Notes

1   The LGA 2002, in particular, took local government strategic plans and recast them as a significant accountability tool by focusing on asset management, long-term financial planning and a range of financial and performance disclosures. A more recent reform, the LGA 2002 Amendment Act 2010, sought to streamline the process but left the fundamental elements intact.

2   Reform reduced the previous 850 local bodies to 86 multi-functional local authorities, and introduced a range of internal reforms intended to strengthen transparency and accountability.

3   'Place-shaping' is the 'creative use of powers to promote the general well-being of a community and its citizens' (Lyons 2007: 60). Among its key features are building and shaping local identity; representing the community, including in discussions with higher levels of government; maintaining the cohesiveness of the community; making the local economy successful to support the creation of new businesses; and working with other bodies to respond to complex challenges – a form of community governance.

4   A 'spatial plan' as defined in the Local Government (Auckland Council) Amendment Act 2010 is meant to contribute to the social, economic, environmental and cultural well-being of the city through a comprehensive and long-term (20- to 30-year) city-wide strategy.

5   Other techniques include corporate planning, contestability and the separation of governance and administration.

6   One of the more symbolic actions of the new government was to insert the word 'community' into the title to reinforce the impression that the plan was not just the council's and that the council worked for the community.

7   Typically outcomes dealt with a desire for better health, safer communities and employment – all issues that are the responsibility of central government more than local government.

8   See: www.cobop.govt.nz (accessed July 2011).

9   It is understood that this requirement is being removed, but community strategies and the associated policy framework are nevertheless instructive examples of strategic planning practice.

10 See the Community Organisers' Toolbox, available at: www.etu.org.za/toolbox/localgov.html (accessed August 2011).

11 The framework has a number of similarities to spatial plans, which have been introduced in New Zealand's largest city, Auckland.

12 For example, councils are required to include future inflation assumptions in their long-term financial strategies, resulting in widespread concern from citizens who expressed their opposition to what appeared to be excessive future rate increases, even though up to half the figures were inflation estimates.

13 The survey was conducted by PricewaterhouseCoopers and had a participation rate of 70 per cent.

14 In 2010, the government made a number of changes to the LTCCP including shortening its title to Long Term Plan (LTP), removing the requirement to use a separate process to identify community outcomes and removing some of the less relevant policies from each plan in a bid to shorten the documents. Unfortunately the changes also added new material in order to improve accountability, which further extended the length of the documents.

References

Boston, J (1991), 'Re-organising the machinery of government: objectives and outcomes', in Boston, J, J Martin, J Pallot and P Walsh (Eds.), *Reshaping the State: New Zealand's Bureaucratic Revolution*, Oxford University Press, Auckland, 233–67.

Boston, J, J Martin, J Pallot and P Walsh (1996), *Public Management: The New Zealand Model*, Oxford University Press, Auckland.

Bryson, JM (2004), *Strategic Planning for Public and Non Profit Organizations: A Guide to Strengthening and Sustaining Organizational Achievement*, 3rd ed., Jossey-Bass, San Francisco.

Burke, K (2004), *Engaging with Communities over Outcomes: A Review of Innovative Approaches to meeting the LGA 2002 Challenge of Identifying Community Outcomes*, Local Government New Zealand, Wellington.

Cabinet Policy Committee (2001), 'Council planning and decision-making processes', POL Min (01) 12/17, 18 May.

Department of Local Government (2010), 'Planning a sustainable future: planning and reporting guidelines for local government in NSW 2010', available at: www.dlg. nsw.gov.au/dlg/dlghome/Documents/Information/IPRGuidelinesJanuary2010.pdf (accessed May 30).

The Economist (2009), 'Reforming the centralised state: the great giveaway', 31 October.

Geddes, M (2005), 'International perspectives and policy issues', in Smyth, P, T Redde and A Jones (Eds.), *Community and Local Governance in Australia*, UNSW Press, Sydney, 13–36.

Hide, R (2009), 'Improving Local Government Transparency, Accountability and Fiscal Management', Cabinet Economic Growth and Infrastructure Committee, Parliament, Wellington.

Leonard, L and A Memon (2008), *Community Outcome Processes as a Forum for Community Governance*, International Global Change Institute, University of Waikato, Hamilton.

Local Futures (2006), *Local Government, Strategy and Communities*, Institute of Policy Studies, Victoria University Press, Wellington.

Local Government New Zealand (LGNZ) (2003), *The Local Government Act 2002: An Overview*, LGNZ, Wellington.

LGNZ (2009), *Costs of Regulation on Local Government: Nature and Size of Compliance Carried by Regional and Territorial Authorities*, LGNZ, Wellington.

Lyons, M (2007), *Place-shaping: A Shared Ambition for the Future of Local Government Final Report*, The Stationery Office, London.

Naschold, F (1997), *The Dialectics of Modernising Local Government: An Assessment for the Mid-90's and an Agenda for the 21st Century*, Science Centre, Berlin.

Office of the Auditor General (2010), *Matters Arising from the 2009–19 Long-term Council Community Plans*, Controller and Auditor General, Wellington.

Office of the Deputy Prime Minister (ODPM) (2004), *The Egan Review: Skills for Sustainable Communities*, available at: www.communities.gov.uk/documents/communities/pdf/152086.pdf (accessed June 2011).

Padarath, R (2006), 'A process of integrated governance for integrated planning in South Africa', *42nd ISoCaRP Congress 2006*, available at: www.isocarp.net/Data/case_studies/871.pdf (accessed June 2011).

Rhodes, R (1997), *Understanding Governance: Policy Networks, Governance, Reflexivity and Accountability*, Open University Press, Buckingham, UK.

Thomas, S and A Memon (2007), 'New Zealand local government at the cross-roads? Reflections on the recent local government reforms', *Urban Policy & Research*, Vol. 25 No. 2, 171–85.

Chapter 11

The Role of Local Authority-owned Companies: Lessons from the New Zealand Experience

Peter McKinlay

This chapter explores the potential for greater use of local authority-owned companies and other council-controlled, arm's-length entities to manage local government assets and services. It looks at the opportunities, risks and implications for accountability and local democracy, with an emphasis on arrangements for post-incorporation governance. These are considered not just from the conventional perspective of good corporate governance including risk management, but also in terms of how they can contribute to strengthening local democracy and community participation in decision-making.

The chapter begins with a brief overview of experiences in Europe, England, Canada and Australia. It then discusses the unique model emerging within New Zealand, where there has been a particular focus on the post-incorporation governance regime. The origins of the New Zealand model are presented, together with a series of case studies and recent developments in the city of Auckland.

The considerable, and potentially beneficial, implications for the role of elected members and for enhanced local democratic accountability are also discussed. The chapter concludes with a discussion of the relevance of arm's-length entities to building local capability and strengthening community governance.

11.1 Local authority-owned companies: global examples

11.1.1 Europe

The use of local authority-owned companies in Europe varies widely between jurisdictions, as do attitudes towards the appropriateness of companies as vehicles for service delivery or other activity within democratically accountable organisations.

A 2005 survey by the European bank Dexia provided an overview of local government use of public companies within the then 25 countries of the European Union (Dexia 2005). It found that only in three countries – Luxembourg, Cyprus and Malta – did local governments not form companies as a means of undertaking part of their activity.

Some relatively common features emerge. It is usual for elected members and/or local civil servants to be appointed to the governing body of such companies. This can be seen as reflecting cultural and constitutional differences, identified by Torres and Pina (2002), between European and Anglo-Saxon jurisdictions, with Europeans being much more comfortable with the concept of elected members or senior managers sitting on the boards of council-controlled companies. Through European eyes this can be a useful way of ensuring appropriate alignment between the council owner and the company. By contrast, through Anglo-Saxon and especially Westminster tradition eyes, current good practice sees appointing elected members to boards as creating an inherent conflict of interest: the performance of the local authority's companies is placed in the hands of the very people who should be responsible for monitoring that performance.

Grossi and Reichard (2008) provide an overview of governance arrangements and practice for local authority-owned companies in Germany and Italy, where it is common for local authorities to own a number of companies: on average, large German cities own nearly 90 companies and large Italian cities own 25. Councils have autonomy in the decision on whether to establish companies, and there are no public sector-specific governance requirements. Instead, governance of council-owned companies is a matter for the general law.

Portuguese local governments only gained the power to establish companies in 1988. Tavares and Camões report that:

> … in Portugal, it is generally accepted that these new forms of local governance are the result of an attempt to improve financial management, relax public procurement rules and circumvent civil service laws and their implications for personnel management, contract agreements and organization. Rigorous controls imposed by national institutions such as the Accounting Court, the General Inspection of Territorial Administration and the General Inspection of Finances, as well as the requirements of civil service laws are avoided by these new forms of governance, even though this does not mean the complete subordination to general labour laws applied to the private sector (2010: 588).

Swedish experience reflects Torres and Pina's (2002) observations on different cultural and institutional understandings. Take for example healthcare services, which in Sweden are the responsibility of county councils. The late 1990s saw a strong emphasis on restructuring health service delivery in order to improve efficiency, increase access and reduce waiting times (Hjertqvist 2002). Central to the process of change, which included both the corporatisation and in a number of instances the contracting out or privatising of the provision of individual services, was that the basic values and individual entitlements of Sweden's public healthcare system should remain unchanged. Reforms were about changing incentives for people working within the system, including opportunities for employees to set up their own healthcare businesses, not about changing values or entitlements. This offers a key lesson for other jurisdictions: it is most important to ensure public confidence that the values on which a service is based will be maintained through the reform process, and the purpose of reform should be to reinforce the core values of the system (Hjertqvist 2002).

11.1.2 British Columbia, Canada

In British Columbia, the *Community Charter 2003* empowers municipalities or regional districts to form or acquire shares in corporations, but only with the consent of the Inspector of Municipalities.[1] In 2006 the Ministry of Community Services published

Launching and Maintaining a Local Government Corporation: A Guide for Local Officials, prepared with the support and direction of the inspector. The purpose of the guide is to assist municipalities in deciding to form a corporation, including whether that is the best means of pursuing the municipality's objective. The guide notes that, over the 30 years until 2005, 78 requests for the formation of corporations were received, of which only two had ultimately been declined. Requests covered a wide variety of activities, as detailed in Figure 11.1.

The guide is written primarily from a compliance rather than a policy/strategic perspective. It provides a useful counterpoint to the emerging New Zealand practice of treating council establishment and ownership of a corporation as fundamentally a matter of relationship management rather than legal compliance, albeit without understating the importance of compliance in its proper place.

11.1.3 England

In England, practice has varied significantly over recent decades. In the 1980s councils used provisions in the *Local Government Act 1972* to create companies for a wide range of purposes (Public–Private Partnerships Programme 2005). However, in the late 1980s the Conservative government established a complex regulatory regime restricting the use of companies, based on a combination of the nature of the company and a control test. The introduction of the 'well-being power', which authorised councils to do anything they believed would promote community well-being, by the *Local Government Act 2000* was seen as extending the ability of local authorities to create companies, but this was subsequently limited by the *Local Government Act 2003*, which restricted the power to form companies to those authorities meeting Best Value standards; in essence, the power to form companies became a reward for good performance. The power was also inhibited by litigation risk, as council decisions were subject to judicial review on the grounds of failure to follow due process.

The recently enacted *Localism Act 2011* includes a 'general power of competence'. This is described by the UK Department of Communities and Local Government as giving 'local authorities the legal capacity to do anything an individual can do that

Figure 11.1 Types of corporations considered by local governments, 1976 to 2005

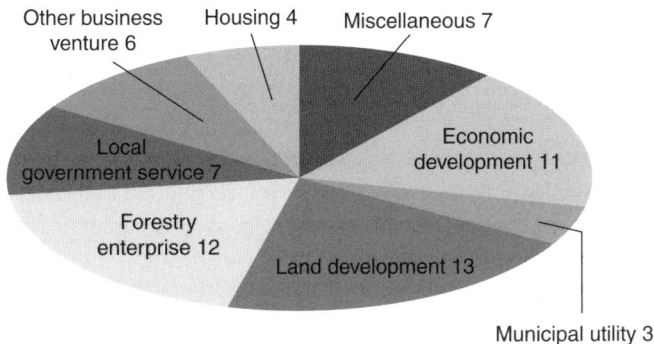

Source: Ministry of Community Services (2006)

isn't specifically prohibited; they will not, for example, be able to impose new taxes, as an individual has no power to tax'.[2]

Notably, the focus in the different legislative and regulatory provisions in England has been on a combination of the power to form companies, and the implications for local government financial management (Public–Private Partnerships Programme 2005). Much less attention has been paid to the governance of those companies, including measures which might be seen as desirable to mitigate potential risks associated with carrying out activities through a company form.

11.1.4 Australia

In Australia the power to regulate local government is reserved to the individual states. Legislation covering the formation of council-owned companies varies from state to state but only one, Queensland, makes any provision for post-establishment governance.

In Queensland two legislative regimes operate, one for the City of Brisbane and the other for local government generally. Both now include a power to establish 'beneficial enterprises'.[3] This requires a judgement by the council on whether any particular activity is 'beneficial', raising the prospect of judicial review, as occurred with the well-being power in England. This may act as a disincentive to use of the 'beneficial enterprise' model, although the responsible state government department does provide extensive guidance, which should minimise the legal risk.

The Queensland legislation is not specific that an enterprise should be a company; indeed it is clear that the local authority has the discretion to choose what legal form a 'beneficial enterprise' should take. In terms of post-establishment governance, the Queensland framework follows in broad terms the long-established New Zealand practice of requiring a statement of corporate intent, which sets out the objectives, operating principles, and reporting and accountability obligations that the entity will observe. However, these provisions have only been in place for a short period of time and it is too early to assess practice and outcomes.

11.2 Local authority-owned companies in New Zealand

Between 1984 and 1990 New Zealand's public sector underwent massive structural, organisational and management changes (Boston et al. 1991). The government embarked upon a comprehensive process of reform across the entire public sector, which included restructuring government trading activities as companies, known as state-owned enterprises (SOEs). At the heart of the reform process for the entire public sector, not just trading activities, was a focus on accountability and on developing incentive arrangements that were both appropriate to the nature of the activity, and which minimised any inherent conflicts.

Government ministers for their part were concerned that they could continue to exercise influence, despite the transfer from departmental to company form. As a consequence, a set of arrangements was designed to ensure that the directors of state-owned enterprises remained strongly accountable to shareholding ministers, and through them to the government. At the heart of these arrangements was what became known as a 'statement of (corporate) intent', negotiated between directors and shareholding ministers. The purpose of this document was to set out the business intentions, performance measures and reporting arrangements under which enterprises operate.

The role of the shareholding ministers is supported by a specialist monitoring and advisory unit located within the New Zealand Treasury.[4] The unit manages an annual cycle of monitoring and reporting (see Table 11.1). This begins with the outlook letter to each SOE board detailing the information requirements, the timing and any specific issues the company is expected to address during the business planning round. The board has to respond with first, a strategic issues letter outlining its perspectives, and later its business plan for the forthcoming financial year, plus a draft statement of corporate intent. Once those are agreed with the shareholder representative(s), the board is required to manage the business in accordance with the statement of corporate intent.

In the late 1980s, the government's reforming zeal turned to the local government sector. The same basic principles were applied, including legislating to enable the use of companies to manage trading activities. Three major categories of local government were affected: harbour boards and electric power boards, both of which were special-purpose authorities, and general-purpose local authorities.

11.2.1 Harbour boards and electricity distribution

The government's agenda reflected an economy-wide approach to reform based on a strongly held set of theoretical beliefs about the proper way of structuring and governing different types of activity. Its reforms of the two sets of special-purpose local authorities, harbour boards and electric power boards, were each part of a broader agenda of reforming a particular sector – transport and electricity respectively. In each case the government of the day was focused on putting in place a set of ownership, governance and accountability provisions which it believed would facilitate the effective governance and management of the business activities involved.

The commercial activities of both harbour boards and electric power boards were vested in new special-purpose companies for each. Ownership arrangements were complex, but for those that remained in public ownership, their governing legislation required broadly the same governance arrangements as for state-owned enterprises (McKinlay 1999).

11.2.2 General-purpose local authorities

The 1989 reforms of local government went much further than simply enabling councils to form companies: they included a substantial rationalisation of the number and scale of local authorities, a shift from cash to accrual accounting, marked changes in accountability and the introduction of a split between elected members, responsible for policy, and a chief executive (as the sole employer of staff), responsible for implementation.

Table 11.1 Accountability model for New Zealand state-owned enterprises

	Outlook letter	Strategic issues letter	Plan	Submit	Agree	Operate
Action	To SOE board From ministers (shareholders)	From SOE board To ministers (shareholders)	SOE completes internal planning	Business plan (draft) Statement of intent (draft)	Business plan Statement of intent	Manage business in accordance with the statement of corporate intent Quarterly reporting Other required meetings
Month	1	2	3 — 4	5	6: FY end	New FY start

Source: Adapted from the Owner's Expectations Manual, available at: www.comu.govt.nz/resources/pdfs/comu-oem12.pdf (accessed 17 February 2012), 18.

In respect of companies, new legislation provided for the formation of what were known as local authority trading enterprises (LATEs): council-owned companies that could undertake what were essentially the business activities of local authorities. The legislation required public consultation on any proposal to establish a LATE, and to transfer an undertaking to it. It also included basically the same requirement as existed for SOEs for the preparation of a statement of corporate intent, with which the board of directors must then comply.

For the most part, the government chose not to require local authorities to corporatise any activities. There were some exceptions, mainly in the transport sector. For example, councils that operated public passenger transport services, and wished to continue receiving government subsidy, were required to corporatise the services. This gave a greater assurance of transparency, which came from establishing the service as a separate entity with its own balance sheet and financial statements.

When New Zealand's Local Government Act was rewritten in 2002, the opportunity was taken to extend the coverage of the provisions affecting local authority-owned companies. Instead of LATEs, the new legislation uses the concept of council-controlled organisations (CCOs). These are defined as any entity in respect of which one or more local authorities owns 50 per cent or more of any equity, or is entitled to appoint 50 per cent or more of any governing body. This brought within the ambit of the legislation bodies such as local authority-controlled trusts, which had previously been established under the exercise of general powers to promote community development.

The SOE requirement for the preparation of a statement of corporate intent (termed simply 'a statement of intent' in the case of CCOs) was carried forward, but with some amendment. The members of a CCO board are required by legislation to run the entity in accordance with the statement of intent. In addition, the parent council or councils may amend the statement of intent by resolution at any time and the board is required to adopt that amendment. The statement of intent thus gives a council significant influence over any CCOs it owns.

11.2.3 Policy implications

Apart from setting the statutory framework, including the provision for the statement of intent, the government did not prescribe how local authorities should manage their relations with any companies that they owned or any other entities they controlled. Rather than requiring that councils should, for example, adopt the same general approach for monitoring and advisory support as the government itself had in place, it was simply left to individual councils to determine what they should do. Issues such as whether or not elected members could be appointed to the boards of council-owned companies or council-controlled trusts, the process for appointment of directors, the nature of dividend and other financial policies, and the nature of any reporting requirements over and above standard financial reporting, were all left to the discretion of individual councils.

With hindsight, this situation has been somewhat problematic. As will be clear from the brief case studies that follow, practice and understandings differed widely.

Few councils had available to them in-house the professional expertise and market knowledge needed to monitor the performance of what were often quite substantial businesses, notably some of New Zealand's largest ports and electricity networks. Instead, there has been considerable 'learning-by-doing', compounded by the fact that many of the most significant council-owned companies had come into existence not because of conscious decisions by councils that this was the appropriate way in which to run an activity, but because the government had directed restructuring as part of its own economic reforms.

Part of the learning process has been a gradual shift from the use of arm's-length entities purely as a presumed means of improving efficiency, to a greater understanding of the public value which different structures can add because of their inherent characteristics, so long as this value is properly understood and appropriate measures are put in place to secure the benefits sought. In this respect, the New Zealand approach can be seen as melding the presumed strengths of 'new public management' with 'public value' considerations.[5] This is emerging more clearly in respect of major local government activities as the result of recent experience in Auckland's CCOs, discussed later in the chapter.

11.3 Case studies

This section considers four New Zealand councils and one multi-council-owned company. The case studies highlight both the variety of approaches different councils have taken to the choice of structure and governance arrangements, and differences of practice in important areas of corporate governance, including managing conflicts of interest. They also illustrate the growing maturity of the model, with recent practice placing a strong emphasis on good corporate governance and relying significantly on the experience of central government with its SOEs, as well as the guidance of bodies such as the Institute of Directors.

11.3.1 Dunedin City Council

Dunedin City Council became the owner of a substantial council-owned company as the result of the *Energy Companies Act 1992*, which required the corporatisation of its then municipal electricity department. As a consequence of financial advice, the council decided to use a holding company structure, Dunedin City Holdings Ltd. At the same time it established Dunedin City Treasury Ltd to manage the council's borrowing and funding activity. This structure gave the council certain financial advantages, and took its borrowing outside the then regulatory arrangements for local authorities.

The energy company was restructured as two separate businesses:

- Aurora Energy Ltd, which owns the city's electricity distribution network and that of Central Electric Ltd (an adjoining company which it acquired by takeover); and

- Delta Utility Services Ltd, which undertakes network and other maintenance services for Aurora Energy and other service providers in the South Island.

Dunedin City Holdings Ltd also holds three other companies:

- City Forests Ltd, the owner of substantial forestry plantation interests;

- a half share of Dunedin International Airport Ltd, a joint venture with the New Zealand government; and

- Citibus Ltd.

The holding company, at the behest of its shareholder, has placed a strong emphasis on providing cash returns, sometimes to the detriment of its subsidiary companies, as its chairman's report in the annual report for the year ending 30 June 2010 makes clear:

> The strategy of the Dunedin City Holdings Limited board has been to pursue opportunities for growth where we see the potential to develop or extend our existing businesses. However, this year with the need to support the shareholder's capital expenditure programme the group's capital expenditure has been down (Dunedin City Holdings Ltd 2010: 4).

In 2011, the city council commissioned a governance review of the holding company and its subsidiaries. The resulting report (Larsen 2012: 9–12) made a number of critical findings, including:

- Conflicts of interest arising from the appointment of councillors on the board of the holding company, and appointment of holding company directors to the boards of subsidiary companies. In each case the central issue was placing people in a situation in which it was their obligation in one role to monitor their performance in another.

- Conflict between the council's objective of extracting maximum cash from the holding company and its subsidiaries, and the long-term needs of the businesses. A specific issue was the implicit challenge to the statutory obligation of directors to act in 'the best interests of the company'.

Recommendations included:

- No one should be both an elected member and appointed director on either the holding company or any subsidiary board. Council managers should be ineligible for director positions.

- The holding company and the council should adopt a standard dividend policy of paying out 50–70 per cent of tax paid profits.

- A review of all council-owned companies with the objective of determining their fit with council cash flow and 'risk appetite' boundaries. Any entity falling outside the boundary should be considered for sale.

- Provision of in-house governance training for elected council members.

The Dunedin experience is an example of what can happen when a council fails to give informed consideration to the good governance issues associated with being the owner of companies undertaking significant business activities (or, if it has given such consideration, to apply it). Dunedin was not the only council in which appointment as a director of a council-owned company was seen as an attractive addition to councillor remuneration, or which regarded its companies as a potential cash flow source to the detriment of the investment needs of the businesses. Arguably the concerns raised in Dunedin can be seen as a consequence of the failure to accompany a statutory framework for local authority-owned companies with adequate guidance on good practice in governance.

11.3.2 Christchurch City Council

As with Dunedin, the Christchurch City Council became the owner of significant council-owned companies through restructuring initiatives required as a result of central government legislation. This included the corporatisation of Christchurch's municipal electricity undertaking (which also absorbed the electricity undertakings of two nearby local authorities); the inheritance of a majority shareholding in the port of Lyttelton; corporatisation of the council-owned public transport undertaking; and ownership of 75 per cent of Christchurch International Airport Ltd (with the New Zealand government as the minority shareholder).

These entities are owned through Christchurch City Holdings Ltd (CCHL). Its website states that 'CCHL was set up in 1993 in response to calls for a confidential independent non-political buffer between the Council and the companies it owned. CCHL therefore ensures that a commercial approach is taken to managing the interface with the Council's companies' (CCHL 2012). Another factor in CCHL's establishment was the same financial analysis as led to the establishment of Dunedin City Holdings Ltd: the recognition that the use of a holding company structure would improve access to capital markets and potentially reduce borrowing costs for the council group as a whole.

Today, the principal companies in the CCHL group include:

- Orion New Zealand Limited (89.3 per cent owned), which owns and operates the electricity distribution network within Christchurch City and surrounding areas;

- Lyttelton Port Company Ltd (79.3 per cent owned);

- Christchurch International Airport Ltd (75 per cent owned);

- Red Bus Ltd (100 per cent owned), a major public transport provider within Christchurch; and

- Enable Services Ltd (100 per cent owned), a broadband provider.

CCHL has the strategic objective of 'playing a more proactive role in supporting the council's aim of making Christchurch a "world class boutique city" by investing in, or promoting the establishment of, key infrastructure assets in a commercially viable manner. Areas such as high-speed telecommunications, water, security of energy supply and integrated transport have been identified as key regional infrastructure priorities' (see CCHL website: www.cchl.co.nz/cchl/about-cchl [accessed 17 February 2012]).

CCHL management argues that long-term council ownership gives it an ability to make future-oriented investments in a way that might not be undertaken by a purely commercial owner. As an example, it supported the redevelopment of Christchurch International Airport five years ahead of the time at which conventional cost–benefit analysis would have suggested making the investment. From the CCHL perspective, and that of the parent council, the early investment was an important initiative in building Christchurch's attractiveness as a destination and point of entry to the South Island. Similarly, CCHL has become a significant investor in ultrahigh-speed broadband, having established Enable Services Ltd in 2007 to develop a broadband network. In 2011, the company became the government's partner in the rollout of its ultrafast broadband project in Christchurch.

11.3.3 New Plymouth District Council

New Plymouth provides an example of a council that has taken a deliberative approach to the use of CCOs, including considering the different reasons why a council might wish to use an arm's-length organisation rather than undertake an activity in-house.

The council's major involvement began with the compulsory corporatisation of its municipal electricity department. This was merged with the energy company serving the surrounding rural area, and the merged company then listed on the New Zealand stock exchange. When the company was first listed, the value of the council's shareholding was NZ$90 million. Ten years later the council sold its shareholding for NZ$259 million. During those years, the council had been supportive of a commercial approach to the management of the business, including its growth through acquisitions.

The sale proceeds were used by the council 'to set up a Perpetual Investment Fund to diversify its investment and retain it for all generations to come – many golden eggs in the basket' (Taylor 2010). To assist with the management of the fund, the council established a CCO, Taranaki Investment Management Ltd (TIML), initially in a purely advisory role, but latterly with an investment management capacity. TIML operates within a corporate governance framework designed to make clear the respective responsibilities of the council and the board. The council has adopted a policy on the appointment and remuneration of directors drawn substantially from private sector practice, and, to avoid conflicts of interest, councillors and managers are precluded from becoming directors.[6]

TIML is an example of a CCO with a structure designed to support and enable a fully commercial approach to the management of a significant activity, in this case an investment fund. The council itself recognises that CCOs may be formed for a number of different purposes, and that commercial performance is only one such purpose and not always the most significant. This reflects the fact that the CCO model is an extremely flexible one which allows elected members to determine what objectives they wish to optimise, and what trade-offs they wish to make; for example, between revenue/value enhancement, delivery of service, engaging the community in the governance of specific activities, or bringing in scarce skills not available through normal recruitment and employment means.

Among the council's other CCOs are special-purpose trusts in areas such as sports and event venues, and arts and cultural activities. One objective of these trusts is to recruit board members with particular skills, commitment and knowledge of the sector, who would not otherwise be part of the governance framework. In some of these activities, the use of a CCO can almost be seen as a means of facilitating co-production, bringing in essentially volunteer but expert people to support the facility concerned. The next case study provides a specific example of this approach.

11.3.4 Horowhenua District Council

Horowhenua is a small district council serving one significant township and an otherwise largely rural and coastal area with a number of smaller townships. Some years ago it acknowledged a resourcing issue with its library services, recognising that they were underfunded.

A decision was taken to create a council-controlled trust, with trustees drawn from the community and with the objective of enabling the library to draw on community resources and support in a way that would not be possible for the council itself. Based on the chairman's report in the trust's annual report for 2010/11 (see: http://issuu.com/joransom/docs/annualreport_2010_2011_final [accessed 12 March 2012]) that objective has been achieved. More importantly, the most significant benefit turned out to be the freedom to operate under its own governance structure, being responsible to people who are committed to the library service itself. As the trust website comments:

> In Horowhenua, library users have benefited from more money being spent on new books, libraries open for longer hours and extensions to the premises of one of our libraries. But the biggest advantage is a different attitude. We now have a more empowered approach to library service – if something is worth doing, we find a way to get it done (Horowhenua Library Trust 2012).

Innovations have included developing new open source software, Kete, for the management of small libraries, which is now in wide use internationally. Overall, Horowhenua's experience confirms that one of the real benefits of using arm's-length entities to undertake services that the community itself values is the unleashing of community and staff energy and commitment.

11.3.5 Bay of Plenty Local Authority Shared Services (BOPLASS Ltd)

BOPLASS Ltd is jointly owned by the eight 'territorial' (local) authorities and Regional Council across the Bay of Plenty region, plus two adjoining areas. It was established to promote the development of shared services among the partner councils. Relationships between council shareholders are governed by a shareholders' agreement.

The company structure was chosen quite deliberately in order to set a different incentive framework from more common local authority shared services arrangements, such as a joint committee. Typically, accountability is directly back to participating councils so that decisions taken around the 'board table' normally require a mandate from each partner. By contrast, BOPLASS operates on the principle that directors are responsible for the management of the company (a statutory provision which courts have held prevents shareholders from intervening in management), and have a duty to act in good faith in the best interests of the company, rather than the best interests of shareholders.[7]

The result is that BOPLASS has real power to act. The board has been developing a culture of decision-making which reinforces the understanding that the directors, who are either the chief executive or his/her nominee from each of the shareholder councils, act in accordance with their directorial responsibilities and not as a shareholder or customer representative. Participants report that this has a major impact on BOPLASS's ability to make decisions, especially in situations where one or more shareholder councils may not have been supportive of a particular course of action. Its ability to develop shared services initiatives has also been helped by other characteristics of the way BOPLASS operates, including:

- Rather than taking service delivery and control away from councils, it has adopted a 'centres of excellence' approach under which individual shared services will be developed by one of the shareholder councils and utilised by all.

- It has conceptualised the essence of shared services as being management of and access to information. Partner councils are linked by high-speed broadband and have real-time access to their own information wherever it is held. This removes the common fear that a shared services approach may result in a loss of control over a council's own information.

- A recognition that, even given the relative strength which directors have in a decision-making capacity, long-term success does depend on taking their council shareholders with them; it is not just a matter of maintaining shareholders' confidence in the board as such, but of retaining their support for utilising the initiatives which result from the company's activities.

11.4 Fast forward: the Auckland Council experience

One of the principal drivers for the recent sweeping reform of local government in the city and region of Auckland was the belief that existing council service delivery arrangements were relatively inefficient, often failed to exploit potential economies of scale and were unduly prone to direct political interference. This was considered by the Royal Commission on Auckland Governance, which without specifying particular services commented that 'the Commission expects that, in future, the Auckland Council's major commercial trading and infrastructure activities will be undertaken through CCOs, to enable the Council to access the best commercial and engineering expertise and resources' (Royal Commission 2009 volume 1: 13).

The government built on this suggestion. In creating a single unitary authority for the whole of the Auckland region, it determined that major commercial activities and major service delivery functions should be placed within council-owned companies.[8] This decision was strongly contested in public submissions on the legislation to establish the new 'super council', and in public debate through the media. Typical of this was an editorial in the *New Zealand Herald* for 14 March 2010, which observed that 'by their very nature, CCOs are designed to take control away from politicians and the public in the interests of greater speed and efficiency' and 'as matters stand, the CCO model is anathema to the idea of democracy and is not what anyone in the region signed up for'.

This reaction reflected an inherent distrust of corporatisation stemming from state sector reforms in the late 1980s and early 1990s. This made it easy for a public and a media, both predisposed to see corporatisation as a first step to privatisation, to assume that this was indeed the government's agenda. Little consideration was given to the possibility that the regulatory framework for CCOs could actually enable elected members to exercise more effective oversight, or to the likely alternative, namely that the activities involved would become large business units within the Auckland Council bureaucracy, reporting to elected members only through a single chief executive.

The remainder of this chapter will explore the details of the Auckland experience to date, including the extensive measures being taken to ensure that the seven CCOs not only remain accountable to the Auckland Council itself, but are also required to be publicly transparent in their deliberations (except when commercial confidentiality requires otherwise), and to engage closely with Auckland's 21 local boards. Lessons will be drawn for the use of this model within other councils and other jurisdictions.

First, however, it is useful to clarify the role of the Auckland Council itself. Despite the fact that much of its service delivery activity is now the responsibility of CCOs, it is the Auckland Council that remains responsible for policy. CCOs are explicitly required to comply with the terms of relevant Auckland Council plans, including its Long Term Plan, which sets out proposed activities, expected outcomes and budgetary arrangements. The legislation establishing the council includes power for it to require a CCO to prepare and adopt a plan covering a period of at least ten years that describes how the organisation intends to:

- manage, maintain, and invest in its assets;

- maintain or improve service levels;

- respond to population growth and other changing environmental factors; and

- give effect to the council's strategy, plans and priorities.

The seven major CCOs are:

- Auckland Council Investments Ltd, which holds the council's 22 per cent shareholding in Auckland International Airport Ltd, and owns 100 per cent of Ports of Auckland Ltd;

- Auckland City Properties Ltd, which owns and manages the council's general property portfolio;

- Auckland Tourism Events and Economic Development Ltd;

- Auckland Transport, a statutory corporation responsible for transport planning, local and regional roads and the delivery of public transport services;

- Auckland Waterfront Development Agency Limited, which holds the council's property interests in the city's downtown waterfront and is responsible for its ongoing development;

- Regional Facilities Auckland Limited, which owns and manages major arts, cultural and recreational facilities, including museums, art galleries, the city's zoo, stadia, event centres and theatres; and

- Watercare Services Ltd, which is responsible for bulk and retail water and wastewater services for the region (with one or two minor exceptions from legacy arrangements entered into by previous councils).

The *Local Government (Auckland Council) Act 2009* defines the seven entities as 'substantive CCOs'. Under the Act the council is required to adopt an accountability policy for substantive CCOs covering matters such as alignment between their activities and council plans, the council's expectations in terms of their contribution to government policy, and accountability to the wider community. The Act also requires that the board of each Auckland Council CCO must nominate two of its meetings during that year to be open to members of the public.

Arguably all of these requirements could have been imposed under the catch-all provision in the standard legislation for statements of intent for CCOs that covers 'any other matter agreed between the shareholder and the board' (clause 9, schedule 8, Local Government Act 2002). However, the government clearly recognised the need to respond to public concern that the CCOs might not be properly accountable, hence the additional legislative requirements.

The Act also prohibits the appointment of any elected member to the board of a substantive CCO, with the exception that two could be appointed to the board of Auckland Transport. Interestingly, it does not prohibit the appointment of any employee of the council.

The establishment of Auckland's seven CCOs is the first instance in which specific major restructuring of local government service delivery through the use of arm's-length entities has been imposed by central government. To ensure continuity of service delivery, the CCOs needed to be in place, with boards appointed, on the same date as the new Auckland Council came into office (1 November 2010). This meant that both the organisational design and the governance arrangements for the CCOs were put in place under government supervision, rather than being dealt with by the new Auckland Council. As a result, there was a strong public expectation that the new council would act to ensure that concerns about lack of accountability were immediately and effectively addressed.[9] The incoming council was aware that the performance of the CCOs would play a major role in the quality of its relationship with residents and ratepayers, because many of their transactions would be with one or more of the CCOs rather than with the council itself. This strengthened the incentive for elected members to ensure that individual CCOs were both responsive to the publics they serve and appropriately accountable. Thus the arrangements made for Auckland's CCOs inevitably saw a strong focus on the governance relationship between them and the council.

The council recognised the need for specialist advisory and monitoring services and established its own internal unit, complemented by a position in the mayor's office advising him on CCO-related matters. It has also largely adopted the practice followed by central government in establishing an annual accountability cycle between the council as shareholder and the CCOs. The annual cycle begins with a letter of expectations to the board of each CCO, setting out what the council expects over the next financial year. The letter serves as the basis for developing the statement of intent, which is to be delivered in draft form by 1 March and agreed by 30 June. The council has also followed central government practice by developing a shareholder's expectations manual, which provides the detailed background and rationale for the way in which the council will work with its CCOs, and the expectations which the council has of the relationships.

However, there is one significant difference from central government practice: a requirement that CCOs provide all necessary information in a timely manner to ensure council planning processes can be completed. CCOs need to provide financial information somewhat earlier than would be the case for SOEs in order to feed into council long-term plans and annual plans, first drafts of which are normally completed by December for the financial year beginning the following 1 July.

The organisational structure for Auckland Council also includes 21 elected 'local boards', which are intended to have an input into decision-making on local matters affecting the communities they represent. Those boards have a keen interest in the workings of the CCOs, and both the letters of expectation and the statements of intent for each CCO reflect a council objective that they will also be accountable to local communities. This applies particularly in the case of roads and transport.

The current letter of expectations for Auckland Transport requires it to have regard to transport-related matters identified in local board plans, and its statement of intent requires the development of a Local Board Engagement Plan.[10] The plan is to show how Auckland Transport intends to:

- support each local board to effectively represent the interests of local communities in local transport issues;

- ensure that Auckland Transport is responsive on local issues;

- contribute to the development of Local Board Engagement Plans;

- give effect to any Local Board Agreement to the extent the agreement requires actions by Auckland Transport; and

- gain input from local boards, via the mayor and councillors, on Auckland Transport's priorities and direction.

In practice it is now usual for a representative of Auckland Transport to attend each meeting of every local board in order to deal with transport-related issues.

11.4.1 Working with CCOs

Although it is still relatively early in the evolution of the relationship between the council and its new CCOs, experience suggests that the CCOs are now significantly more accountable to the communities they serve than were their predecessor councils. This is more than a function of the practices outlined above; it flows from the fact that, rather than being individual business units with financial statements and performance data often 'buried' within that for the council as a whole, each CCO now has its own separate financial statements and its own performance requirements against which it reports.

None of these provisions erase the difficulties of dealing with 'wicked issues' – for example, decision-making over a major infrastructure investment that may be beneficial for the region as a whole, but will have significant negative impacts on some localities. The processes in place for resolving those challenges lie outside individual CCOs themselves. They are found within the planning and accountability processes of Auckland Council, including its spatial plan and Long Term Plan. Complex challenges of necessity require a political response: structural change cannot by itself resolve inherent differences within a community.

Enhanced accountability is evidence of Auckland Council's constitution placing a strong emphasis on ensuring good governance. One possibly unanticipated consequence is the way in which this has changed the skills that both councillors and CCO board members need in order to function effectively within the new environment. The recent controversy surrounding Ports of Auckland Ltd (POAL), still unfolding at the time this chapter was written, illustrates this point.

POAL is wholly owned by Auckland Council Investments Ltd (ACIL), the council's investment CCO. As part of its statement of intent with the council, ACIL has agreed to quite aggressive targets for increasing port revenues and productivity. The board of POAL has determined that, in order to do so, it needs to put in place different employment arrangements for a large number of its staff – traditional waterside workers who have carried out the port's stevedoring work for many years. It is unclear whether the council was aware when it agreed to the statement of intent that the port company would see shifting to contracting-out to be an integral part of its strategy for meeting targets.

The immediate result of POAL changing its employment arrangements has been a serious and ongoing industrial dispute with the Maritime Union of New Zealand. The usual response within a council-owned business would be for political pressure to force a settlement protecting the status quo. In this case, however, Auckland Council has made it clear that dealing with the dispute is the responsibility of ACIL, and ACIL in turn has made it clear that managing the port business to achieve the required improvement in profitability and productivity is the responsibility of the POAL board.

Both those responses are consistent with the formal requirements of the CCO model, and both may be creating difficulties for elected members and directors respectively. It seems clear that elected members, including the mayor, had not foreseen the industrial dispute, or the widespread public support for the view that the council has an ultimate 'good employer' responsibility to the staff of its CCOs. It also seems that elected members may not have fully understood the powers they have to change the mandate for a CCO board, by amending the statement of intent either to rule out particular practices or to require changes in the way in which they are implemented.[11] Equally, it seems clear that the board of POAL has not sufficiently understood the sensitivities associated with public ownership. These include an emerging public value expectation that even commercial businesses owned by a council should act somewhat differently and in a more employee-friendly manner than private companies.

11.5 Reflections on the New Zealand experience

There are four separate elements of the New Zealand experience which merit reflection, both for the ongoing development of the CCO regime within New Zealand and to offer lessons for local government in other Westminster jurisdictions. These relate to corporate governance; monitoring and support; accountability; and flexibility/co-production and capability development.

11.5.1 Corporate governance

The private sector has evolved its understanding of best practice in corporate governance over a number of years, beginning with the UK's Cadbury Report (Cadbury et al. 1992). The result is that expected practice and understanding of the separate roles of shareholders, directors and executive management are now well embedded in the sector. Issues such as conflict of interest, the obligation of directors to act in the best interests of the company and the importance of accountability are all now part of 'this is how we do things around here' for well-performing boards.

In New Zealand, that practice has been largely embedded in the SOE environment. This is in part because of the use of a specialist monitoring and advisory unit, and in part because the shareholder's representatives (government ministers) are common for all major SOEs. In contrast, there is no consistency of practice as yet within local government.

As noted earlier, New Plymouth District Council's *Director Remuneration and Appointment Policy* prohibits the appointment of elected members or staff as directors on the grounds of conflict of interest. In contrast, Dunedin City Council's policy allowed the appointment of elected members or staff, and the appointment of elected members has been a common practice.

New Plymouth has benefited significantly through the high performance of its fund manager, Taranaki Investment Management Ltd, and its recruitment of independent directors. Dunedin City Council encountered something of a crisis in the management of its CCOs as the result of a policy of treating the parent council's cash requirements (including minimising property tax increases) as a priority over and above the need for the CCOs to invest in the continuing development of their businesses. This approach was seen to be facilitated by the presence of elected members on the board of Dunedin City Holdings.

However, local government practice does appear to be evolving towards recognising the importance of good corporate governance. As a result of the Larsen review (Larsen 2012), Dunedin has moved away from appointing elected members. In Auckland, there is a statutory prohibition in respect of substantive CCOs.

Related to the question of good corporate governance is that of how monitoring and advisory services are provided, especially in terms of reconciling the broader objectives councils may have with the demands of running a commercial enterprise. The need for appropriate training for elected members is also now being recognised – it was one of the recommendations to the Dunedin City Council in the Larsen review.

This need is emphasised by the Auckland Council's experience with the POAL dispute. It seems clear that elected members are still on a relatively steep learning curve in terms of the powers they have, and how they should be exercised. It is also clear that at least some CCO directors need to better understand how best to operate in a public ownership environment.

None of this is to suggest that the model itself has any inherent defects. Rather, because the very purpose of the CCO model is to put a much greater emphasis on the nature and quality of performance, it needs to be complemented by ensuring that the people involved, especially elected members, have the necessary understanding and experience.

11.5.2 Monitoring and support

Monitoring of CCOs and support of shareholder councils in managing their relationships with them is a highly skilled and specialist activity. Frequently CCOs are engaged in activities that are at the leading edge in terms of technology, regulatory innovation or business practice. Examples within the local government environment include electricity undertakings, investment management and transport.

The central government recognised early on that monitoring and support of SOEs (including advice on the appointment of directors) required specialist capability and a critical mass of activity, both to attract and retain skilled advisors, and to ensure that they remained aware of developments within their areas of responsibility. It also recognised the merits of applying a consistent approach across a portfolio of SOEs to minimise, for example, the potential for conflicts of understanding about required performance and how that might be measured.

There is no equivalent for local government, in part because the central government simply left it to local authorities to establish whatever arrangements they saw fit. This helps explain why different councils have different approaches on issues such as conflict of interest, the eligibility of elected members to be appointed to boards, and how to measure the performance of entities that may undertake similar activities but have different local government owners.

One lesson from the New Zealand experience is that other jurisdictions contemplating a similar approach should consider establishing a monitoring and support service for councils. This will help provide the critical mass required for effective performance of the role, which most councils would find difficult to support as a stand-alone activity. It would also ensure a useful measure of independence from any one council.

11.5.3 Accountability

Accountability has been one of the most interesting and in many ways exciting aspects of New Zealand's CCO regime. The conventional wisdom has been that placing public sector activity within a company structure undermines community accountability. In the words of the *New Zealand Herald* editorial, 'by their very nature, CCOs are designed to take control away from politicians and the public in the interests of greater speed and efficiency' (*New Zealand Herald* 14 March 2010). This comment reflects both public understanding of the nature of companies as a means of undertaking activity, and experience from New Zealand's state sector corporatisation and privatisation in the late 1980s and early 1990s.

In contrast, a close examination of the CCO model suggests that it may be the best option for combining production efficiency with a public value approach. The CCO model provides comprehensive provisions for public accountability. It requires that councils have a good understanding of corporate governance, and of the reasonable measures that need to be in place for the monitoring and oversight of arm's-length entities. This should result in greater accountability, including the strengthening of local democracy. Reasons for this improvement include:

- The CCO activity, rather than being a business unit potentially buried within 'whole-of-council' reporting, has its own separate legal identity, balance sheet, financial statements and performance measures, both financial and non-financial. The result is an improvement in transparency.

- The CCO is directly accountable to elected members, rather than being accountable through the council chief executive, along with all the other matters for which the chief executive is responsible. The terms of the statement of intent are negotiated between elected members and the CCO board (typically with the support of advice from officials, as in the case of the Auckland Council with its specialist governance and monitoring unit).

- The statement of intent process provides the means for elected members to look not just at standard financial/commercial performance, but also at other potentially non-commercial outcomes. Additionally, the process ensures that any non-commercial outcomes are transparent and appropriately costed.

- The statement of intent can, as with Auckland's CCOs, include specific requirements for involvement with local communities.

- Finally, the incentives that elected members face are quite different between CCO structures and council business units. With a business unit the incentive for elected members is to resist transparency, because they are likely themselves to be held responsible for any shortcomings in performance. In a CCO structure the incentive is reversed. Elected members become accountable for ensuring that CCOs either achieve expected performance or explain to the council and the public why they have not done so.

11.5.4 Flexibility/co-production and capability development

Not all CCOs are inherently commercial in their purpose, or responsible for the management of large assets on behalf of a council. CCOs also include a number of trusts and other non-commercial entities responsible for managing services, where there is a strong public or merit good element. Often the rationale for using a CCO structure is to engage the community itself, both in terms of governance and other involvement (such as volunteering to help with arts, cultural or recreational facilities), and to strengthen resourcing (as with the Horowhenua Library Trust). CCOs can play an important role in developing capability within the community by providing an opportunity for people to take part in the governance of community-focused entities.

Finally, as the BOPLASS case study shows, CCOs can help bring about much needed change in the culture of engagement within and between local authorities, and thus help break down persistent barriers to new ways of delivering services.

11.6 Conclusion

The New Zealand experiment with the use of CCOs is still in its early stages. There are obvious areas for further development in terms of building common understandings of corporate governance, accountability and what is required for effective monitoring and support. Despite this, it represents the most successful regime among Westminster jurisdictions for post-establishment governance of local authority-owned entities, not just in the commercial sphere but as a means for improving community engagement and facilitating co-production. It is well worth close examination by other jurisdictions considering whether to create, extend or review the power of local authorities to undertake activity through companies or other arm's-length entities.

Understanding the New Zealand process depends on recognising that the focus of the post-establishment regime should be on separating political and performance accountability. It is the elected members who make the political judgements about the operating objectives and framework for the CCO. It is the board of the CCO that has the performance accountability for determining how to deliver within the framework established in agreement with elected members. The model is both flexible and relationship-based. Fully understanding its potential requires setting aside conventional perceptions of the operation of the different corporate forms which an arm's length-entity may take (especially the company form), and focusing instead on the potential of the model to balance political and performance accountability in a way which reinforces both.

Notes

1 A statutory official who has a variety of approval and oversight functions in relation to local government.
2 See: www.communities.gov.uk/localgovernment/decentralisation/localismbill/keymeasures/ (accessed 12 March 2012).
3 The original City of Brisbane Act gave the council a power of general competence, which enabled it to form companies without further authority. The rewritten Act is accordingly more restrictive.

4 Formerly the Crown Companies Monitoring and Advisory Unit; now the Crown Ownership Monitoring Unit.

5 It should be noted that a public value approach has been much more evident, although not necessarily clearly articulated, in the use of council-controlled trusts than in council-controlled companies. For a useful discussion of the shift from new public management to public value see O'Flynn (2007).

6 See the council's policy on Appointment and Remuneration of Directors of Council Organisations, available at: www.newplymouthnz.com/CouncilDocuments/Policies/AppointmentAnd RemunerationOfDirectorsOfCouncilOrganisations.htm (accessed 20 February 2012).

7 Interpretation of the duty has been a matter of case law rather than statute. For a recent discussion of the duty as it applies in Australia (and would in New Zealand), see: http://corporatelawandgovernance. blogspot.co.nz/2008/11/australia-directors-duty-to-act-in-best.html (accessed 21 November 2012). In England the law was recently and controversially changed so that a director of a company must act in a way that he considers, in good faith, would be most likely to promote the success of the company for the benefit of its members as a whole, and in so doing, to have regard to a number of other interests, including those of stakeholders (see Keay 2010).

8 This still left the Auckland Council itself with a significant range of functions, including spatial, environmental, transport and land-use planning, local regulation, building control, libraries, local and regional parks and overall corporate and strategic planning for the Auckland Council group, including CCOs.

9 In some respects this was a less daunting task than it may have appeared, because a number of the concerns were relatively ill founded – largely because the public did not understand the full range of tools that the council had available to it for ensuring effective control over its CCOs.

10 These requirements are common to each of the seven CCOs.

11 At the time of writing the advice that elected members had received was still confidential, so these comments are necessarily somewhat speculative.

References

Boston, J, J Martin, J Pallot and P Walsh (Eds.) (1991), *Reshaping the State: New Zealand's Bureaucratic Revolution*, Oxford University Press, Auckland.

Cadbury, A et al. (1992), *Report of the Committee on Financial Aspects of Corporate Governance*, available at: www.ecgi.org/codes/documents/cadbury.pdf (accessed 23 February 2012).

Christchurch City Holdings Ltd (2012), CCHL website, available at: www.cchl.co.nz (accessed 17 February 2012).

Crown Company Monitoring and Advisory Unit (2007), *Owner's Expectations Manual*, available at: www.comu.govt.nz/resources/pdfs/oem-soe-07.pdf (accessed 17 February 2012).

Dexia, C (2005), *Local Public Companies in the 25 Countries of the European Union*, available at: www.lesepl.fr/pdf/carte_EPL_anglais.pdf (accessed 27 January 2012).

Dunedin City Holdings Ltd (2010), Annual Report for year ending 30 June 2010, available at: www.dunedin.govt.nz/__data/assets/pdf_file/0010/167680/DCH-annual-report-2010.pdf (accessed 11 March 2013).

Grossi, G and C Reichard (2008), 'Municipal corporatization in Germany and Italy', *Public Management Review*, Vol. 10 No. 5, 597–617.

Hjertqvist, J (2002), *The Health Care Revolution in Stockholm; A Short Personal Introduction to Change: Timbro Health Care Unit*, available at: www.timbro.se/ bokhandel/health/pdf/75665263.pdf (accessed 15 February 2012).

Horowhenua Library Trust (2012), Horowhenua Library Trust website, available at: http://kete.library.org.nz/trust/topics/show/270-horowhenua-library-trust-and-trustees (accessed 17 May 2012).

Keay, AR (2010), 'The duty to promote the success of the company: is it fit for purpose?', University of Leeds School of Law, Centre for Business Law and Practice Working Paper, available at: http://papers.ssrn.com/sol3/papers.cfm?abstract_id=1662411 (accessed 21 November 2012).

Larsen, W (2012), *Governance Review of All Companies in which Dunedin City Council and/or Dunedin City Holdings Ltd Has an Equity Interest of 50% or More*, available at: www.dunedin.govt.nz/__data/assets/pdf_file/0018/208053/Larsen-Report-February-2012.pdf (accessed 17 February 2012).

McKinlay, P (1999), *Public Ownership and the Community*, Institute of Policy Studies, Victoria University of Wellington, New Zealand.

Ministry Community Services (2006), *Launching and Maintaining a Local Government Corporation: A Guide for Local Officials*, available at: www.cscd.gov.bc.ca/lgd/infra/library/Local_Government_Corporations_Guide.pdf (accessed 16 May 2012).

New Zealand Herald (14 March 2010), 'Editorial: CCO plan mocks democracy', available at: www.nzherald.co.nz/boards-and-governance/news/article.cfm?c_id=133&objectid=10631829 (accessed March 2013).

O'Flynn, J (2007), 'From new public management to public value', *Australian Journal of Public Administration*, Vol. 66 No. 3, 353–66.

Public–Private Partnerships Programme (2005), *Local Government Powers*, available at: www.google.co.nz/#hl=en&cp=36&gs_id=57&xhr=t&q=%22Local+government+powers%22+%2B+Pinsents&pf=p&sclient=psy-ab&source=hp&pbx=1&oq=%22Local+government+powers%22+%2B+Pinsents&aq=f&aqi=&aql=&gs_sm=&gs_upl=&bav=on.2,or.r_gc.r_pw.,cf.osb&fp=b5292a12d630202&biw=939&bih=583 (accessed 26 January 2012).

Royal Commission on Auckland Governance (2009), *Auckland Governance Report, Volume 1*, available at: http://ndhadeliver.natlib.govt.nz/delivery/DeliveryManagerServlet?dps_pid=IE1055203 (accessed on 11 March 2013).

Tavares, A and P Camões (2010), 'New forms of local governance', *Public Management Review*, Vol. 12 No. 5, 587–608.

Taylor, S (2010), '"CCOs: governance at a distance – how close is close enough?": the Taranaki Investment Management Limited story', Governance – Panel Presentation at New Zealand Law Society Local Government Intensive, 20 August.

Torres, L and V Pina (2002), 'Delivering public services – mechanisms and consequences: changes in public service delivery in the EU countries', *Public Money and Management*, Vol. 22 No. 4, 41–8.

Chapter 12

The Evolving Role of Mayors: An Australian Perspective

Graham Sansom

This final chapter[1] revisits some of the principal themes of this book through the lens of the role of mayors. In so doing it reflects Quirk's (2011: 137) view that:

> *Elected politicians set the tone for public institutions. The style and substance of their leadership is central to how public institutions are viewed by their staff, their service users and their stakeholders. Their conduct and their behaviour set the atmosphere, the microclimate in which the institution functions. Their role in governing the institution is vital – they lead, they speak for the public, and they choose direction and strategy. They set the intent of policy and they also choose the instrument of policy. They decide what is to be done and often how it is to be done.*

The early years of the twenty-first century have seen significant developments in the role of mayors in several Commonwealth countries. For example, legislation has provided for mayors with substantial executive powers in both England and South Africa; in New Zealand, the mayor of the new Auckland 'super city' has been handed considerably greater responsibilities and authority than his counterparts across the rest of the country; while in Australia recent or proposed legislative amendments in three states have reflected emerging ideas on this issue.

Discussion here focuses on the Australian experience, but with reference also to recent practice and debates in England and New Zealand. The chapter draws on literature, case studies and interviews with mayors,[2] senior local government managers and commentators in each of the three countries, and seeks to:

- place emerging practice within a conceptual framework of governance, strategic planning and leadership;

- summarise the 'state of play' in Australia;

- consider the lessons to be learned from recent developments in England and New Zealand; and

- develop a model for directly elected, (semi)executive mayors that would be appropriate across Australia and might usefully be applied elsewhere.

Over recent decades, Australian local governments have been subject to wide-ranging reforms imposed or urged by the state governments that establish and control them (e.g. Marshall 2008; Australian Centre of Excellence for Local Government [ACELG] 2011). These have focused on structure and efficiency (amalgamations, regional collaboration and resource sharing); aspects of the New Public Management (separation of powers between the body politic and management, councillors as a 'board of directors'); strategic and corporate planning (requirements for long-term strategic plans and 'delivery programmes', improved asset and financial management, workforce plans); greater community engagement and accountability (in part through community-focused and place-based strategic planning); and corporate governance (probity, risk management).

However, little attention has been given to how the intended direction of these reforms – especially the pursuit of efficiency, effectiveness and community engagement through strategic and corporate planning – interacts with frameworks for political and community governance. Changes to local government Acts over the past two decades have largely adopted (and adapted) the managerialist provisions of equivalent New Zealand legislation. There too the issue of political governance appears to have received scant attention, at least until the recent creation of the Auckland 'super city' (see below).

This contrasts markedly with the strong focus on trends in local politics evident in the United States, United Kingdom and Europe. In those countries, particular attention has been given to the role of directly elected mayors, and there has been extensive debate about, among other things, how the functions of mayors should be structured and evolve, as well as the relative merits of different models of governance (e.g. Svara 2006; Borraz and John 2004; Elcock and Fenwick 2007).

12.1 Governance, planning and leadership

Recent trends in the election and role of mayors have reflected the widening international discourse on local governance and civic leadership. New functions and enhanced authority for mayors are part of broader changes sweeping through local government. These include the increasing emphasis on *governance* as opposed to *government*; the introduction of new forms of strategic and corporate planning; the growing importance of closer engagement with a broad range of stakeholders – notably local communities, nearby councils and central governments; and the perceived need for stronger political and community leadership. There is now an extensive literature on these issues, some of which has been canvassed in previous chapters. What follows is a brief summary of some key themes that are taken up in later sections of this chapter.

In Australia, an early discussion of local and community governance was provided by Sproats (1997). He argued that the 'largely instrumental reform agenda' of the time – focused on local government's role as a service deliverer, efficiency and effectiveness in achieving outcomes, performance excellence and value for money – needed to be balanced by 'engagement of an informed citizenry in collectively solving community problems' (ibid.:3). Better local management should thus be matched by better local governance, with greater emphasis on local people and social, as well as physical and financial, capital. Sproats applied Osborne and Gaebler's (1993: 24) definition of community governance as 'the process by which we collectively solve our problems and meet our society's needs'. His ideas are summarised in Figure 12.1.

More recent thinking about governance has focused on the increasing fragmentation of public and democratic institutions (Borraz and John 2004: 110) and the perceived

Figure 12.1 Sproats' components of local governance

Better local management	
Corporate governance	+ Community governance
Customers/clients	+ Citizens
Management	+ Leadership
Public opinion	+ Public judgement
Financial and physical capital	+ Social capital
	= Better local governance

Source: Modified from Sproats (1997: 5)

inability of governments to address all the complex issues and 'wicked' problems facing modern societies, especially in a globalised world. Hambleton (2011: 13) thus argues that 'governance'

> ... involves government plus the looser processes of influencing and negotiating with a range of public and private sector agencies to achieve desired outcomes. A governance perspective encourages collaboration between the public, private and non-profit sectors ... Whilst the hierarchical power of the state does not vanish, the emphasis in governance is on steering, influencing and co-ordinating the actions of others.

This view of governance, in turn, highlights the importance of partnerships, planning and leadership. Collaboration – partnerships – requires a foundation, a basis for agreement on what needs to be done and how to go about achieving agreed objectives: in other words, a plan. At the local level, the tenets of urban and regional planning, environmental conservation and the New Public Management were already being applied in the later years of the twentieth century to require local governments to prepare a range of strategic and corporate plans. It was a short step to apply such planning concepts to a partnership approach to governance, thus giving rise to mechanisms such as long-term 'whole-of-community' and 'whole-of-government' strategic plans, and multisector partnerships. Previous chapters have outlined initiatives such as New Zealand's Long-Term Council Community Plans and 'Community Outcomes' process; South Africa's Integrated Development Plans; and Local Strategic Partnerships and 'Total Place' in the UK.

These models suggest a need for what has been described as local 'facilitative leadership' (Stoker et al. 2007) in order to:

- engage the community and other local stakeholders in the planning process;

- negotiate with central government agencies and neighbouring local governments;

- secure political support within the council for the adoption and concerted, consistent implementation of strategic plans and associated budgets; and

- maintain ongoing partnerships with others involved in implementation, especially sound intergovernment relations in which the local voice is heard and respected.

Hambleton (2011) has added the notion of 'place-based leadership'. This refers to the importance of concerted action by a range of players at the local level to counterbalance potential adverse impacts of 'place-less' leadership: globalised corporations and central governments that may care little for community well-being and the qualities of local places. Hambleton (2009: 538) has also set out indicators of good political leadership that draw together the various concepts of governance and leadership outlined above (Box 12.1).

A further consideration is how the different players in local governance each contribute to civic leadership. Hambleton (2009: 522–523) argues that civic leadership comprises three important groups: political (elected), managerial and community (civil society) leaders. However, as Sproats (1997: 8–9) makes clear, while management and leadership should be complementary, the central tenets of the two are quite different. Managers may be good leaders, but the skills of community leadership – even when exercised in part by managers – are inherently political (see Figure 12.2).

This leads to the question of whether a 'separation of powers' is meaningful and appropriate in the local government context – the idea that elected members should

---

Box 12.1 Indicators of good political leadership

- **Articulating a clear vision for the area**

Setting out an agenda of what the future of the area should be and developing strategic policy direction; listening to local people and leading initiatives

- **Promoting the qualities of the area**

Building civic pride, promoting the benefits of the locality and attracting inward investment

- **Winning resources**

Winning power and funding from higher levels of government and maximising income from a variety of sources

- **Developing partnerships**

Fostering a range of partnerships, both internal and external, working to a shared view of the needs of the local community

- **Addressing complex social issues**

Taking the broader view and bringing together the right mix of agencies to tackle a particular problem

- **Maintaining support and cohesion**

Managing disparate interests and keeping people on board

Source: Adapted from Hambleton and Bullock (1996)

Figure 12.2 Comparing management and leadership

Management	Leadership
Plans and budgets	Vision and strategy
Organising and staffing	Communicating and aligning
Controlling and problem solving	Motivating and inspiring
Minimising risk	Taking risks

Source: Based on Sproats (1997: 9)

set policy and strategy and monitor performance, while management should be otherwise left alone to deal with implementation of policies and plans and service delivery. It is debatable whether such an approach is either workable or desirable given the often fine line between policy and practice across many local government functions, the often small scale of local authorities, the representative role of elected members in addressing specific community and individual needs, and the valuable skills and local knowledge elected members may offer in support of management (e.g. Munro 2000; Sansom 2001; Svara 2006). Hambleton (2009: 532–533) provides a brief overview of recent research on this issue and describes the idea of a sharp separation of roles between politicians and officers as a 'longstanding myth'. Following Peters (1995), he suggests that the 'dichotomy idea shields administrators from scrutiny and serves the interest of politicians who can pass responsibility for unpopular decisions to administrators'.

12.2 Australian context and practice

A key distinguishing feature of Australian local government is its diversity. Australia currently has around 560 local councils: the count varies slightly depending on whether or not some non-elected special purpose bodies are also included. Because Australia is a federation, those councils are divided into seven different systems: one for each of the founding states plus an emerging system in the Northern Territory.

Over time the total number of councils has fallen dramatically due to amalgamation and/or restructuring of local government areas. As a result, the average population of Australian local governments is now around 40,000 – small by comparison with the United Kingdom or South Africa, but considerably larger than across much of Europe. However, this masks a huge diversity in size of both populations and geographical areas: there are still many rural and remote local government areas with populations of fewer than 5,000, but also some 50 large urban centres with populations in excess of 120,000, including Gold Coast City with more than 500,000 and Brisbane City with more than 1 million. This diversity militates against 'one size fits all' approaches to issues of roles, responsibilities and governance, even within state or territory systems.

Since the 1990s, increasing emphasis has been placed on the potential for larger units to improve the capacity and viability of local governments, notably in relation to the widespread restructuring that took place in Queensland in early 2008 (Local Government Reform Commission 2007). This is linked to a growing expectation that local government will contribute to the achievement of national- and state-level policy goals, such as regional development, addressing climate change, reducing indigenous disadvantage etc. Since the late 1970s, the federal government has been the largest external provider of funding for local government, and there has been progressively closer engagement between the two. Local government is now represented on the peak federal forum, the Council of Australian Governments, alongside the federal government, states and territories. It also has a seat in a number of intergovernment ministerial councils dealing with different aspects of public policy. This implies a need for more capable local governments that can make a substantial contribution to tackling complex local, regional and intergovernment agendas.

As noted earlier, a great deal of attention has been given to what these changing expectations of local government might mean in terms of structures, strategic planning and various aspects of corporate management, but the need for new approaches to political governance has received little consideration. Here too, the Australian scene is marked by enormous diversity: ratios of electors to councillors vary greatly (from fewer than 100:1 to more than 40,000:1); councillors may be elected 'at large' in a single electorate across the whole local government area, or by wards (local electoral divisions); the number of councillors per ward may be one, two, three or more; elections may be conducted for the whole council every four years, or for half the councillors every two years; voting may be compulsory or optional, in person or by post; mayors and deputy mayors may be elected directly by all voters, or indirectly by and from the councillors; the term of mayors varies from one to four years; the legislated role of a mayor may be largely ceremonial or semi executive; and so on.

Table 12.1 provides a summary of how mayors (and their equivalents) are elected in each state and the Northern Territory, as well as their designated roles and responsibilities and how they relate to those of the other councillors. Substantial variations are evident both between and within states.[3] In Queensland and Tasmania, plus urban areas of the Northern Territory and most of the central capital cities, mayors must be directly elected. In New South Wales (NSW), South Australia, Western Australia and the rest of the Northern Territory, local councils or their electors can choose between popular and indirect election – but only in South Australia has a large proportion favoured popular election. In Victoria, legislation generally specifies indirect election and only two councils – the central capital city of Melbourne and the large regional centre of Geelong – have directly elected mayors. Thus popular election is compulsory or available by choice in all states except Victoria, but operates in fewer than 40 per cent of all Australian councils.

The role of mayors – as defined by legislation – is clearly strongest in Queensland, where all mayors are directly elected and voting is compulsory. This is reinforced in many cases by the relatively large size and budgets of the local governments they lead. The *Queensland Local Government Act* was amended in 2009 and again in 2012 to extend to

Table 12.1 Election and roles of Australian mayors

State or territory	Method of election and term	Designated role
New South Wales	• Direct or indirect (Sydney Lord Mayor must be directly elected) • Local referendum required to introduce popular election • Popular election is for the full four-year term of the council; indirect election takes place annually	• Principally that of chairperson plus civic/ceremonial duties • Policy decisions if required between council meetings • Councillors collectively direct council affairs and provide civic leadership • Council may delegate additional functions to mayor
Northern Territory	• Less than 20 per cent are directly elected • Mayors of municipal (urban) councils are directly elected • Presidents of rural shires may be either directly or indirectly elected	• Chairperson and civic/ceremonial duties, plus 'principal representative' and spokesperson of the council • Councillors collectively direct council affairs and provide civic leadership

Queensland	• All mayors are directly elected for the full four-year term of the council	• Semi-executive role plus civic and ceremonial duties:
		  ○ leading and managing meetings;
		  ○ preparing a budget to present to the council;
		  ○ leading, managing and providing strategic direction to the chief executive officer (CEO);
		  ○ directing the CEO and other senior executives in accordance with the council's policies; and
		  ○ ensuring provision of information to the minister about the local government area

South Australia	• Directly elected for the full four-year term of the council, or indirectly elected for up to four years • Council decides which method to adopt • Almost three quarters are directly elected	• Lord Mayor of Brisbane has additional executive responsibilities • Preside at meetings, principal spokesperson of the council, civic and ceremonial duties • If requested, provide advice to the CEO on the implementation of council decisions • Councillors collectively direct council affairs and provide civic leadership • Council may delegate additional functions • Lord Mayor of Adelaide has additional responsibilities

(continued)

Table 12.1 Election and roles of Australian mayors (continued)

State or territory	Method of election and term	Designated role

Tasmania	• All mayors and deputy mayors are directly elected for two-year terms
	• If no nomination, the councillors elect one of their number
		• Substantial leadership role:
		  ○ leader of the community of the municipal area;
		  ○ chairperson and spokesperson of the council;
		  ○ liaise with the general manager on the activities of the council and its performance; and
		  ○ oversee the councillors in their functions

Victoria	• Nearly all are indirectly elected for a term of up to two years • Mayors of Melbourne and Geelong are directly elected for full four-year term of the council	• Chair council meetings and take precedence at all municipal proceedings within the municipal district • No other functions specified for either the mayor or councillors • Melbourne City Council may delegate limited additional powers to the Lord Mayor
Western Australia	• Directly or indirectly elected • Council may decide to move to popular election • Local referendum required to go back to indirect election • Lord Mayor of Perth must be directly elected	• Preside at meetings and speak on behalf of the local government • Liaise with the CEO on the local government's affairs and the performance of its functions • Civic and ceremonial duties • Councillors collectively provide leadership and guidance to the community

all mayors a modified version of the established powers and responsibilities of the Lord Mayor of Brisbane. The Lord Mayor's powers are truly executive in nature; they extend to leading *and controlling* (emphasis added) the business of the council; implementing the policies adopted by the council; and developing and implementing other policies.

Tasmania is the only other state where legislation gives all mayors an added degree of authority within the body politic. Again, all mayors are directly elected, but voting is optional.[4] Section 27 of the Local Government Act requires Tasmanian mayors, among other things, to:

* act as a leader of the community of the municipal area;

* liaise with the general manager on the activities of the council and the performance of its functions and exercise of its powers; and

* oversee the councillors in the performance of their functions and in the exercise of their powers.

Elsewhere in Australia, local government Acts typically limit the prerogatives of the mayor to presiding at council meetings, having the right to sit on any committee, and carrying out civic and ceremonial duties. This applies whether mayors are directly or indirectly elected. Moreover, only in NSW, South Australia and the City of Melbourne do councils have an explicit power to delegate additional functions to the mayor. In practice, however, mayors often play a significantly greater role and exercise more authority than the legislation implies.

First, the mayors of the seven 'capital city' councils[5] in Australia's metropolitan regions are well-known, high-profile figures and to varying degrees exercise power or influence significantly greater than indicated by the relevant provisions of the Local Government Act – even in the case of Brisbane, where the mayor's legal powers are already considerable. This reflects their personal mandates – all are directly elected – as well as the importance of their councils as home to the country's major business centres and public facilities of state and sometimes national importance. The Lord Mayors of Melbourne and Sydney are especially prominent, although lacking specific powers under the relevant Acts. In the case of Melbourne, the council's power to delegate additional responsibilities to the Lord Mayor is very limited. However, under the NSW Local Government Act, councils may delegate a wide range of functions to the mayor, and current delegations to the Lord Mayor of Sydney confer what might be described as semi-executive status (see Box 12.2). In addition, the Lord Mayor is ex officio chair of the Central Sydney Planning Committee (a joint committee of the council and the state government).

The City of Adelaide Act gives two additional responsibilities to the Lord Mayor 'as the principal elected member of the council representing the capital city of South Australia'. These include a unique (in Australia) reference to intergovernment relations:

* to provide leadership and guidance to the City of Adelaide community; and

* to participate in the maintenance of intergovernmental relationships at regional, state and national levels.

Box 12.2 Examples of council delegations to the Lord Mayor of Sydney

(to be exercised in a manner consistent with council's policies and decisions as applicable from time to time)

- Exercise, during recesses of council, the powers, authorities, duties and functions of council other than those reserved to the council itself or delegated to the Chief Executive Officer

- Direct the Chief Executive Officer, except as otherwise provided by the Local Government Act

- Review, approve and implement governance and accountability structures and processes for the performance of the organisation, and oversee the performance of the Chief Executive Officer

- Make changes to the organisational structure which the Lord Mayor reasonably considers to be minor

- Approve all expenditure from contingency funds (excluding the Chief Executive Officer's contingency fund) provided it is within the terms of the budget adopted by council, and after consultation with the Chief Executive Officer

- Determine who should represent council on external organisations and committees and inter-agency working parties, and at civic ceremonial and social functions

- Direct that council's internal auditor to carry out a review or audit

- Obtain direct and independent advice (including legal advice) relevant to council functions

- In respect of the Office of the Lord Mayor, determine the structure, allocate expenditure, and direct staff and allocate tasks in consultation with the Chief Executive Officer

Source: City of Sydney Delegations to the Lord Mayor, current at August 2012

Second, there are many other mayors across Australia who, regardless of their method of election, exercise considerable authority and provide forceful leadership, irrespective of the precise wording of legislation. This may be as the strong leader of a dominant party-political or other grouping of councillors, or by dint of their personal qualities and acknowledged skills and experience. Some have occupied the position of mayor for a decade or more.

A third significant factor is the emergence of influential groupings of mayors. Two stand out: the Council of Capital City Lord Mayors (CCCLM) and the South East Queensland (SEQ) Council of Mayors. CCCLM has a small secretariat based in the national capital, Canberra, and represents the seven councils mentioned earlier, plus the government of the Australian Capital Territory.[6] It also includes a few large regional cities as 'associate' members. In particular, CCCLM has sought to develop a close relationship with the federal government on matters of urban policy. In that regard, it is to some extent a rival of local government's 'official' peak national organisation, the Australian Local Government Association, which is a joint body of the seven state and territory associations.

The Council of Mayors (SEQ) was established in September 2005. It covers Australia's fastest-growing metropolitan region, centred on Brisbane, comprising 11 local government areas with a combined population of around 2.7 million. The organisation is chaired by the Lord Mayor of Brisbane, and most of its members are high-profile mayors of (by Australian standards) very large councils: South East Queensland contains Australia's four most populous councils. Like CCCLM, the primary goal of the Council of Mayors is political – to influence federal and state government policy and funding priorities – and it plays a significant role in intergovernment relations.

Nevertheless, despite these developments there has been minimal discussion about the status and role of Australian mayors and how that role appears to be changing. This may reflect an assumption on the part of most people that mayors already exercise considerable authority; this would be reinforced by popular election and the regular appearances of prominent mayors in the media. However, one recent issue that did generate considerable debate was the move by the state government of Victoria to legislate for popular election of the mayor of Geelong, Victoria's largest regional city, with a population of around 220,000. The government issued a discussion paper in March 2011 proposing a directly elected mayor on the grounds that (Victoria Department of Planning and Community Development [DPCD] 2011a: 2):

- allowing the voters of Greater Geelong to directly elect their mayor will recognise the state and regional significance of the city;

- a directly elected mayor will have a high public profile and clear public endorsement, and this allows him or her to provide strong leadership for the council and the community; and

- a mayor elected for the full four-year term of the council can also contribute to providing stability of government for the city.

The proposal attracted considerable public and media interest. Most responses, especially those from business groups, favoured a directly elected mayor in some form (DPCD 2011b: 2). In its submission, the Geelong Chamber of Commerce (2011: 4–5) also set out what it regarded as the key expectations of the mayor in office. These included:

- setting up an effective governance structure and presiding over decision-making;

- managing the councillors and building a cohesive team;

- providing motivation and leadership to the administration to convey a strong sense of what is important (but not managing the staff, which is the chief executive officer's role);

- effectively positioning the council in its strategic relationships with federal and state governments, key agencies and institutions, community organisations and stakeholders;

- bringing people together around a specific vision for the future and acting as a catalyst for finding the best solutions to issues;

- aiding co-ordination and cohesion; and

- being the spokesperson for the council and making public statements which project a positive image.

The Committee for Geelong, also strongly business-based, argued that the mayor should be given additional powers, at least commensurate with those of the Lord Mayor of Melbourne, but preferably also including the power to establish a 'small decision-making executive', perhaps comprising the chairs of major committees.[7] The Committee for Geelong asserted that this would free up other councillors to be community representatives, rather than being expected to function as a 'board of directors' (Committee for Geelong 2011: 9).

By contrast, the two main representative bodies for local government, the Municipal Association of Victoria (MAV) and the Victorian Local Governance Association (VLGA), adopted a cautious approach, arguing that the case for change had not been made and that further research and/or an inquiry was required. The MAV sought 'a clear and detailed discussion of the benefits and any disbenefits on democracy and governance, and the additional cost to the community and council...' (MAV 2011: 1). However, the state government announced in November 2011 that it would be going ahead with the change (DPCD 2011c).

In summary, and apart from Queensland, approaches to the role of mayors across Australia could best be described as ambivalent. There is an evident reluctance to institutionalise strong local leadership through the office of mayor. Only in Tasmania, Western Australia and the City of Adelaide are mayors specifically tasked with community leadership. In NSW, Queensland, the Northern Territory and the rest of South Australia, that role is given to all the councillors individually and collectively. In Victoria it is not mentioned at all. Yet calls for more effective local leadership abound. The remainder of this chapter considers how they might be answered.

12.3 Developments in England and New Zealand

Governments in both England and New Zealand have recently addressed the role that mayors should play and amended legislation accordingly. A move to introduce directly elected mayors with semi-executive powers was part of broader reforms of English local government undertaken by the Blair Labour government around the turn of the century. The prompt for similar action in New Zealand was a decision in

2007 by the then Labour-led government to hold a Royal Commission into the future governance of Auckland.

12.3.1 England

In England, the decisive step towards new forms of mayoral leadership was the creation in 2000 of the Greater London Authority (GLA), headed by a directly elected Mayor of London. This followed a successful referendum to establish the new arrangements. The GLA is a regional authority that operates at a strategic level in conjunction with the 32 London borough councils. The mayor is answerable to an assembly of 25 elected members which scrutinises the authority's activities, spending and performance, and can – by a two-thirds majority – amend the mayor's proposed budget.

The mayor exercises the executive functions of the GLA. His/her role encompasses:

- promoting a vision for economic, social and environmental improvement;

- formulating plans and policies covering transport, planning and development, housing, economic development and regeneration, culture, health inequalities, and a range of environmental issues including climate change, biodiversity and environmental quality;

- ensuring those plans and policies contribute to sustainable development and the health of Londoners;

- responsibilities for culture and tourism, including managing Trafalgar Square and Parliament Square;

- setting the annual budget for the Greater London Authority and the wider GLA group, which includes the Metropolitan Police, Transport for London and the London Fire Brigade;

- appointments to the boards of the Metropolitan Police Authority, Transport for London, and the London Fire and Emergency Planning Authority, and chairing those boards if s/he so chooses.[8]

Subsequently, the Local Government Act 2000 introduced new governance options for all local authorities, including one of a directly elected, semi-executive mayor – as opposed to the previously universal model of a 'leader' elected by and from the councillors, with decision-making in the hands of a series of committees. The position of mayor had previously been essentially ceremonial and subservient to that of the leader. Local authorities were required to hold a local referendum if they wished to adopt the new mayoral model: only 37 out of 353 did so, and only 12 succeeded. The overwhelming majority of authorities selected a governance option that retained or was similar to previous arrangements (Stevens 2010).

The 2000 Act did not detail the role and powers of elected mayors, beyond those of appointing a deputy and members of an executive group of councillors that would manage the local authority in conjunction with the mayor, chief executive and senior officers. The underlying concept here was that of a ministerial and cabinet system, with other 'backbench' councillors acting as community representatives and scrutinising the work of the executive – a major departure from previous practice and one aimed at more decisive, innovative and responsive local leadership.

The specific functions and decision-making powers of the mayor and executive were to be the subject of ministerial regulations and/or individual council constitutions. Thus they can and do vary considerably from one authority to another. In the London Borough of Lewisham, for example, the council constitution sets out the role of the mayor as follows (London Borough of Lewisham 2011: 47):

- to be the council's principal spokesperson;

- to give overall political direction to the council;

- to appoint (and dismiss) the executive;

- to decide on a schedule of delegation of executive functions;

- to chair meetings of the executive;

- to represent the council on external bodies that deal with executive functions; and

- to be the council's lead member for children's services.

The key point here is the mayor's power to allocate and delegate 'executive functions', i.e. the wide range of decision-making powers vested in himself and the executive. In Lewisham, he may delegate any of those powers to:

- the executive as a whole or a committee of the executive;

- an individual member of the executive;

- an officer;

- an area committee;

- a joint committee;

- an individual ward councillor, to the extent the function is exercisable within the ward; or

- another local authority.

The mayor is also responsible for leading the preparation of a number of key strategic and corporate plans, and of the annual budget. The council as a whole may amend the budget submitted by the mayor and executive, but requires a two-thirds majority to do so.

Debate continues in England over the merits or otherwise of elected mayors: Stevens (2010) provides a pithy summary:

> *Depending on your preference or affiliation, elected mayors are, like reform of local finance, destined to remain either a desirable panacea for declining rates of participation and underperformance by local councils, or an aspirin in search of a headache. What has been shown is that mayors, like council leaders possibly, have mostly been capable of*

putting their local authority on an improvement journey, which in some cases has shown dramatic turnarounds (Hackney, North Tyneside) and in other cases simply steady progress (Lewisham). Whereas some mayors have provided stability after considerable chaos (Hackney) or underperformance (Torbay), others have simply got on with the job and been recognised for it (Hartlepool, Middlesbrough). And where they haven't, the electorate have had their say (Doncaster, Stoke on Trent). Either way, they've got people talking about local government, which remains in most people's eyes a municipal theme park of mayors' chains of office, dull committee meetings behind closed doors and possibly even irrelevance.

Interestingly, the key point for debate has not been the concept of replacing the old committee system with a strong council executive, but rather whether the head of that executive should be a directly elected mayor or an indirectly elected leader. Amendments to the Local Government Act since 2000 have given leaders similar roles and powers to those of mayors, and this is used by some to argue that there is no need for popular election. The central issue thus becomes one of whether the presiding member of a council should enjoy a popular mandate, and the value to a locality of having a clearly identified 'first citizen' with significant political and executive authority.

Further fuel was added to the debate by the decision of the Conservative–Liberal Democrat government elected in 2010 to seek to extend the system to another 12 major city councils across the country. Two of those councils (Liverpool and Salford) voluntarily adopted the model; referenda were held in the other 10 cities in May 2012, but only one (in Bristol) succeeded. Elsewhere majorities against elected mayors ranged from 53 to 63 per cent (Wilks-Heeg 2012). This may represent a decisive rejection of the model, although voter turnout was very low (nowhere more than 35 per cent) and a number of other contributing factors can be identified (ibid.). These include the lack of an effective 'yes' campaign, especially by the government itself; the wording of the question, which appeared to favour the status quo; the lack of clarity around the proposed powers of a mayor; and the failure to pursue a metropolitan regional model like the GLA.

12.3.2 New Zealand

All mayors in New Zealand have been directly elected for many years, but they have had no specific powers beyond chairing council meetings. Even when the Local Government Act was comprehensively reviewed and rewritten in 2002 it seems that little or no thought was given to moving away from the prevailing 'weak mayor' model. The 2002 Act does contain a provision (section 40) for 'governance statements' that, together with the use of delegations, could be used to codify and extend the mayor's role, but the provision does not appear to have been used in that way (Local Government New Zealand undated: 51–52). As in Australia, lack of formal powers does not necessarily preclude the emergence of 'strong' mayors, and New Zealand provides many examples of forceful and effective civic leadership based on the mayor's popular mandate and personal qualities (Royal Commission on Auckland Governance 2009: 423).

However the Royal Commission, established in October 2007 to review the governance of the Auckland metropolitan region, saw a need for a much more structured approach. In recommending establishment of a 'super city' council covering the entire metropolitan area and with a population of around 1.4 million, and drawing to a significant extent on the English model of elected mayors, it argued as follows (ibid. p. 8):

> Auckland needs an inspirational leader, inclusive in approach and decisive in action. Auckland needs a person who is able to articulate and deliver on a shared vision, and who can speak for the region, and deliver regional priorities decisively.
>
> The Auckland Council will be led by a mayor who is elected by all Aucklanders. The Mayor of Auckland will have greater executive powers than currently provided under the Local Government Act 2002, although these additional powers will still be more modest than in many international models of mayoralty. The additional powers will be limited to three key abilities:
>
> * appointment of the deputy mayor and committee chairpersons
>
> * proposal of the Auckland Council budget and initiation of policy
>
> * establishment and maintenance of an appropriately staffed Mayoral Office.
>
> The Mayor will be expected to chart and lead an agenda for Auckland. To ensure the Mayor remains fully accountable, all policy will need to be approved by the full Auckland Council. There will also be additional obligations on the Mayor to engage with the people of Auckland through regular 'Mayor's Days' and an annual 'State of the Region' address.

In the event, the government decided to go somewhat further. It rejected the Royal Commission's recommendation for six 'sub-councils' and instead further strengthened the role of the over-arching 'super city'. The functions of the mayor were also expanded, and articulated in section 9 of the Local Government (Auckland Council) Act 2009 as follows:

* articulate and promote a vision for Auckland;

* provide leadership for the purpose of achieving objectives that will contribute to that vision;

* lead the development of council plans (including the LTCCP[9] and the annual plan), policies and budgets for consideration by the governing body;

* establish processes and mechanisms to engage with the people of Auckland, whether generally or particularly (for example, the people of a cultural, ethnic, geographic or other community of interest);

* appoint the deputy mayor, establish committees of the governing body and appoint the chairperson of each committee; and

* establish and maintain an appropriately staffed office of the mayor, with an annual budget not less than 0.2 per cent of the council's total budgeted operating expenditure for that year.

While this set of powers and functions falls short of creating an executive mayor (McKinlay 2011), it clearly establishes a new benchmark for New Zealand local government, in the same way that the powers of the Lord Mayor of Brisbane were seen as a point of reference for other Queensland mayors. In March 2012 the New Zealand Government (2012) launched a new wave of local government reform proposals under the banner 'Better Local Government'. Those proposals included the following statement on mayoral powers (ibid.: 8):

> Mayors are the public face of councils and publicly carry the responsibility for their decisions. The problem is that there is a mismatch in the current local government framework between the high level of public interest, scrutiny and engagement in mayoral elections, where they are elected for an entire city or district, and their limited formal powers over the governing body of a council. Mayors need the capacity to provide clearer and stronger leadership.

> This was recognised with the Auckland council reform. The Local Government (Auckland Council) Act 2009 provides Auckland's mayor with governance powers not available to other mayors, although substantial decision-making remains with the full council. It makes good sense for mayors across New Zealand to have similar governance powers.

Subsequent amendments to the Local Government Act mean that from late 2013 all mayors will be able to lead the development of council plans, policies and budgets; appoint the deputy mayor; establish council committees; and appoint chairpersons to council committees. However, councils will be able to reverse mayoral decisions on establishing committees and appointing chairpersons, thus requiring a consensus approach.[10]

12.4 A future model

We now turn to the central issue of defining a model for the future role that mayors could and should play in the Australian context, but one that might also be applied elsewhere. Based on the literature overview and other material presented above, six key dimensions have been identified for further consideration. These comprise:

- the merits of popular election;
- the need for stronger community leadership;
- ensuring effective strategic and corporate planning;
- enhancing political governance;
- the respective roles of mayors and chief executives; and
- intergovernment relations.

12.4.1 The merits of popular election

In New Zealand, Queensland and Tasmania, there is no evident debate about whether mayors should be directly elected, and all the mayors interviewed in those jurisdictions affirmed the value and importance of having a personal mandate. Even though mayors may not enjoy specific additional powers, and may sometimes find themselves in a minority within the elected council, a personal mandate was seen to enable them to appeal directly to constituents, to represent a diverse range of community interests, to work more effectively with central governments, business and other key partners, and to exercise more influence within the council organisation, both in negotiations with other councillors and with senior management. Similar arguments were advanced by all the other directly elected mayors interviewed.

In England, debate still rages on the merits of popular election. Some claim that elected mayors have provided more visible and accountable 'facilitative leadership', improved the performance of their councils and established a platform for devolution of authority from central government (Kenny and Lodge 2008). Fenwick and Elcock (2005: 64) similarly concluded that the English mayoral system was beginning to exhibit gains in terms of clear local leadership, a concentration on strategic issues and an engagement with the wider governance role. The contrary view is that an indirectly elected 'council leader' (the head of the controlling political party or group) can and does achieve similar results; that indirect election avoids personality politics and ensures leaders have sound local government experience; and that effective devolution requires broader systemic change (Kemp 2006). Elcock and Fenwick (2007: 236–237) found a lack of evidence that directly elected mayors increase public interest and involvement in local government.

In a similar vein, some of those opposed to the popular election of the mayor of Geelong pointed to the dangers of personality politics and the potential for candidates with greater resources to 'buy' the mayoralty. Other concerns were that the mayor might veer 'out of control', running a purely personal agenda, or conversely that there could be gridlock between the mayor and an opposing majority of councillors. Such concerns reflect the need to ensure that the mayor's powers and responsibilities are articulated in sufficient detail to establish clear 'rules of the game' – either by statute or through a mechanism such as a council constitution or specific delegation of decision-making authority. This is recognised most clearly in Brisbane (and to a lesser extent the rest of Queensland), Sydney (in terms of the delegation from the council) and England (through council constitutions). Also, in Tasmania section 27 (1A) of the Local Government Act requires the mayor to 'represent accurately the policies and decisions of the council' in performing his or her functions.

Where a popularly elected mayor exercises considerable executive authority, regular and effective scrutiny of his or her performance is also essential. This is normally inherent in the way Australian local governments operate, but more structured and rigorous processes may need to be introduced if there is a risk of corruption (Elcock and Fenwick 2007: 236), or that the representative role of other councillors may be unduly impaired. National or subnational (state or provincial) governments commonly exercise close oversight and supervision of local councils, and such processes could be extended to monitoring the performance of directly elected mayors and intervening when necessary. Another option would be to introduce 'recall' provisions, empowering the electors and/or the councillors to remove the mayor by referendum or, say, a two-thirds majority vote, but such provisions may introduce unwarranted disruption and instability.

An alternative approach favoured by some is for the mayor to be indirectly elected, but with a guaranteed term of not less than two years or possibly the whole of the council's term. This would ameliorate the problem of mayors having to be re-elected every 12 months, with the attendant risks of inaction or instability in the lead-up to each annual election, as well as that of deals being done to share the role of mayor among three or four councillors over the life of the council, diminishing the authority and effectiveness of the position. However, unless the mayor is the unqualified leader of a dominant political grouping within the council, as often occurs in the UK, it is difficult to see how indirect election for extended periods would be democratically justified or work in practice.

12.4.2 The need for stronger community leadership

Entwined with the issue of popular election is the commonly perceived need for decisive and effective community leadership (Denters and Rose 2005: 254). There appears to be widespread agreement on this point: it was an explicit objective of government moves to introduce elected mayors in England, Auckland and Geelong, and is supported by the literature on facilitative and place-based leadership. The question that arises, however, is how best to construct such leadership: to what extent should the power to lead be vested in the mayor as opposed to a broader collective of councillors and indeed other non-elected community representatives. This was a key issue raised in the Geelong debate. Certainly, the provisions of Australian local government Acts, apart from Queensland, suggest a reluctance to move away from the collective council decision-making model, even though councils are frequently criticised for indecision and lack of strategy.

All the mayors interviewed for this study emphasised the need to build consensus and none saw any value in operating as a 'one man band'. However, they also agreed that someone had to be responsible for taking the lead, both in proposing action and in seeking consensus. All saw themselves as playing a leadership role in liaising with a broad range of government and non-government stakeholders to promote the interests of their locality and its communities. Again, few local government Acts explicitly confer such responsibilities on the mayor.

Of special relevance here is the increasing emphasis placed on community consultation and engagement. This may be linked specifically to preparation of plans and policies (discussed below) or expressed more broadly. The wording of the Auckland City Act is particularly interesting, requiring the mayor to 'establish processes and mechanisms to engage with the people of Auckland, whether generally or particularly'. The Mayor of London is similarly charged with consulting Londoners. By contrast, no Australian local government Act gives mayors any special role in community engagement: where communication or consultation with the local community is mentioned, it is listed as one of the responsibilities of all councillors. The inherent risk is of this loose approach that engagement becomes largely ad hoc and administrative: what should be seen as a continuous political function is instead treated as a matter of compliance when specified plans and policies are being prepared, and is conducted principally by managers.

A further issue is whether or not central governments are serious about enabling local leadership. One of the arguments put forward by those opposed to elected mayors in England is that they cannot make any real difference unless there is genuine devolution of authority from central to local government (Kemp 2006). To a significant extent, that may be a chicken-and-egg issue: devolution (legislative or de facto) may be more likely if local leadership is more effective and better able to exercise greater authority. The experience of Brisbane City Council and more recently the Greater London Authority and Mayor of London appears to support such an argument.

Interestingly, the head of the UK's New Local Government Network recently linked the need for devolution to a call for compulsory voting in local elections (Parker 2012). He argued that:

> This is a way to solve the localist's dilemma: councils complain that nobody votes for them because they have no power, but Whitehall refuses to pass down more power because councils are not fully accountable. Compulsory voting would transform the practice of local politics, forcing parties to appeal to a much wider range of voters.

In Australia, voting in local elections is already compulsory in the three largest states and there is little doubt that this adds significantly to the authority of directly elected mayors.

12.4.3 Ensuring effective strategic and corporate planning

Following the New Zealand model, recent amendments to most Australian local government Acts have placed considerable emphasis on the importance of long-term strategic plans, typically linked to goals of well-being and sustainability, and prepared in consultation with a broad range of stakeholders. These strategies are then to be translated into a series of shorter-term corporate plans; in NSW the term 'delivery programme' is used to make the purpose clear. The purpose of all this is to make councils more policy- and future-focused, committed to the ongoing pursuit of agreed community objectives and to sound management of assets, finances and human resources.

However, only in NSW and Tasmania does the legislation indicate explicitly that one of the functions of councillors is to involve themselves in the preparation of strategic plans, and none of the Acts suggests leadership by the mayor in this regard. Only the Queensland Act gives mayors associated functions: to give strategic direction to the CEO and to prepare the budget. In the case of the City of Brisbane, these functions are extended to developing policies.

This situation contrasts markedly with New Zealand and England, where mayors (and now also indirectly elected council leaders) are variously charged with formulating and promoting a vision for their city or area, and with leading the preparation of plans and budgets – in part to give effect to that vision. Like community engagement, strategic planning is fundamentally political rather than technical: it is about community preferences and expectations, setting objectives and balancing competing claims on resources. If legislation requires such planning but does not require and enable elected representatives to lead the process, then it is not difficult to understand why plans prepared largely by officials are adopted by councillors without sufficient consideration of their implications and with little solid commitment to their implementation. The same applies to annual or multi-year budgets.

12.4.4 Enhancing political governance

An underlying theme in the evolving role of mayors is the need for enhanced political governance. This relates to the goal of effective leadership discussed earlier and involves issues of 'good governance': the way the body politic of the council organises and conducts itself to ensure sound decision-making.

A number of interesting developments are apparent. First, mayors in England, Auckland and (subject to the necessary delegation) Melbourne are variously responsible for appointing their deputy, delegating decision-making, determining the committee structure, and appointing councillors to internal committees (including as chair) and as representatives of the council on outside bodies. In other words, the mayor is empowered to set up the structure of political governance in such a way as to reflect his or her vision and priorities (and potentially, of course, to reward his or her supporters).

From interviews with mayors, the selection and role of deputies emerged as particularly important. All emphasised the need for a close and trustful working relationship: having a deputy they could rely on to 'fill in' where necessary and, importantly to liaise with other councillors and help secure votes in the council on key issues. While some thought that removing the right of councillors to elect the deputy could prove counterproductive, the majority felt that the benefits of being able to appoint a trusted colleague or strategic ally outweighed the risk. In the case of Melbourne, the requirement for candidates for mayor and deputy to stand for election together is designed to ensure an effective leadership team, although relationships may not always last the distance.

Second, the mayor may be expected to take the lead in ensuring probity and appropriate behaviour on the part of all councillors. In Tasmania, for example, the Local Government Act requires the mayor to 'oversee the councillors in their functions', and the mayor plays a key role when complaints are made against councillors. This can be seen as an important element of civic leadership: in its submission supporting a directly elected mayor, the Geelong Chamber of Commerce (2011) identified a need for the mayor to 'manage' the councillors and build a cohesive team.

12.4.5 The respective roles of mayors and chief executives

The relationship between mayors and chief executives is a complex and often vexed issue: it lies at the heart of the debate about whether and to what extent mayors should exercise executive powers. This is a particularly sensitive question in Australia, where the general trend of local government legislation over the past two decades has been to apply the concept of 'separation of powers'. The responsibilities and prerogatives of chief executives are described in as much detail as those of mayors and councillors, or more, typically such that they become (officially at least) the sole point of contact between the body politic and the administration, entrusted with all aspects of the 'day-to-day' management of the organisation, including appointment of all staff, and allowed considerable discretion in the implementation of council policies.

In legal terms, the only significant departures from this model in Australia are Queensland, where the Act now empowers mayors to direct senior staff and prepare the budget, and Sydney, where the Lord Mayor may direct the chief executive under a delegation from the council, together with the power to make 'minor' adjustments to the organisation structure. Elsewhere, legislation limits mayors to 'advising' or 'liaising with' their chief executives. However, this does not necessarily prevent a politically powerful mayor from exercising a considerable measure of de facto executive authority, especially when senior managers are employed under fixed-term, performance-based contracts.

The situation in New Zealand is generally similar to that in Australia: even the new mayor of Auckland has not been given explicit executive powers. However, as noted earlier, he or she does 'lead the development' of strategic and corporate plans and, perhaps most importantly, the budget. Moreover, the mayor has dedicated support staff and a guaranteed minimum budget to maintain that office.

In England, elected mayors (and indirectly elected council leaders) may have much more explicit and extensive executive authority, depending on their council's constitution and scheme of delegations. The London mayor is also able to exercise powerful influence, if not executive authority as such, by appointing and chairing the boards of key service-delivery organisations, such as Transport for London.

None of the mayors interviewed for this study expressed a desire to administer the day-to-day operations of their council organisation: all saw their primary focus as on the one hand looking outward (formulating strategy, engaging the community and stakeholders and working with partner organisations); and on the other 'political management' (creating an enabling environment within the council so that agreed objectives are achieved). However, in most cases it was evident that this 'hands-off' approach to administration was conditional on having a chief executive who appreciated the mayoral role and mandate, and did not seek to apply 'separation of powers' in a literal and rigid manner. In this regard, there appears to be considerable merit in the English concept of a council constitution that can be negotiated and updated after each election, and that sets out the important 'rules' governing operations and key relationships. This would apply equally to issues of political governance discussed previously.

While having a separate chief executive remains the norm, some English councils are now experimenting with the 'mayor as CEO' model (Stevens 2011), and downgrading the position of chief executive to 'chief operating officer' or 'head of paid service' or the like. In some instances this follows the advent of a mayor or council leader who wishes to be the dominant authority, but elsewhere it may reflect a view that the head of the body politic ought to deal directly as required with all the senior officers (as is now the case with all Queensland mayors), and that granting the title 'chief executive officer' to an appointed official is inappropriate (although Queensland retains that terminology). In the UK, the need to reduce expenditure is also a significant factor: eliminating the separate position of CEO and making one of the senior officers 'head of paid service' may be seen as a worthwhile saving in the current environment of severe cuts to local government budgets.

12.4.6 Intergovernment relations

A necessary corollary of community leadership and strategic planning is involvement in intergovernment relations. All the mayors interviewed spoke about their role in dealing with and advocating to central governments on behalf of their local area. As noted earlier, the Auckland Royal Commission highlighted the need for someone to 'speak for the region'.

Only two Australian local government Acts specifically mention intergovernment relations. The City of Adelaide Act includes the strongest reference, making it a duty of the mayor 'to participate in the maintenance of intergovernmental relationships at regional, State and national levels' (section 21). The Queensland Act includes a somewhat odd requirement for the mayor to provide information to the minister about the local government area. In addition, the Northern Territory Act makes the mayor the 'principal representative' of the council, while, as noted earlier, Sydney's Lord Mayor chairs the joint state–council Central Sydney Planning Committee, an important intergovernment mechanism.

Regardless of legislation, it is evident that Australian mayors are generally expected to play a significant role in intergovernment relations. When the Rudd federal government established an 'Australian Council of Local Government' in 2008, its nominal membership (and annual plenary gathering) consisted of all the country's mayors (or equivalents). Similarly, a recent move by the NSW government to launch ongoing reform and revitalisation of local government began with a meeting of all the state's mayors and council general managers (chief executives). This suggests that some codification of the mayor's intergovernment role, along the lines of the Adelaide Act, would be appropriate.

12.5 Conclusion: a framework for legislation

This concluding section builds on the lessons drawn in this chapter about key elements of the evolving role of mayors, to suggest a framework of legislative provisions that might be applied in Australia and perhaps elsewhere. Its starting point is that the evidence reviewed points to the value of mayors who are directly elected and thus enabled to exercise strong, facilitative community leadership. At the same time, however, popular election of mayors makes it more important that their roles be defined in some detail so that their powers and responsibilities are clear and suitably balanced, and in order for them to be held to account by their fellow councillors and constituents. Based on that approach, Table 12.2 proposes a set of principal mayoral functions and prerogatives, and legislative provisions that would give effect to them. The suggested provisions draw principally on those contained in Australian local government Acts, as previously summarised in Table 12.1, plus some from New Zealand.

While the legislative provisions suggested in Table 12.2 would considerably strengthen the role of most Australian mayors, they are by no means radical in the international context and stop short of conferring executive powers in the commonly accepted sense of the term. Indeed, it may well be that greater executive authority is seen as desirable in some cases, such as currently applies in Brisbane and Sydney (the latter under delegation).

Table 12.2 Suggested framework of mayoral roles and legislative provisions

Function or prerogative	Legislative provision (and origin)
Principal member of the council	• Lead and control the business of the council (Brisbane) • Chair and manage meetings (all Australian Acts) • Speak on behalf of the council as the council's principal representative (Northern Territory) • Conduct civic and ceremonial functions (all Australian Acts)
Community leadership provisions of various Australian and New Zealand and engagement	• Articulate and promote a vision for the area (Auckland) • Provide leadership and guidance to the community (Adelaide) • Establish processes and mechanisms to engage with the community (Auckland)
Selection of deputy mayor	• Appoint the deputy mayor (New Zealand) or • Mayor and deputy to stand for election as a team (Melbourne)
Effective political governance	• Establish committees of the governing body and appoint the chairperson of each committee (New Zealand) • Oversee the councillors in the performance of their functions and in the exercise of their powers (Tasmania) • Represent accurately the policies and decisions of the council (Tasmania)
Strategic and corporate planning	• Lead the development and implementation of council plans, policies and budgets (New Zealand/Queensland) • Prepare the budget (Queensland)
Guiding the chief executive	• Lead, manage and provide advice and strategic direction to the chief executive officer on the implementation of council policies (Queensland/South Australia) • Direct the chief executive officer and senior staff in accordance with council policies (Queensland) • Exercise, in cases of necessity, the policy-making functions of the governing body of the council between meetings (New South Wales) • Liaise with the chief executive officer on behalf of the other councillors (Tasmania) • Conduct performance appraisals of the chief executive officer (Queensland)
Intergovernment relations	• Participate in intergovernmental relationships at regional, state and national levels (Adelaide)
Exercise delegated authority	• Exercise such other functions as the council determines (New South Wales/South Australia)

On the other hand, there is perhaps little need for change in many of Australia's thinly populated rural and remote local governments that discharge only limited functions. Such distinctions might well apply in other Commonwealth countries.

Nevertheless, packaging existing provisions of various Australian and New Zealand local government Acts in the manner suggested would probably be seen as a significant change of direction, particularly granting mayors powers to appoint their deputy, to establish committees and appoint chairs, and to direct the chief executive and other senior staff. As discussed earlier, such changes would need to be accompanied by arrangements to ensure effective scrutiny of the mayor's actions by the council as a whole, plus, if necessary, external oversight (perhaps by an independent local government board or commission). This might also involve enabling councillors to overturn some mayoral decisions: in England mayoral budgets can be amended by a two-thirds majority, and in New Zealand councils can reverse mayoral decisions on establishing committees and appointing chairpersons.

If mayors are to do more, they will need increased resources and support. The Auckland model, under which there is a legislative guarantee that the mayor will have an adequately resourced personal office, appears desirable in the case of large urban local governments. Mayoral offices have been established in a number of Australian city councils.

Essentially, what is being suggested here is that the functions of mayors – who are already generally acknowledged as the principal member of their councils – should be updated and recodified to match other changes that have occurred in local government structures and processes. The Australian experience is that, with the exception of Queensland, the frameworks and norms of political governance have largely failed to keep pace with the expanded functions of local government, and especially the growing expectation that councils will act more strategically to reflect and represent the needs and aspirations of their communities. These goals cannot be achieved unless the political arm of local government has the capacity to discharge its responsibilities effectively alongside those of management. To build that capacity, the role of the mayor seems a good place to start.

Notes

1 An earlier version of this chapter was released by the Australian Centre of Excellence for Local Government under the title 'Australian Mayors: What can and should they do?' Comments received and issues raised in ensuing discussions on that paper have been incorporated into the chapter.
2 Nine semi-structured interviews were conducted with mayors and former mayors, along with numerous informal discussions.
3 Henceforth 'states' should be read to include the Northern Territory.
4 At the time of writing, the Tasmanian government had introduced legislation to extend the term of mayors and deputy mayors to the full four-year term of the council, and to introduce the option of compulsory voting where supported by the council concerned. See: www.dpac.tas.gov.au/__data/assets/pdf_file/0007/186685/SummaryOfAmendments_LocalGovernmentAmendment_Elections_Bill2013.pdf (accessed 10 June 2013).
5 Brisbane, Sydney, Melbourne, Hobart, Adelaide, Perth, Darwin. Except for Brisbane, these councils cover only the central business district and, to varying degrees, adjoining inner suburbs. Metropolitan governance is a state responsibility. There is no local council for the national capital, Canberra, which is administered directly by the government of the Australian Capital Territory (ACT).
6 The ACT consists largely of the city of Canberra and is a 'city-state' of around 400,000 people with no separate local government.
7 This would be a similar arrangement to the City of Brisbane's longstanding 'civic cabinet' structure.
8 See: www.london.gov.uk/who-runs-london/mayor/role (accessed 19 August 2012).
9 Long-Term Council Community Plan – a wide-ranging strategic and financial plan.
10 See: www.dia.govt.nz/pubforms.nsf/URL/BLG-Fact-Sheet-Mayoral-Powers-November-2012.pdf/$file/BLG-Fact-Sheet-Mayoral-Powers-November-2012.pdf (accessed 10 June 2013).

References

Australian Centre of Excellence for Local Government (ACELG) (2011), 'Unfinished business? A decade of inquiries into Australian local government', Working Paper No. 4, September, University of Technology, Sydney.

Borraz, O, and P John (2004), 'The transformation of urban political leadership in Western Europe', *International Journal of Urban and Regional Research*, Vol. 28 No. 1, 107–120.

Committee for Geelong (2011), *Submission: Mayor of Greater Geelong – Direct Election*, May, available at: www.dpcd.vic.gov.au/__data/assets/pdf_file/0018/64701/GGM-36.pdf (accessed 19 August 2012).

Denters, B, and RE Lawrence (2005), 'Towards local governance', in B Denters and RE Lawrence (Eds.), *Comparing Local Governance: Trends and Developments*, Palgrave Macmillan, Basingstoke.

Department of Planning and Community Development (DPCD) (2011a), *Mayor of Greater Geelong – Direct Election: Discussion Paper*, March, DPCD, Victoria.

DPCD (2011b), *Direct Election of the Mayor of Greater Geelong: Consultation Summary*, June, DPCD, Victoria.

DPCD (2011c), *Geelong Voters to Elect Mayor*, November, available at: www.dpcd.vic. gov.au/localgovernment/news-and-events/news/geelong-voters-to-elect-mayor (accessed 19 August 2012).

Elcock, H, and J Fenwick (2007), 'Comparing elected mayors', *International Journal of Public Sector Management*, Vol. 20, No. 3, 226–238.

Fenwick, J, and H Elcock (2005), 'The elected mayor and local leadership', *Public Money and Management*, Vol. 18, No. 3, 15–21.

Geelong Chamber of Commerce (2011), *Directly Elected Mayor for Greater Geelong: Consultation Submission*, available at: http://geelongchamber.com.au/app_cmslib/media/lib/1108/m3961_v1_submission%20to%20dept.%20p&cd%20re.%20 directly%20elected%20mayor%202011.pdf (accessed 19 August 2012).

Hambleton, R (2009), 'Civic leadership for Auckland', *Report of the Royal Commission on Auckland Governance*, Vol. 4: Research Papers, Auckland, available at: www. royalcommission.govt.nz (accessed 19 August 2012).

Hambleton, R (2011), 'Place-based leadership in a global era', *Commonwealth e-Journal of Local Governance*, No. 8/9, May–November, 8–32, available at: http://epress. lib.uts.edu.au/ojs/index.php/cjlg (accessed 19 August 2012).

Hambleton, R, and S Bullock (1996), *'Revitalising Local Democracy – The Leadership Options* Local Government Management Board, London.

Kemp, R (2006), 'Directly elected mayors are not an effective model for England', *CityMayors*, available at: www.citymayors.com/politics/uk_mayors_anti.html (accessed 1 February 2011).

Kenny, M, and G Lodge (2008), 'Mayors rule', *Public Policy Research*, Vol. 15, No. 1, 12–21, available at: http://onlinelibrary.wiley.com/doi/10.1111/j.1744-540X. 2008.00502.x/pdf (accessed 19 August 2012).

Local Government New Zealand (undated), *The KnowHow Guide to Governance: Under the Local Government Act 2002*.LGNZ, Wellington, available at: www.lgnz. co.nz/library/files/store_021/Governance.pdf (accessed 19 August 2012).

London Borough of Lewisham (2011), *Constitution*, Lewisham Council, London, available at: www.lewisham.gov.uk/mayorandcouncil/aboutthecouncil/how-council-is-run/Pages/constitution.aspx (accessed 19 August 2012).

Local Government Reform Commission (2007), Report: Volume 1, State of Queensland, Brisbane.

McKinlay, P (2011), 'Can others learn from Auckland's restructuring?', in G Sansom (Ed.) *Second International Roundtable on Metropolitan Governance, Brisbane, 19–20 August 2010: Summary Report*, Australian Centre of Excellence for Local Government, University of Technology, Sydney.

Marshall, N (2008), 'Local Government reforms in Australia', in B Dollery, J Garcea and E LeSage (Eds.), *Local Government Reform: A Comparative Analysis of Advanced Anglo-American Countries*, Edward Elgar, Cheltenham.

Municipal Association of Victoria (2011), *MAV Submission: Mayor of Greater Geelong – Direct Election*, May, available at: www.dpcd.vic.gov.au/data/assets/pdf_file/0010/64738/GGM-57.pdf (accessed 19 August 2012).

Munro, J (2000), 'Hand in glove or boxing gloves? The interface between elected representatives and managers', *Local Government at the Millennium Conference*, February 2000, NSW Local Government and Shires Associations, Sydney.

New Zealand Government (2012), *Better Local Government*, Department of Internal Affairs, Wellington, available at: www.dia.govt.nz/better-local-government (accessed 19 August 2012).

Osborne, D and T Gaebler (1993), *Reinventing Government: How the Entrepreneurial Spirit is Transforming the Public Sector*, Penguin, New York.

Parker, S (2012), 'Can Labour learn to love localism?', *Guardian Professional*, 17 August, available at: www.guardian.co.uk/local-government-network/2012/aug/17/can-labour-learn-to-love-localism (accessed 10 June 2013).

Peters, BG (1995), *The Politics of Bureaucracy*, Longman, White Plains, NY, 177–178.

Quirk, B (2011), *Re-imagining Government: Public Leadership and Management in Challenging Times*, Palgrave Macmillan, Basingstoke.

Royal Commission on Auckland Governance (2009), *Volume 1: Report*, The Commission, Auckland.

Sansom, G (2001), 'Blurring the line: sensibly blending the roles of councillors and managers can produce better local government', National Congress of Local Government Managers Australia, Brisbane.

Sproats, K (1997), 'Local management or local governance', Understanding the Region Paper 5, Regional Planning Partnership for the Inner Metropolitan Region of Sydney.

Stevens, A (2010), 'England's elected mayors have performed rather well', *City Mayors*, available at: www.citymayors.com/government/uk-elected-mayors-2010.html (accessed 19 August 2012).

Stevens, A (2011), 'Local leaders: mayors vs chief executives', *Guardian Professional*, 23 May, available at: www.guardian.co.uk/public-leaders-network/2011/may/23/international-localism-models (accessed 19 August 2012).

Stoker, G, F Gains, S Greasley, P John and N Rao (2007), *The New Council Constitutions: the Outcomes and Impact of the Local Government Act 2000*,

Department of Communities and Local Government, London, available at: www.elgnce.org.uk/docs/main_report_13_07_07.pdf (accessed 19 August 2012).

Svara, JH (2006), 'The search for meaning in political–administrative relations in local Government', *International Journal of Public Administration*, Vol. 29, 1065–1090.

Wilks-Heeg, S (2012), 'The widespread rejection of elected city mayors is a spanner in the works for the government's localism agenda', British Politics and Policy Blogs, London School of Economics and Political Science, 5 May, available at: http://blogs.lse.ac.uk/politicsandpolicy/archives/23394 (accessed 19 August 2012).